Still I Rise

THE PERSISTENCE OF
PHENOMENAL WOMEN

D1508707

Marlene Wagman-Geller

Cover Design: Marija Lijeskic and Elina Diaz
Layout Design: Elina Diaz

For permission requests, please contact the publisher at:

Mango Publishing Group
2850 Douglas Road, 3rd Floor
Coral Gables, FL 33134 USA
info@mango.bz

For special orders, quantity sales, course adoptions and corporate sales, please email the publisher at sales@mango.bz. For trade and wholesale sales, please contact Ingram Publisher Services at customer.service@ ingramcontent.com or +1.800.509.4887.

Still I Rise : The Persistence of Phenomenal Women

Library of Congress Cataloging
ISBN: (paperback) 978-1-63353-596-1, (ebook) 978-1-63353-595-4
Library of Congress Control Number: 2017908614
BISAC category code : BIO022000 BIOGRAPHY & AUTOBIOGRAPHY / Women

Printed in the United States of America

PREVIOUS BOOKS

Behind Every Great Man: The Forgotten Women Behind the World's Famous and Infamous

And the Rest is History: The Famous (and Infamous) First Meetings of the World's Most Passionate Couples

Eureka! The Surprising Stories Behind the Ideas That Shaped the World

Once Again to Zelda: The Stories Behind Literature's Most Intriguing Dedications

Dedication

To the women who helped me rise:

My Mother, Gilda Wagman
My daughter, Jordanna Shyloh Geller

Author's Note: The title of this book, STILL I RISE is a tribute to Maya Angelou's 1978 poem, STILL I RISE, where in the first stanza reads:

You may write me down in history,

With your bitter, twisted lies,

You may trod me in the very dirt

But still, like dust, I'll rise.

"Still I Rise" can be found in AND STILL I RISE: A BOOK OF POEMS by Maya Angelou, a Random House book.

TABLE OF CONTENTS

Foreword   **13**

Prologue: Hell, I'm Still Here   **17**

Chapter 1: The Worst of Times (1761)   **27**

Chapter 2: It is Warm (1880)   **37**

Chapter 3: The Stepping Stone (1891)   **47**

Chapter 4: Steel Gardenia (1895)   **57**

Chapter 5: "Where Your Treasure Is…" (1903)   **67**

Chapter 6: The Black Sky (1910)   **77**

Chapter 7: This Little Light of Mine (1917)   **87**

Chapter 8: Phenomenal Woman (1928)   **97**

Chapter 9: Dance All Night (1928)   **107**

Chapter 10: Can We Talk? (1933)   **117**

Chapter 11: Under the Bus (1939)   **127**

Chapter 12: No Color (1940)   **137**

Chapter 13: The Female David (1945)   **147**

Chapter 14: A Miracle Worker (1946)   **157**

Chapter 15: My Mother's Daughter (1952)   **167**

Chapter 16: My Beloved World (1954)   **177**

Chapter 17: The Force (1956)   **187**

Chapter 18: The Boomerang (1959)   **197**

Chapter 19: The Glass Castle (1960)   **209**

Chapter 20: The Light (1965)   **219**

Chapter 21: Unbroken (1967)   **229**

Chapter 22: Hooah! (1968)   **239**

Chapter 23: A Butterfly (1981)   **249**

Chapter 24: Sin and Salvation (1982)   **259**

Chapter 25: The Best Revenge (1989)   **269**

Epilogue   **278**

Acknowledgements   **281**

Bibliography   **284**

About The Author   **323**

FOREWORD

Some things stagger the mind—the size of the universe, or the trillions of atoms in a single grain of sand or cells in a newborn's little fingernail. As much beyond our grasp is the estimated one hundred billion human beings who have ever lived. This means that fifty billion women have watched the sun rise and set and the seasons pass since our species came into being.

Millions of women, we can therefore safely say, have lived what Western culture has defined as the appropriate female experience—the helpmate, the subordinate, the one who stirred the pot and darned the socks at home. Though women in our culture have far greater opportunities than in the past, a significant degree of gender stereotyping still clings to our society and rattles around unbidden and unwanted in our brains. Women have put up with mansplaining and gender bias far longer than there have been words for either, and have sold themselves short for centuries, as so many still do today. Here, in these stories of twenty-five women who overcame incredible personal and societal adversity, Marlene Wagman speaks not just for these women's heroism, but for all the rest whose stories we will never know, and for the next generation of female heroes whose voices are better heard in classrooms, on playing fields, and in workplaces today because of the women who have come before.

Many of the stories recounted in *Still I Rise* are bigger than gender, though gender limitations are woven inextricably throughout. Helen Keller and Annie Sullivan struggled to overcome the ravages of a disease that couldn't have cared less if Helen was a girl or boy. Hattie McDaniel, the first African American to win an Oscar for her portrayal of Mammy in *Gone with the Wind*, sat in the same separate waiting rooms and drank from the same "colored" water fountains as African American men. Having an addicted spouse, as Lois Burnham Wilson, the wife of the founder of Alcoholics Anonymous did, is devastating whether the spouse is a husband or wife. Nevertheless, there is no question that being female compounds immeasurably the other burdens and struggles of life, as Wagman shows here.

The twenty-five essays are replete with details that show evidence of Wagman's deep research. Did you know, for example, that Keller's eyes were replaced with glass ones for cosmetic and medical reasons? Or that McDaniel successfully pleaded with Clark Gable not to "make a scene" by boycotting the gala opening night, which she could not attend because of her race? Or that Lois Wilson endured her husband's many other addictions, while they struggled to make the Twelve Step AA program, which had freed him from dependence on alcohol, the household word it is today? All the details are here in these thoughtful, touching, and well written essays, sprinkled throughout with signature doses of Wagman's wry humor.

Still I Rise serves as a shout-out to all of us and our stories. I am proud to share my gender not just with the women about whom Wagman writes, but with Wagman herself, and all my sister authors who put their hearts, intelligence, creativity, and hard work into telling the stories of women who can no longer speak for themselves.

Laurel Corona

Author of *Finding Emilie* and *The Mapmaker's Daughter*

San Diego, 2017

PROLOGUE: HELL, I'M STILL HERE

"A woman is like a teabag; you never know how strong it is until it's in hot water."

— **Eleanor Roosevelt**

Anyone who has managed to survive to mid-mark of the biblically allotted three score years and ten has had occasion to cast one's eyes heavenward and mutter, "Ya know, God, there are other people." Amidst these litany of woes can be discerned cries of betrayal, illness, lost illusions. After all, part and parcel of living means treading the Boulevard of Broken Dreams, navigating the Canal of a Shattered Romance. What eases the thorny path is the belief we do not have a monopoly on grief, that loss is a universal condition. Another weapon in the arsenal of endurance is the hope we can rise from our knees. In the words of Oprah, *"Turn your wounds into wisdom."*

In a nod to the sweet is sprinkled with the bitter; while celebrating the launch of my fourth book, *Behind Every Great Man,* was the pain I experienced from watching a lady I love grappling with a tsunami of *tsoris* that through solidarity became my own. For solace I turned to women who had conquered their own emotional Everest—who not only refused to crumble, but prevailed. The first of these possessors of indomitable spirit I investigated was Hattie McDaniel. She was the thirteenth child born to former slaves and her life was a struggle against grinding poverty, racism, four failed marriages, and a hysterical pregnancy. Rather than bow to defeat, she arm-wrestled Jim Crow and broke the color barrier in film to become the first African American to win an Academy Award for her portrayal of Mammy in *Gone with the Wind*. In her emotional acceptance speech, she stated she hoped she was a credit to her race. She was—and not just to her race, but the human race.

Aung San Suu Kyi went from two decades of house arrest in Burma to Sweden's Nobel Peace Laureate. Rather than vow vengeance on the regime who had stolen her life, she sought to negotiate with the junta; however, so far it has chosen to ignore her. She stated with her indefatigable humor sweetened with temperance, "I wish I could have tea with them every Saturday, a friendly tea. And, if not, we could always try coffee."

Nobody feels sorry for British-born Joanne Rowling, the most staggering successful author in the world. Yet her earlier life was a prologue far removed from her present golden years. She was in Portugal, trapped in a physically and emotionally abusive marriage, mother of an infant, when she fled penniless to her sister's Scottish home. Had she succumbed to the depression and contemplation of suicide, the world would never have met its beloved, bespectacled wizard.

At the age of eleven, Malala Yousafzai took on the Taliban by giving voice to her dream of obtaining an education. They responded with bullets. In 2014, she became the youngest winner of the Nobel Peace Prize. She stated of her historic win, "I am pretty certain that I am the first recipient of the Nobel Peace Prize who still fights with her younger brothers."

Although these ladies hail from different climes and chronologies, they share a common denominator. Life had thrust them to their knees, but they refused to remain in that position—with the result they not merely stood, but soared.

I have a connection with one of our era's great ladies. Gail Devers had been a student at Sweetwater High School in National City, CA where I currently teach. After graduating from UCLA, she was on her way to becoming an Olympic track and field star when smitten with Graves' disease. The girl who was always running was reduced to crawling, and doctors suggested amputating her feet. Her husband, feeling it was not what he had signed up for, declined to live up to "the in sickness and in health." An embodiment of true grit, Gail went on to become a three-time Olympic champion.

The parable of the donkey in the well is a metaphor for the power of persistence, of surviving against the proverbial odds. One day an old donkey fell into a well and the farmer decided, as he had outlasted its usefulness, to let him die. He grabbed a shovel and began to toss dirt into the well. At first the cornered animal let out piteous cries followed by silence. Every time the dirt hit his back he shrugged it off; soon he was level with the ground and walked away.

Although this volume showcases the women who left imprints on the face of history, we must remember the unsung women who embody the face of fortitude. A metaphor for these ladies is Mary Tyler Moore tossing her iconic blue-knit beret into the air to the accompaniment of "Love is in the Air"—a thumbs up gesture to life. The freeze frame captures her megawatt smile, a testimony to one can endure bell-bottoms, bad dates, institutionalized sexism, and still retain faith.

Recently I met "Rebecca," who could have qualified as a contestant on the 1960s television show *Queen for a Day*. For the younger-than-baby boomer generation, it was the precursor to reality television. Every week it featured four desperate housewives whose criteria for appearing on the air were lives of unmitigated horror. Each contestant turned the show into a public confessional, wherein they would relate their litany of sorrows. Each of the ladies' faces wore expressions reminiscent of the figure from the painting *The Scream*. The studio audience would buzz in for the tale of greatest grief and the "winner" would be gifted with tiara, sash, and prize, and pronounced Queen for the Day. When "Queen Rebecca" shared what she was up against—every day a Sisyphus struggle for survival—I marveled how someone could take what her life was dishing out. However, what resonated far more than Rebecca's pain were her words, *"Hell, I'm still here."*

In addition to writing the book as a paean to the ladies who, rather than letting all obstacles smash them, smashed all obstacles, was the fact that historically men seem to have garnered the monopoly on transcending suffering. One needs only to think of the Bible and the men engaged in epic struggles: Jonas adrift in the whale's belly, Job as the archetypal whipping boy, Christ on his cross. From the modern era are the images of the jailed freedom fighters: Mandela in South African, Gandhi in India, King in America. Their female counterparts have somehow been obscured, although their sufferings were no greater, their courage no less.

The Grimm brothers did not help matters when they portrayed princesses as damsels in distress—unable to save themselves, they depended on the auspices of the prince: to find the glass slipper, to awaken with a kiss, to climb the golden tower of hair. As a little girl, my favorite record was Thumbelina, the enchanting fairy no bigger than a thumb, who, trapped on a lily pad and fearful of the advances of an unwelcome toad, plaintively cried out, "Oh hear, my plea/And rescue me..." Walt Disney, in his early films, perpetuated this stereotype—Snow White sang in her little girl voice, "Someday my prince will come." His studio later gave feminism some teeth when it made their royal maidens the possessors of backbone. One of these rough and tough ladies was Megara (Meg,) who nailed it when she proclaimed, "I'm a damsel. I'm in distress. I can handle this. Have a nice day!" At the end she overcomes her fear of heights and saves strong-man Hercules. Pixar piggybacked on this with *Brave*—a film which lives up to its name. Merida, the red-haired archer, is the first animated princess in a major American film who did not fall in love, who refused to get married, and does not depend on a handsome mate to save the day. And, in 2013, we had *Frozen's* Elsa, freed by the love of her sister. Unfortunately, Anna accomplished this feat in the stereotypical heroine attire—in revealing dress which showcased a body of anatomically unrealistic proportion and high heels. One icy step forward—one icy step back.

This paradigm shift can partially be attributed to the shoulders' of the historic women on which we stand: Susan B. Anthony casting a ballot when it was illegal for women to vote, Germaine Greer's *The Female Eunuch,* Helen Reddy's lyric "I Am Woman." It is females of this intrepid ilk which made for modern heroines who are far from the mythological maidens chained to a rock, helplessly and hopelessly waiting to be devoured by the Minotaur. Thanks to a growing multitude of kick-ass heroines, the damaging damsel in distress paradigm is receding into the Disney distance, a conceit antiquated and unenlightened. These days, our daughters experience gals such as the non-animated archer Katniss Everdeen and other fearless femmes who are holding down the fictional fort and making Princess Poor Me a phenomena of the past. These non-shrinking violets fortunately do so without loss of pheromones. Their anthem is poet Maya Angelou's own,

Does my sexiness upset you?

Does it come as a surprise

That I dance like I've got diamonds

At the meeting of my thighs?

In my inbox I receive emails from friends concerning female empowerment, of the solidarity of sisters. *Still I Rise* is an extension of these cyber-hugs. By sharing these stories of courage, it is my hope it will give faith to those who falter, for there is truth to the might of the pen. Nelson Mandela, while a prisoner of apartheid on Robben Island, kept in his cell an inspirational poem from 1875, "Invicitus." It was a kind of Victorian *My Way,* about one's head being bloody but unbowed, of remaining captain of one's soul. The verse from which I took the title of this volume was inspired by the intrepid Maya Angelou, whose life was a patchwork quilt of challenges. She had been the victim of a childhood rape whose trauma left her without a voice for several years, failed marriages, and racism. Yet, through the elixir of words, she broke free from the solitude of silence and became the poet laureate at President Clinton's inauguration. Through her travails, she discovered why the caged bird sings—it sings because though imprisoned, it never loses the vision of a life free from bars. In an ode to her indomitable spirit, she wrote an anthem of fortitude:

You may write me down in history

With your bitter, twisted lies,

You may tread me in the very dirt

But still, like dust, I'll rise.

In the following chapters are the stories of intrepid women who, when the going got tough, kept going, which enabled them to cross the finish line. Their lives prove that the possessors of estrogen are not just "the fairer sex" because of outer beauty but inner strength. They refused to let go of Emily Dickinson's hope is the thing with feathers and subsequently blazed trails. By reading of their power of persistence, their determination that dreams do not just have to remain in the realm of sleep, we can glean succor. Rather than view their sisters as competitors, they became the shoulders on which others can stand. Strong individuals are usually the possessors of uneasy pasts. However, heroines are defined not by their wounds, but by their triumphs. It is my hope that my readers will draw strength from reading of these great ladies' struggles, and *like dust, shall rise.*

CHAPTER 1:
THE WORST OF TIMES (1761)

Charles Dickens' epic novel, *A Tale of Two Cities,* is a love story set against the fiery backdrop of France and England during the Reign of Terror. A nonfictional heroine whose life was likewise enacted in Paris and London during the same epoch is equally riveting, though it has been regulated to an obscure chapter of this tumultuous time.

There are many exclusive clubs which dot the glitterati capitals of the world which provide open sesame solely to the possessors of blood of blue or pants with deep pockets. And yet there is one such rarefied enclave where entry is even more exclusive: billions of dollars cannot buy entry. Membership is by invitation only; Mother Teresa is one of the few who have declined. British royalty and rock royalty, as well as American presidents, have long entered. In our more liberal milieu, admittance is less conventional. *Orange is the New Black* actress Laverne Cox became its first transgender inductee. In answer to where is this place, the answer is its establishments are found throughout the world; in answer to who began this novel emporium is a woman whose life was as fantastical as her glittering guests.

Anne Made Grosholz had to deal with the twin challenges of becoming a new mother and a widow when Joseph, her German husband, died from gruesome wounds incurred in the Seven Year War two months before his daughter Marie was born. To add to the dire situation, her spouse's salary had been her sole source of income. To provide for herself and her infant, she obtained a position as a housekeeper to Dr. Philippe Curtius in her hometown of Strasbourg. The physician became so fond of Anne—he claimed to be a big fan of her casseroles—he brought mother and daughter along when he left France to return to his native Switzerland. There developed a lifelong bond between Marie and Curtius, who she called Uncle, and he served as surrogate father.

Like many medics of the time, Curtius made anatomical waxes, but his were exceptionally skillful, especially when it came to replicating the textures and hues of human skin. Hence, Marie was raised in a household where it was not unusual to see random body parts. Word of his talent spread, and Louis XV's cousin, the Prince de Conti, offered patronage. Finding the royal opportunity too great a position to pass up, Dr. Curtius, Anne, and six-year-old Marie left for Paris.

From her earliest years, Marie was enraptured with the art of wax works and became an eager protégée. The minion ultimately supplanted the master, and at age seventeen, she was creating her own models. While other teenaged girls were courting eligible boys, Marie was busy immortalizing contemporary luminaries, such as Jean-Jacques Rousseau and Benjamin Franklin. Her first complete sculpture was of Voltaire, who joked that at his age every mask was likely to be a death-mask. She liked to remark the three men were frequent dinner guests at the Curtius table, and that Rousseau enjoyed her mother's cooking.

By the early 1780s, Curtius and Marie had so impressed the French populace he set up a *cabinet de circe*—wax exhibition—at the Parisian entertainment hotspot: the Palais Royal. It featured the crowned heads of Europe, so visitors felt the thrill of mingling with the upper echelons. This proved such a resounding success, he staged another at the Boulevard du Temple, the *Caverne des Grands Voleurs*. This one, an echo of the growing violence in the country, was more a chamber of horrors than a portrait gallery. On display were figures of murderers and thieves; ever the tabloid journalist, Curtius bathed them in a blue light and fake blood was liberally applied. The master wax magicians intuitively understood the public's voracious appetite for both glitz and gore.

News of the woman who wrought marvels in wax spread, and Marie received a summons to serve as art teacher to King Louis XVI's sister, Madame Elizabeth. Consequently, she spent nine years in the Royal Court in the bosom of the royals. During her stay, she modeled the Bourbon family; the hair used in the display came from the horses of the royal stable. To complicate matters, while Marie was ensconced in the grandest estate in Europe, Phillippe was playing host to the Salon de Circe, whose members were dedicated to the destruction of the family in whose estate Marie resided.

Outside the palace a tidal wave was fast approaching, and on a July afternoon an infuriated mob marched on Versailles; at the front of the procession were the wax heads—raided from Dr. Curtius' exhibit—of those who had proved hostile to the tri-color. The rabble arrested King Louis, Marie Antoinette, and the rest of the blue-bloods—along with Marie Grosholz. She was incarcerated in La Force Prison where she shared a cell with Josephine de Beauharnais, future consort of Napoleon.

Although Marie tried to reason with her captors—she had been merely an employee of the Bourbons and was the daughter of a housekeeper—her pleas fell on deaf ears. The architects of the Reign of Terror were not known for their powers of reason. She and Josephine had their heads shaved in preparation for their rendezvous with the guillotine. Dr. Curtius intervened on her behalf and the revolutionaries agreed; however, the price of her release was a Faustian bargain.

While Madame Defarge sat in the shadow of the guillotine knitting the names of its victims in her garment, Made Grosholz had a more gruesome task. In exchange for her freedom, Marie had to create death masks from the seemingly endless piles of guillotined heads. The grisly souvenirs were hailed as revolutionary victories and were paraded through the streets of Paris by the frenzied rabble. For a woman in her mid-twenties to sit with bloodied heads in her apron, many of which had belonged to those of whom she had lived for almost a decade, made for an agonizing, artistic endeavor.

Marie was one of the few who had befriended both the revolutionaries and the royals and lived to tell the tale, one which was to have many more twists. When the Reign of Terror ended, she married a much younger man, Francois Tussaud, with whom she had sons Joseph and Francois. Her husband squandered the inheritance Curtius had left upon his death, leaving her without means. Rather than succumb to a woe-is-me outlook, Marie's fiery spirit adhered to the *still I rise* spirit. At a time when the only independent businesswomen were those who sold their flesh, she decided to peddle another form of flesh, one made of wax.

Madame Tussaud left the France that had been the architect of her imprisonment, murder of her friends, and disappointing marriage. In 1804, having just turned forty, she took advantage of a lull in the Napoleonic War and crossed the Channel. She left with her prized wax heads, eldest son (age four,) and a steely determination to succeed. This was to be a daunting task, as she was setting sail to a country in which she had no friends and did not speak its language. She never saw her homeland or Francois again. Indeed, other than with her mother, Dr. Curtius and her sons (her younger one joined her at age twenty-one,) she formed no close personal attachments. After all she had witnessed, she felt more at ease with those of wax than those of flesh.

Madame Tussaud toured Britain and Ireland for thirty-three years in a travelling show, "Curtius' Cabinet of Curiosities." They consisted of the doomed royal family, Marat's death-mask as he had appeared when Charlotte Corday had stabbed him in his bath, and Napoleon, amongst dozens of others. On one occasion, her ship capsized in a storm and the decapitated, waxed heads floated on the waves. Marat had once again met a watery grave. It was this which served as an impetus for the itinerant show-woman to establish a museum that would permanently showcase her unique collection. In addition, a stationery venue would allow for the creation of elaborate backdrops. While Sir Arthur Conan Doyle chose Baker Street for his fictional detective, Marie chose the same road to house her wares. The public was thrilled with the opportunity to mingle with the mighty who had left an imprint on history. It proved so lucrative, P. T. Barnum made an unsuccessful bid. The Duke of Wellington often toured to enjoy the effigies of himself and Bonaparte. Marie's greatest artistry was when she made backdrops for her figures, and one of the most spectacular was of Queen Victoria's 1837 coronation. In Britain, as in France, the lowly-born woman walked amongst royalty.

Like the life of its founder, Madame Tussaud suffered tragedy as well as triumphs. In 1925, a fire raged through the building, and during the Blitz a bomb from the Luftwaffe destroyed 350 head molds. Safe from the devastation was the 1930 wax figure of Adolf Hitler; in 2008, it suffered decapitation when a German man—

shades of Madame Guillotine—attacked it.

Madame Tussaud was to become the British equivalent of
Hollywood's Wall of Fame; however, while the latter is comprised
of stars, hers houses anatomical likeness of startling verisimilitude.
Her one-of-a-kind exhibit was met with great acclaim, one that
eighteenth century women rarely achieved in the business world.
Along with displaying the newsmakers of the time, she included
death-heads from the guillotine, replete with an authentic blade.
In a nod to her beloved Uncle Phillippe, she recreated his Parisian
chamber of horrors. Although emotionally scarred by the ravages of
the French Revolution, the astute businesswoman knew how to milk
its horrors, thereby proving, unlike her figures, she was no dummy.

At age seventy-seven, Marie wrote her memoirs; a fantastical
life in which, while others were literally losing their heads, she
contrived to keep hers—making her the greatest star amongst
her gallery of guests. Yet, like all magicians, she kept her secrets
close. A master at fashioning wax to look like life, Madame
Tussaud was also able to fashion fiction to look like fact. Most of
her autobiography dealt with the famous people and events that
had made her live in interesting times. When it came to her own
story, Madame was more reticent. Except for her two sons, mother,
and adopted uncle, she had not formed any other significant
attachments. Regardless of what degree of artistic license she
took in her autobiography, it was a story that could have come
from the pen of Dickens. Indeed, the Victorian author wove her

into a thinly disguised character of Mrs. Jarley in his novel *The Old Curiosity Shop*. The poorly educated French girl survived the Reign of Terror to become the iconic figurehead of one of the most visited entertainment establishments in the world, with branches found everywhere from Bangkok to Berlin. In 2007, the Tussauds Group was acquired for one billion pounds by Merlin Entertainments, and remains the crown jewel in British tourism. Of the multitudes who pass through its doors, many do not realize the iconic establishment encompasses a history of a bloody revolution, gruesome death masks, and a nineteenth century indomitable woman.

In the entrance of her London museum, Marie had created a self-portrait of herself at age eighty-one in the act of taking tickets from customers. The exhibit is still on display—so real, one is tempted to inquire the price of admission. She is dressed head to toe in black crepe, with round glasses partially obscuring her eyes. Her waxen features bear no trace of a smile; she had witnessed too much.

On vigil at her deathbed were her two sons. Her last words to Joseph and Francois proved that her wisdom was not confined to the world of wax: "I divide my property equally between you, and implore you, above all things, never to quarrel." Taking their mother's words to heart, they continued to run her museum as equal partners. Their own sons continued the family business, and they moved the museum from Baker Street to its current location on Marylebone Road.

The contemporary emporium continues the tradition of enshrining the famous, but many of the exhibits are of the ilk the straitlaced businesswoman would not approve. Although she encouraged her guests to stand side by side with those of wax, she would take exception of the exhibit of President Clinton, whose impeccable suit always has its zipper down, compliments of overzealous fans. She would have been especially mortified of the seminude figure of Nicki Minaj, on whose wax body men have simulated sex.

The commonality between Marie Grosholz and her creations is they both achieved immortality; the difference is she was one never to melt under any flame. Madame Tussaud's larger than life existence was, like the classic novel, a tale of two cities, and echoed its opening line, "It was the best of times, it was the worst of times..."

CHAPTER 2:
IT IS WARM (1880)

If anyone were ever entitled to indulge in a pity party, it would have been the woman who fate had locked in a world of silence and darkness. Yet, instead of dwelling on her misery, she dedicated her life to the spreading of light. She remains a testament to what a possessor of courage can overcome.

Born in Tuscumbia, Alabama, a woman would have remained as unknown as her hometown had she not contracted a mysterious illness at nineteen months. Although she survived, it left her blind and deaf; unable to hear, she was also denied the power of speech. The toddler, who had just been learning to talk, behaved like a feral child. Her devastated parents grieved the world was lost to her. Unable to communicate, she grew up giving vent to uncontrollable rages: she locked her mother in a closet, overturned her baby sister's cradle. Relatives suggested the girl be sent to an institution. Although saddled with two younger children, this is something the Sullivans refused to countenance. In the nineteenth century, homes for the disabled were not geared for fostering; the unfortunate residents were viewed as useless feeders until death mercifully ended the nightmare.

Serendipity stepped in when Kate Keller read an article by Charles Dickens about Laura Bridgman, a deaf-blind girl he had met at the Perkins Institute for the Blind in Boston. At age two, scarlet fever had also rendered her blind and deaf; and she had also lost the sense of smell and touch. Through its teacher, Dr. Samuel Gridley Howe, the husband of the author of "The Battle Hymn of the Republic," Laura had made significant strides. Kate was also in contact with Alexander Graham Bell. By then, the invention of the telephone was well behind him, and he was working to teach the deaf to speak in an intelligible fashion. He had been inspired in this endeavor as both his mother and wife were unable to hear. When he met the six-year-old Helen, he took her on his lap and calmed her by letting her feel the vibrations of his pocket watch as it struck the hour. Locked in her isolated world, she did not respond. He advised her father to contact his son-in-law, the director of the Perkins Institute, for a teacher to come to Tuscumbia.

The woman selected for the daunting task was twenty-year-old Anne Sullivan. She was visually impaired and hailed from a far different background than her young charge. Helen's paternal grandmother was the second cousin of Robert E. Lee, and father Arthur had fought as a captain for the Confederacy, was a gentleman farmer, and a newspaper editor. The Kellers lived in a stately country home "Ivy Green" where they lavished love on their children. Anne had suffered bouts of blindness and had been raised in a poorhouse after the death of her mother and abandonment by her alcoholic, abusive father. Their meeting was to prove the defining moment of their lives, and was to bestow on Anne Sullivan the moniker "the miracle worker."

The new teacher, hired for the sum of twenty-five dollars a month, arrived in a household which the disabled child had rendered chaotic. Helen used cutlery as projectiles, pinched, grabbed food off dinner plates, and sent chairs tumbling when she did not get her way. Upon their first meeting, the child rummaged in the stranger's bag for candy, and when she found none, flew into a rage. Her parents, who walked on eggshells, were unable to impose any control. This was a situation Anne knew she had to change if she were to make headway, but Helen was not a willing participant. Her first act on meeting her teacher was to knock out one of her front teeth. Sullivan moved into a guest cottage with Helen in order to separate the child from a mother and father who could not bear to see their disabled daughter disciplined.

Anne tirelessly made Helen feel objects and then placed her fingers on the child's palm in the hope she would make the connection that the gestures represented words. This endeavor bore no results until a revelatory moment in 1887. Helen stood at a pump while her teacher poured water and immediately afterwards signed. Helen's epiphany was the remembered word "wa." She suddenly realized that everything has a name; the pump had become her version of the Tree of Knowledge. Ms. Keller later recalled of the magical moment, "I knew that w-a-t-e-r meant the wonderful cool thing that was flowing over my hand. That living word awakened my soul, gave it light, hope, joy, set it free. There were barriers still, it is true, but barriers that in time could be swept away." In the course of a single month, Helen was transformed from the family despot into a docile and affectionate child with an unquenchable thirst to learn the names of everything. The young girl then pointed to Anne, who spelled "teacher," and teacher she was called till the end.

News of her remarkable achievement spread, and Helen became a child celebrity in both the United States and Europe. At age eight, she visited President Cleveland at the White House, and in Boston met many of the luminaries of the period, such as Oliver Wendell Holmes. Journalists and photographers gathered in droves when she took trips to Niagara Falls and to the World's Fair in the company of Dr. Bell. People with five senses were in awe of the remarkable child who could accomplish so much with only three.

If Helen had been less far-reaching, she would have spent her life in Tuscumbia, eventually becoming the maiden aunt for the children of her brother Phillips and sister Mildred. However, as a teen, her quest for knowledge remained unabated, and she entered Radcliff (Harvard at the time did not admit women.) Her education was paid through the intervention of Mark Twain, who had introduced her to Standard Oil magnet Henry Huttleston Rogers. In college she distinguished herself as the only deaf-blind student in the school's history, as well as its only published author.

At age twenty-one, she wrote on her Braille Hammond typewriter
The Story of My Life, which she hoped would prove a beacon
for those struggling with their own demons; the autobiography
was translated into fifty languages. She graduated cum laude
with honors in German and English, an accomplishment made
possible by steely determination and Anne's selfless assistance.
What set Miss Keller apart was that no similarly afflicted person
had done more than acquire the simplest skills. Helen reminisced
of her college years, "I slip back many times. I fall, I stand still.
I run against the edge of hidden obstacles. I lose my temper and
find it again, and keep it better. I trudge on, I gain a little. I feel
encouraged. I get more eager and climb higher and begin to see
widening horizons."

Post-graduation, the two women toured the world, where
Helen served as a distinguished lecturer, advocating the rights
of the disabled. Although her high-pitched voice was not easily
understood, everywhere she went there was an outpouring of
praise. After her formal talks—interpreted sentence by sentence
by Miss Sullivan—Miss Keller answered questions, even when
they were inane: "Do you close your eyes when you go to sleep?"
to which she answered, "I never stayed awake to see." She took
great pride in her appearance and was always impeccably dressed.
Due to her protruding left eye, she was generally photographed
in profile. Both her eyes were replaced in adulthood with glass
replicas for both medical and cosmetic reasons. She went on to

pen thirteen other books as well as countless articles; her passport listed her occupation as "author." Winston Churchill called her "the greatest woman of our age." Mark Twain compared her to Napoleon and Shakespeare. The *Tom Sawyer* author described her as "quick and bright" and "almost certain to send back as good as she gets, and almost as certainly with an improvement added." She was no flash in the pan: Helen's hold on the public imagination continued unabated throughout her life. Gallup polls consistently showed her to be one of the world's most admired women, edging out such notables as Queen Elizabeth, Princess Grace, and Golda Meir. Despite her fame and acclaim, Miss Keller remained unaffected and believed to the end her optimism was justified: "I believe that all through these dark and silent years, God has been using my life for a purpose I do not know. But one day I shall understand and then I will be satisfied."

The world views Helen Keller as one of its guardian angels, but under the icon was a woman who longed for romance. In 1916, she fell in love with Peter Fagan, a committed socialist who had served as Helen's secretary when Anne had taken ill. Fearing the disapproval of both her teacher and mother, the couple planned an elopement. However, when a Boston reporter discovered a newspaper entry of the marriage license, his article on the romance alerted Kate Keller, who ordered Fagan out of the house and ended the love affair. This may have been because she believed there had to be an ulterior motive for a younger man to wed her deaf-blind daughter. Another reason was the prevailing belief that a wife's job was to be caregiver to her husband and child, and Kate assumed this was a role her daughter could not fulfill. Helen wrote of her loss, "The love which had come, unseen and unexpected, departed with tempest on his wings. A little island of joy surrounded by dark waters." Years later her enforced spinsterhood remained a painful wound, and she said that if she could see, "I would marry first of all."

Rather than dwell on what she had been cruelly cheated, Helen lived life to the fullest. In this way, she had no time to dwell on her misfortunes and steadfastly shunned pity. None was needed. She performed improbable feats, such as riding horseback, and became an example of unquenchable will. She stated, "My life has been happy because I have had wonderful friends and plenty of interesting work to do. I seldom think about my limitations, and they never make me sad. Perhaps there is just a touch of yearning at times, but it is vague, like a breeze among flowers. The wind passes, and the flowers are content."

What brought her the most satisfaction was her advocacy of social issues, even when they brought umbrage in its wake. She criticized fellow Southerner Margaret Mitchell's *Gone with the Wind* for overlooking the brutality of slavery and cheered the protestors for better conditions for workers. She was a suffragette and birth control advocate, a supporter of the NAACP and co-founder of the ACLU. In the 1950s, she made an enemy of Senator

Joseph McCarthy as an ardent advocate of the right to practice whatever ideology one chose.

Helen was an ardent opponent of fascism prior to World War II and worked with soldiers who had been blinded, her life a testament of hope despite disability. Her remarkable achievements flew in the face of Adolph Hitler's Aktion T4, a Nazi-run program of involuntary euthanasia for those afflicted with physical or mental handicaps. Her outspoken denunciation of the dictator was why his Minister of Propaganda, Joseph Goebbels, included Keller's works in his book-burnings, which *Time* termed a "bibliocaust."

One of Helen's darkest days came in 1936 when her beloved teacher passed away at their shared home in Forest Hills, Queens. After a half-century, she had to say goodbye to the woman whose hands had been her bridge to the world. The depth of her devotion was apparent with her tribute: "Teacher is free at least from pain and blindness. I pray for strength to endure the silent dark until she smiles upon me again." The many who loved Helen feared with her beloved teacher's loss she would fall apart, but Anne had taught her well—she determined to *still rise*.

Helen's prayer was answered, and she persevered after Anne's passing. She continued to lecture and travel, helped by her secretary Polly Thompson, touching the faces of kings, presidents, and world leaders, such as Winston Churchill and Golda Meir. In 1966, Lyndon B. Johnson presented her with the Presidential

Medal of Freedom, honoring her as a model of courage and determination. But most important to her was her campaign devoted to improving the lives of the handicapped.

Helen's life ended just before her eighty-eighth birthday in 1968 at her Connecticut home, Arcan Ridge. A service was held in her honor at the National Cathedral in Washington, DC, where her ashes were laid to rest next to her constant companion, Anne Sullivan. Her home state of Alabama honored their distinguished daughter by putting her likeness on their state quarter, the only circulating US coin to feature Braille. She is portrayed sitting on a chair, book in lap, with a ribbon emblazed with the words Spirit of Courage.

From a childhood that seemed destined to cage her forever in a sightless and soundless world, her indomitable dedication to the spirit of *still I rise* made her one of the world's most respected and revered of women. She remains an enduring symbol of triumph over crushing adversity. Perhaps her biography can be encapsulated by her first spoken sentence, "It is warm."

CHAPTER 3:
THE STEPPING STONE (1891)

When a bride pledged "for better or for worse, in sickness or in health," she never imagined how strongly she would be tested in honoring her vows. Her roller coaster marriage made her the most famous anonymous woman of her era, and though childless, she was the mother of thousands. Throughout her long life, she remained a paragon of selflessness, content to serve as a stepping stone.

Contrary to Andy Warhol's prediction that everyone has fifteen minutes of fame, most people are consigned to oblivion, their triumphs and tragedies turn to sand, washed away by the waves of time. Lois Burnham would have likely had a metronome existence had she not met the man who became both her lover and destroyer. She was the eldest of six raised on Clinton Street in Brooklyn Heights, the daughter of a respected physician. The family were staunch believers in the Swedenborgian faith that counted among its followers Hellen Keller and Robert Frost. During the year the children attended the Quaker's Friends School and in the summers, they vacationed in Vermont, where Dr. Burnham catered to his wealthy New York patients. The word Lois used in reference to her childhood was "idyllic."

When one wakes up, it is with the expectation it will be an ordinary day, but sometimes an event occurs which changes the trajectory of life. While summering in Vermont, a local teen knocked on her door, trying to sell kerosene lamps that were slung across his shoulder on a pole. She recognized Bill Wilson as her brother Rogers' friend, but was not interested in either boy or product. Wilson, who had a chip on his shoulder, felt the rich, city girl looked at him with condescension. Later on, when he saw her sailing on Emerald Lake, he decided it was payback time. He refurbished his grandfather's old rowboat and fastened it with a makeshift sail made from a bedsheet. A gust of wind capsized his craft, and Bill was flung into the lake, wrapped in the sheet, a watery mummy. Lois rescued him—the beginning of a life-long pattern.

Although the Burnhams would have preferred a more suitable match for their college educated daughter—such as a male descendent of Abraham Lincoln who lived next door—they accepted the couple's engagement. Lois proudly wore her twenty-five dollar small, amethyst ring. They wanted to marry when Bill was financially stable; however, with his imminent departure for Europe to serve in World War I, they wed in the Swedenborg Church, followed by a reception in Clinton Street. After his departure, Lois was devastated when she miscarried. She asked her superiors at her job in the YMCA to ship her overseas in the hope of being stationed near her husband and to be part of the war effort. She was turned down on the basis of her faith that they did not consider Christian.

In Brooklyn, Lois grappled with the pain of losing her baby and missing her husband; in England, Bill grappled with his own demons. To dull his insecurities and social inadequacy, he turned to the bottle. It was an instant love affair; Wilson claimed he had found "the elixir of life." Because of his addictive personality, no matter how much alcohol he consumed, it never slayed his thirst.

While thousands of soldiers returned shell-shocked from the horror of trench-warfare, Bill returned with the burden of alcoholism. Lois, unfamiliar with disease, did not understand the depth of his illness, and what a devastating toll it would take.

Through her friend's husband, Bill obtained a job on Wall Street. However, he found it soul-sucking, and felt that contributed to his ever escalating inebriation. To add to the mix of misery, Lois suffered another miscarriage that entailed a hysterectomy. Her husband arrived at the hospital, so lost in his own grief he could not help with hers. The Wilsons turned to adoption, but because of Bill's alcoholism, every agency turned them down. No one would have cast aspersions had Lois walked away; the message in the bottle was clear. However, she could have given Tammy Wynette a run for her money in the stand-by-your-man department.

To save themselves, Bill came up with the plan to travel the country on a Harley to study lucrative companies, and send back telegrams to his former bosses. When Wall Street gave his first report a thumbs up, he felt it was a call for a celebration. He left Lois on the side of a country road on their broken-down motorcycle while he walked to the nearest town to get hammered. While most wives would have attempted to run over his retreating figure with the Harley, Lois patiently awaited his return. She believed if she could just love him enough, Bill would be saved. Penniless and in despair, they moved into her parents' home on Clinton Street.

Lois worked as a salesclerk in Macy's, and when she returned home Bill pilfered from her purse; when she hid her money, he panhandled. In despair, one rainy night she almost succumbed to adultery, but her faith and her love for her husband stopped her from succumbing. Filled with self-loathing, when she entered the house it was to the sound of a lamp crashing as Bill used it to help him stand. Lois—also at a breaking point—screamed, "You don't even have the decency to die!"

During these years on Kenny Rodger's "train bound for nowhere," there were endless arguments followed by desperate reconciliations where Bill promised to stop drinking. He even wrote one of his pledges in the family bible. Lois found her unanswered prayers "turning to ashes in my mouth." Her life had become the antithesis of idyllic.

After seventeen torturous years, Bill had his epiphany: only a drunk could help another drunk. Armed with the knowledge, he conceived the principles for Alcoholic Anonymous. It should have been the time when Lois had the better rather than the worse, the health rather than the sickness, portion of her wedding vows. But it was never smooth sailing as the wife of Bill Wilson.

The Clinton house Lois had once envisioned filled with children overflowed with the local Bowery drunks who she fed while Bill initiated meetings: "My name is Bill W. and I'm an alcoholic." Ironically, while her husband found his calling, Lois began to flounder. She was devastated she had not been the instrument of her husband's salvation, and the purpose that had sustained her for decades—saving her husband—was now out of her hands. She recalled, "He was always with his A.A. cronies. I guess I was jealous and resentful that these strangers had done for him what I could not do." The turning point came when she threw her shoe at him as hard as she could. Although this was a case of quid pro quo—Bill had once hurled a sewing machine at her—she was so ashamed she walked around the block several times. It was then she realized she needed some therapy herself. Rather than succumb to bitterness, as always, she determined *to still rise*. It was then she had her own revelation—one that was to save herself, along with thousands of strangers. She realized for every man in her smoke-filled home, there was a woman waiting outside in her car, with her own story, her own struggle with an alcoholic husband. She invited them inside, and Al-Anon was born. It was set up under the same principle as her husband's, with its same conformity to anonymity, and to her group she was known as Lois W. And to those who were familiar with her life, she was also a member of SA—Saints Anonymous. Just as Rapunzel wove straw into gold, Lois used her experience to form a group with universal healing power.

Fired with enthusiasm for their respective causes, Bill and Lois started to rebuild their lives and marriage until they were felled with a terrible blow. Dr. Burnham had left the house on Clinton Street to his daughter, but in 1939 they could no longer make payments. In desperation, Lois sold her engagement ring and family heirlooms, but it did not ward off foreclosure. For the following two years, they couch-surfed, and the life of a nomad was especially hard for Lois, who ironically loved interior decorating and possessed a nesting spirit.

In 1941, a permanent home came when a fan of AA offered her sprawling home in Bedford Hills to the Wilson's at a price far below market value. It had taken twenty-three years, but at last Lois had her own home and to share it with her now sober spouse. Perched on a hill, the property could only be accessed from the driveway by a series of stone steps that led to its double entendre name: Stepping Stones.

A reversal of their always shaky finances occurred when Bill published *The Big Book*, one of the best-selling of all time, his 12-step principle escape from purgatory. With its release, it knocked F. Scott Fitzgerald from his perch as the most prolific, alcoholic writer.

During the first half of their marriage, the couple had been known as the drunk and his long-suffering spouse; however, post *The Big Book*, they were fêted as the royal couple of recovery. Eventually the world came to recognize Bill Wilson as the great man his wife always knew him to be. Aldous Huxley proclaimed him "the greatest social architect of our time," and he was chosen as *Time*'s top 100 heroes of the twentieth century. True to the feminist slogan, behind the great man was a great woman, though she was obscured by his shadow. Although a lifelong addict, he never became addicted to fame, and refused to have his portrait on the cover of *LIFE Magazine*, even with the offer to photograph him from the back. Part of his modesty came from Lois, who, when his head began to swell, teased, "Sweetheart, your halo's on crooked." In tribute to her unflagging devotion, on their 1954 wedding anniversary he wrote on a card, "Come any peril, we know that we are safe in each other's arms because we are in God's."

It would have been a nod to poetic justice had Bill and Lois W. spent their twilight years relaxing in their beautiful retreat, secure in their satisfaction they had weathered the storm and been instrumental for thousands doing the same. But it was never easy to navigate the rocky road as the wife of Bill Wilson.

Although he had overcome his addiction to alcohol, he became addicted to sex, and he took to chasing skirts as fervently as he had once chased bottles. At AA meetings, after talking about his 12 steps, his 13th was hitting on recovering young women. And the older he got, the younger they became. These flings crossed the threshold from physical to emotional adultery when he began an affair with actress Helen Wynn that lasted fifteen years. Fortunately for him, bottles had been banned from Stepping Stones, or Lois would have smashed one over his head. In his will, Wilson bequeathed 10 percent of royalties from his book to his mistress.

In addition to slipping into non-marital sheets, other crosses Lois had to bear were Bill's experimentation with LSD and the occult. But she took to heart the advice of the gambler: she knew what she wanted to keep and it was the man she had met through kerosene lamps. Upon his retirement from head of the powerful organization he had birthed into existence, he wrote, "Clearly my job henceforth was to Let Go and Let God. Alcoholics Anonymous was safe—even from me." But Bill Wilson was not safe from himself.

In his final years he began his final addiction, this time to nicotine. Lois now had to ferret out his secret stash of smokes, just as she had once done with his bottles. Although suffering from emphysema, he alternated between inhaling from his oxygen tank and inhaling from his cigarettes. When Bill passed away, many

feared Lois would soon follow, but, as always, she soldiered on, devoting her life to Al-Anon.

At age ninety-seven, Lois passed away and was laid to rest beside her husband in a Vermont cemetery. Her *Los Angeles Times* obituary stated that she "left no immediate survivors." In a sense, through Al-Anon, she had left thousands. In her will she bequeathed her hilltop home to her foundation in the hope that it would educate and inspire future generations. Lois' at-long- last home is now listed on the National Register of Historic Places and is open to tours. Every June, hundreds of AA members undertake the pilgrimage where the faithful pay tribute. The site is a shrine to memorabilia: there is the letter to Mr. Wilson from Carl Jung and a photograph of Richard M. Nixon receiving the millionth copy of *The Big Book*. With its mahogany antiques, including the desk on which Bill wrote his great work, it seems as if the Wilsons had just stepped out. In the master bedroom, a can of Perma Soft hairspray still rests on the vanity, along with a single bobby pin. In another area, a box of Wash 'n Dri and a can of lighter fuel sits alongside books.

Alcoholic Anonymous is the Holy Grail to millions. The name on its spine is Bill Wilson, and yet it would not have been written without Lois, his ever present stepping stone.

CHAPTER 4:
STEEL GARDENIA (1895)

The Civil Rights timeline has witnessed significant Afrcan-American firsts, each a step closer to Dr. King's "We shall overcome." In sports, Althea Gibson competed at Wimbledon in 1951; in music, Marion Anderson sang at the Metropolitan in 1955; in literature, Toni Morrison received the Nobel Prize in 1993. Another woman who succeeded in the proverbial against-all-odds arena was a Southern "belle" whose achievements made for a quilt of the bitter, of the sweet.

After winning the 2010 Oscar for Best Supporting Actress for *Precious*, Mo'nique stated she was wearing a royal blue dress, along with gardenias in her hair, because Hattie McDaniel had dressed in that fashion seventy years earlier when she had become the first African American to receive an Academy Award. The event was met with shock, as everyone felt her *Gone with the Wind* co-star Olivia de Havilland was a shoe-in. Mo'nique thanked her predecessor "for enduring all that she had to, so that I would not have to." Mo'nique's praise was unequivocal; however, this had not been the case when Hattie had become a card-carrying member of the be-careful-of-what-you-wish-for club.

Hattie McDaniel, who created a tempest in a celluloid teacup, was the youngest of thirteen, born to former slaves in 1895 in Wichita, Kansas. Her father, Henry, had fought for the Union in the Civil War and later became a Baptist minister who moonlighted as a banjo player in minstrel shows. Her mother, Susan, was a gospel singer. While Forest Gump spent every spare moment of his childhood running, Hattie spent hers singing, to such an extent Susan sometimes bribed her with spare change to buy a moment of silence.

In 1901, the family moved to Colorado, where she was one of only two black children in her elementary school; she ended her education in her early teens to join her father's troupe. It seemed a more palatable path than domestic work, the most likely career path for blacks in the early twentieth century. A natural entertainer, she became popular in the African American theater scene in Denver, and her gift of pantomime led to her reputation as the black Sophie Tucker. Acclaim likewise followed for her sexually suggestive renditions of the blues, many of which she penned. However, even after a nationwide tour of vaudeville houses, McDaniel was often forced to supplement her income with work as a domestic. By age twenty, she was also a widow. Her marriage abruptly ended in 1922 when her husband of three months, George Langford, was reportedly killed by gunfire. The same year her father died and, devastated by the back-to-back losses, she took solace in performing. In 1925, she appeared on Denver's radio station that garnered her the distinction of being the first African American woman to perform in this medium.

In 1929 her booking organization went bankrupt as a result of the Great Depression, and Hattie found herself stranded in Chicago with no job and meager savings. On a tip from a friend, she departed for Milwaukee and obtained a position at Sam Pick's Club Madrid as a bathroom attendant. The club engaged only white performers but, an irrepressible singer, she belted out tunes from the restroom, a unique venue for showcasing her talents. Patrons took notice of her voice and good nature, which led the owner to allow her onstage. After her rendition of "St. Lois Blues," she became a wildly popular attraction. She remained in the club for a year until her siblings Stan and Etta invited her to join them in Los Angeles. Like other Hollywood hopefuls, in Tinseltown she had dreams of becoming what twinkled in the firmament, but finding her way in Hollywood was not easy. Black actors' choices consisted of: African savage, singing slave, or obsequious employee. Stan was able to throw her a life-preserver, and she found work in the radio show "The Optimistic Do-Nuts." She earned the nickname Hi-Hat Hattie after showing up in evening attire for her initial broadcast.

Hattie's long-dreamed of screen debut occurred in 1931 when she played a bit part as a maid, for which she was able to draw on firsthand experience. Her breakthrough was as Marlene Dietrich's domestic in *Blonde Venus*, and three years later as Mom Beck in *The Little Colonel* that starred Shirley Temple and Lionel Barrymore. With her perfect comic timing, she appeared alongside the biggest stars of the silver screen—Clark Gable, Jean Harlow, Henry Fonda. She was so successful that MGM did not allow her to play anything other than as a domestic or to lose an ounce, though she tipped the scale at three hundred pounds. Mammy had to be fat. Firmly typecast as the woman with the apron, she was one of the logical candidates to secure the coveted role of Mammy in David O. Selnick's 1939 production, *Gone with the Wind*. The competition for the part was as fierce among black hopefuls as the part of Miss Scarlett was for whites. First Lady Eleanor Roosevelt had recommended her own maid for the part; however, Hattie had her own patron—the King of Hollywood, Clark Gable. She nailed the audition when she appeared in a plantation maid uniform and so impressed Selznick he called off other tryouts with the words, "Save your overhead boys. We can start shooting tomorrow." What further helped was she fit the stereotypical perception of the Southern domestic as she was the doppelganger of Aunt Jemima, which proliferated on Quaker Oats boxes. During the epic film, clad in trademark apron and bandanna, she delivered lines in antebellum lingo: "What gentlemen says and what they thinks is two different things," "I ain't noticed Mr. Ashley askin' for to marry you." Although cast as the servant, she refused to be subservient. She told Selznick she would not utter a racial epithet or employ the caricature phrase "de Lawd."

The premiere of *Gone with the Wind* at the Loew's Grand Theater was the apogee celebration of 1939, and the night of its premier Atlanta resurrected its plantation past: the women attended in hoop skirts, the men in breeches, and Confederate flags flapped in the Southern breeze. However, absent from the revels were the black performers, as Jim Crow held sway. Clark Gable threatened to boycott the gala unless Hattie was permitted to attend; however, he relented under her insistence he not create a scene. A second salve was a telegram from Margaret Mitchell, the celebrated author of *Gone with the Wind*, who said of Hattie's absence from the premier's festivities, "I wish you could have heard the cheers when the Mayor of Atlanta called for a hand for our Hattie McDaniel."

If McDaniel's exclusion from opening night was not enough, she was sharply criticized by blacks who viewed the epic film as a valentine to the slave-owning South and a poison-pen letter to the anti-slavery North. Walter White, head of the National Association for the Advancement of Colored People, singled her out for reproach, arguing she was an Aunt Tom. She lashed back by asking, "What do you expect me to play? Rhett Butler's wife?" However, her most memorable comeback: "I'd rather play a maid and make $700 a week than be a maid and make $7.00." One can only wonder how she would have reacted to the fact that seventy-two years later, Octavia Spencer won an Academy Award for Best Supporting Actress for her role in *The Help*—as a maid. On top of the back-to-back backlash from whites and blacks, Hattie had to deal with the demise of her second marriage to Howard Hickman that both began and ended in 1938.

In 1940, *Gone with the Wind* garnered ten Academy Awards; predictably Best Actress went to Vivien Leigh; unpredictably, Best Supporting Actress went to Hattie McDaniel, the first time an African American had been honored and an event which was not to occur for another fifty years when Whoopi Goldberg received the tribute for *Ghosts*. Although the more liberal North allowed her to attend the Hollywood gala at the Ambassador Hotel and personally receive her award, she and her African American escort were seated at a segregated table. In her sixty-seven second emotional acceptance speech, she stated she "hoped to be a credit to her race." Gossip columnist Louella Parsons for once put down her poisoned pen:

If you had seen her face when she walked up to the platform and took the gold trophy, you would have had the choke in your voice that all of us had when Hattie, hair trimmed with gardenias, face alight, and dressed up to the queen's taste, accepted the honor in one of the finest speeches ever given on the Academy floor.

Hattie, overcome with emotion, returned to her seat by the kitchen to thunderous applause.

After *Gone with the Wind*, Hattie suffered a reversal of fortune, partially due to the demise of stereotypical roles. With the advent of World War II, Hollywood came under pressure to portray blacks in a more positive light to encourage their patriotism. As a result, a new black star emerged, Lena Horne, who was everything Hattie McDaniel was not: young, sexy, and not a maid (stipulated in her contract). Turning once more to love to fill the gaping career hole, she married third husband, Lloyd Crawford, in 1941. She was ecstatic when she confided to gossip columnist Hedda Hopper she was expecting a long-awaited baby. With nesting instinct in full gear and wealth from acting, Hattie purchased her dream house in a wealthy enclave in Los Angeles. The white, two-story estate boasted seventeen rooms, decorated in a Chinese theme. She celebrated the purchase with a huge party, where one of the guests was Clark Gable. However, the joy of first-time home ownership came with an expiration date. Her neighbors launched a campaign to evict her on the basis of a white-only ordinance. This time she decided to make a scene. It resulted in a Supreme Court decision that eliminated "restrictive covenants" which had kept African Americans from residing in certain areas. Her joy at the victory was quashed when Hattie discovered the pregnancy was a hysterical one. The truth threw her into a tsunami of depression. On top of that, her marriage ended in 1945, and Hattie cited one reason was her husband had threatened to kill her. Her fourth and final walk to the altar was with Larry Williams, in Yuma, Arizona, that was only of a few months duration.

Hamlet had said when sorrows come they come not in single spies but in battalions, and Hattie had weathered hers: white and black slings, aborted marriages, hysterical pregnancy, curtailed career. However, *like dust she rose.* She returned to radio, a medium which knew no color, the one where she had reigned as Hi-Hat Hattie. However, after taping several episodes of *The Beulah Show*, she met the one foe she was not able to overcome. By 1952, she was too ill from breast cancer to work, and died in the hospital situated on the grounds of the Motion Picture House in Woodland Hills. At the church service she received a variation of her Academy ovation when thousands of mourners turned out to celebrate her life and its singular achievement of breaking the color barrier in film.

Through her bequest, her Oscar was given to the predominantly black Howard University for their drama department in remembrance of having honored her with a luncheon after her historic win. It was a small plaque rather than the current gold-plated statue. Mysteriously, it vanished during the 1960s racial unrest, and to this date its whereabouts remains unknown. One theory claims it was tossed by rioting students into the Potomac in protest against racist stereotyping.

Even in death Ms. McDaniel could not escape the long shadow cast by Jim Crow. In her will she had stated, "I desire a white casket and a white shroud; white gardenias in my hair and in my hands, together with a white gardenia blanket and a pillow of red roses. I also wish to be buried in the Hollywood Cemetery." She had always loved being amongst the stars, and the cemetery held the remains of Rudolph Valentino, Douglas Fairbanks, and other silver screen immortals. Though the flowers, clothing, and casket were fulfilled, her desired final resting place did not come to pass because of its segregationist policy.

Posthumously, the Old South did become a civilization gone with the wind. In 1999, the new owner of the cemetery offered to have Hattie's remains transferred, though her family declined the offer. Instead she was honored on its grounds with a monument. A further tribute was two stars on Hollywood's Walk of Fame and her image on a 2006 postage stamp. The latter was fitting, as she had left her stamp on American history. Hattie McDaniel had proved not just a credit to her race, but to the human race, truly a steel gardenia.

CHAPTER 5:
"WHERE YOUR TREASURE IS..." (1903)

I n his final days, Frederick Chopin, the supreme poet of the piano, requested his body be interred in his adopted city of Paris while his heart be laid to rest in his native Poland. His organ resides in Warsaw in the Holy Cross Church. Another posthumous act surrounding the composer is he saved a woman's life, 165 years after his own passing.

Alice—nicknamed Gigi—was born in Prague in what was then Austria-Hungary, the city that served as a cultural and intellectual melting pot of Germans, Czechs, and Jews. She was the fourth of five children, including twin sister Marianne (Mizzi), of Friedrich and Sophie Herz. The German Jewish family had enjoyed a comfortable life through her father's factory that supplied the Hapsburg Empire with precision scales, but lost most of their wealth in the First World War. Faced with economic deprivation, young Alice said, "And so we realized, as little children, what is war." Her diminutive height—she was five feet—was a cause of parental concern, and for a while Friedrich paid for her to be stretched in an orthopedic machine. It had no effect—other than to cause pain.

Although money was in short supply, they had something they valued more than materialism: an appreciation for the arts. Sophie had been a childhood friend of the conductor Gustav Mahler and socialized with poet Rainer Maria Rilke. Through the eldest sister Irma's husband, Felix Weltsch, they were introduced to a reclusive young man who the children called Uncle Franz, author Franz Kafka. The writer once attended their family's Passover Seder and lent his voice to "Dayenu." Sometimes he took Alice and Marianne into the woods and entertained them with make believe. Alice recalled, "Stories which I've forgot, but I remember the atmosphere. It made a deep impression." One can imagine. She reminisced about the literary giant that he had "great big eyes" and was "a slightly strange man." He also once made a comment that she did not understand until much later: "In this world to bring up children—in this world?"

Alice's magical moment from childhood was when she first sat in front of the piano at age five. Her initial lessons were from Irma, and she played duets with her violinist brother. Her parents, recognizing she was a child prodigy, arranged lessons with Vaclav Stephan, who had studied in Paris with Marguerite Long. For three years she was under the tutelage of Conrad Ansorge, who had been a student of Liszt, a living link she would mention with pleasure almost a century later. "Liszt got a kiss from Beethoven, Ansorge got a kiss from Liszt and I got a kiss from Ansorge!" She also admitted of the latter, "as a pianist, extraordinary, as a teacher, not so good." This was because he would often absent himself and come back smelling of alcohol, so lessons were arranged first thing in the morning to catch him when sober. Her final instructor was Arthur Schnabel, who told her—after accepting a large fee—her prowess was of a standard that he could not improve. Such was her talent; Alice entered the German Academy of Music and Drama in Prague, headed by Alexander von Zemlinsky, a former pupil of Brahms. Her formal concert debut came at age sixteen—the youngest person to have been so honored—when she performed Chopin's Concerto in E minor with the Czech Philharmonic to a sold-out hall, eliciting rave reviews. She continued to perform regularly in Prague and also built up a solid roster of private students. Max Brod, Kafka's publisher, sang her praise. By her late teens, she was performing in concerts throughout Europe.

While music was Alice's first love, another arrived in 1931 when she met Leopold Sommer, an amateur violinist, who she married a fortnight later. She said that she was bowled over by his compendious knowledge of art and music. At the height of her career, married with son Stephan, her world of privilege began to crumble. Everything changed when Hitler, casually tearing up the Munich Accord of a year earlier, marched his troops into Prague. Alice was in Wenceslas Square on March 13, 1939, watching the invasion, when an open-topped vehicle came past bearing Adolf Hitler, his right arm lifted in the Nazi salute. The anti-Semitic edicts began: Jews were forbidden to perform in public, own telephones, or to purchase sugar, tobacco, or textiles. The Sommer's neighbor offered to buy these forbidden goods for the family—at double the price. In addition, their movement about the city was restricted, and they were compelled to wear the Star of David. Failure to comply with the latter was to summon execution. Alice was devastated at the hatred, especially as from a young age, she had looked up to Germany, the land of Goethe, Schiller, Bach, and Beethoven. Her sisters and their husbands had bought visas for Palestine and left just prior to the takeover. Alice had decided against immigration as her widowed mother was too frail to travel. The Sommers were allowed to remain in their apartment, Nazi neighbors on every side.

Even worse than the deprivations and the sanctions were the deportations for "resettlement," where people headed east into oblivion. The SS required Leopold to work for the Jewish Community Organization, where he was given the task of drawing up the names for removal from Czechoslovakia. Because of his mother-in-law's advanced age, he was eventually required to add the name of Sophie Herz. It was after Alice escorted her sickly, seventy-two-year-old mother—permitted only to bring a small rucksack—to the deportation center that she was at "the lowest point of my life." Of her mother's fate she said, "Till now I do not know where she was, till now I do not know where she died, nothing." She was on the brink of a breakdown when an inner voice urged her to learn Chopin's Etudes, the set of twenty-seven solo pieces that express the ultimate sorrow and raptures of human existence and are some of the most technically demanding and emotionally impassioned works in piano repertory. The Etudes provided a consuming distraction at the loss of her adored mother and the hovering web of doom that hung over the city's remaining Jews. She said, "They are very difficult. I thought if I learned to play them, they would save my life." And so they did.

In 1943, the inevitable came to pass, and Leopold, Alice, and five-year-old Stephan received their deportation notice. Leopold comforted his wife, telling her from his position in the Jewish council he had heard they staged concerts at what the Czechs called Terezin, the Germans called Theresienstadt. She replied, "How bad can it be if we can make music?" Of that horrific time Alice recalled, "The evening before this we were sitting in our flat. I put off the light because I wanted my child to sleep for the last time in his bed. Now came my Czech friends: they came and they took the remaining pictures, carpets, even furniture. They didn't say anything: we were dead for them, I believe. And at the last moment the Nazi came—his name was Hermann—with his wife. They brought biscuits and he said, 'Mrs. Sommer, I hope you come back with your family. I don't know what to say to you. I enjoyed your playing—such wonderful things, I thank you.' The Nazi was the most human of all."

Terezin, northwest of Prague, was an eighteenth century garrison town converted into a Jewish ghetto, used as a front for what was in reality Hitler's ante-chamber for the death camps. It was touted as a "show camp"—"The Fuhrer's gift to the Jews"— and was advertised as a place where Jews might find a welcome haven. Indeed, a few deluded souls had applied for admission, paying extra for a room with a view. It was used as a propaganda tool for Nazi officials seeking to demonstrate to the Red Cross that European Jewry was not, as rumor had it, mistreated. It had a library, an art studio, and lecture hall—all of which could be used after performing back-breaking labor.

The Sommers arrived in Terezin and found a city of disease, death, and starvation. Upon arrival, she was separated from Leopold, and she and Stephan were herded with one hundred other mothers and children into a freezing room with filthy mattresses spread on the floor. Alice recalled, "We didn't eat. In the morning we had a black water named coffee, at lunchtime a white water called soup, in the evening a black water called coffee, so my son didn't grow a millimeter..." The following year, Leopold was forced onto a train; just before departure, he made Alice promise never to volunteer for anything. The advice saved her life: a little later the authorities asked if the ghetto wives wanted to rejoin their husbands, and they climbed into the cattle cars that took them to their deaths. Alice remembered her promise, and she and Stephan remained behind; at the end of the war, he was one of only 123 children to survive, of the 15,000 who had passed through Terezin. Leopold perished in Dachau, probably from typhus, a few weeks before liberation. A fellow prisoner later brought Alice her husband's battered camp spoon—his only remaining physical memento.

After Leopold's departure Alice, despite the horror, found the strength to *still rise*. She had to remain strong for Stephan. Music also helped her, both spiritually and literally. Throughout her two years in Terezin, through the hunger and cold and death all around her, through the loss of mother and husband, Alice was sustained by a Polish man who had died long before—Frederick Chopin. It was that composer, Alice averred, who let her and Stephan survive. She performed at one hundred concerts, playing from memory. What moved her audiences the most were the Etudes.

Terezin had an orchestra, drawn from the ranks of Czechoslovakia's foremost figures in the performing arts, whose members literally played for time before audiences of prisoners and their Nazi guards. Mrs. Herz-Sommer, who performed on the camp's broken, out of tune piano, was one of its most revered members. Even though many of the concerts were charades for the Red Cross, she said the healing power of music was no less real. "These concerts, the people are sitting there—old people, desolated and ill—and they came to the concerts, and this music was for them our food. Through making music, we were kept alive." One night, after a year's internment, she was stopped by a Nazi officer who told her, "Don't be afraid. I only want to thank you for your concerts. They have meant much to me. One more thing.

You and your little son will not be on any deportations lists. You will stay in Theresienstadt until the war ends."

After their Russian liberators arrived, Alice and Stephan returned to their former city. "When I came back home it was very, very painful because nobody else came back. Then I realized what Hitler had done," she stated. A midnight concert she gave on Czech radio was picked up on short-wave in Jerusalem that alerted her family to the fact she was still alive. In 1949, with postwar anti-Semitism still swirling around Prague and with the Communists tightening their grip, Alice and Stephan joined her family in the new nation of Israel. She became a member of the teaching staff at the Jerusalem Conservatory, learnt Hebrew, and performed to audiences that included Golda Meir and Leonard Bernstein. For almost forty years she enjoyed "the best period in my life...I was happy." Stephan took the name Raphael, and proved himself an exceptionally talented cellist. It was his appointment to a teaching post at the royal Northern College of Music in England that prompted Alice to move to Britain in 1975. There she obtained a flat in London's Belsize Park, in apartment number 6. Her resilience was tested again in 2001 when Raphael, on a concert tour of Israel, collapsed with a ruptured aorta and died on the operating table. She found solace in her two grandsons, David and Ariel.

Apartment number 6 was dominated by lovely paintings, her Steinway piano; it also included a battered silver spoon. Alice

ing based on religion. When thugs attacked

e defaced her card that allowed her to sit in

or the infraction, she was suspended for three

ement, she became a member of the Socialist

yslaw Sendler, and obtained a position as a

e was irrevocably altered in 1939 when the

into Poland. Waves of bombers, tanks, and

forced Poland to her knees, and the first

he Occupation was to force the Jews to wear

ar of David and to deprive them of basic

, the German Governor Ludwig Fischer

hetto, into which the country's Jews were

a, roughly the size of Central Park, was

t high walls, topped with broken glass.

,000 unfortunate souls, and starvation,

led the streets while corpses lay on the

newspaper, makeshift shrouds. Sendler

he Ghetto, it was pure hell beyond

in, Irena decided to "sit" with the Jews. She

orkers gathered in Irena's second floor flat.

nd glasses of cordial, they decided it was

war against Goliath. All they needed was a

ed when typhus ravaged the Ghetto.

k spreading to the Aryan sector, the

medical groups to enter the arena of

---

faithfully practiced, and after her advanced age had immobilized one finger on each hand, she reworked her technique so she could play with eight.

In her later years, Alice received acclaim for being the oldest Holocaust survivor, and due to her remarkable life, she became a beacon to journalists. But though her hands were failing, her musical acumen remained sharp. On her one hundred-and-tenth birthday, the *New Yorker*'s music critic, Alex Ross, called on her. Because Mrs. Herz-Sommer could find journalists wearying, he presented himself as a musician. When she asked Ross to play something, he gamely made his way through some Schubert before Alice stopped him, "Now, tell me your *real* profession."

In 1879, Chopin's heart was interred in Holy Cross behind a memorial slab that bore a citation from the Book of Matthew—and one that could serve as Alice Hertz-Somner's epitaph, "Where your treasure is, there your heart will be also."

T

"Keynn
the
plea was for the
Poland's Jews.
of those who fo
diminutive wo

A proverb—
in interesting
as a curse—to
the only child
The Roman (
Warsaw, in t
of morality t
who told he
drowning y
you can swi
treated pat

Irena st

had segregated seat
her Jewish friend, s
the Aryan section. F
years. After reinsta
Party, married Miec
social worker. Her li
Nazis goose-stepped
Wehrmacht divisions
order of business of t
armbands with the S
human rights. In 194
created the Warsaw (
concentrated. The are
surrounded by ten-fo
It overflowed with 45
disease, and despair r
sidewalks covered wit
said, "If you had seen
description." Once aga
and her fellow social w
In-between cigarettes
time for David to wage
slingshot, and it appea

Fearful of the outbre
Germans allowed Polis

faithfully practiced, and after her advanced age had immobilized one finger on each hand, she reworked her technique so she could play with eight.

In her later years, Alice received acclaim for being the oldest Holocaust survivor, and due to her remarkable life, she became a beacon to journalists. But though her hands were failing, her musical acumen remained sharp. On her one hundred-and-tenth birthday, the *New Yorker*'s music critic, Alex Ross, called on her. Because Mrs. Herz-Sommer could find journalists wearying, he presented himself as a musician. When she asked Ross to play something, he gamely made his way through some Schubert before Alice stopped him, "Now, tell me your *real* profession."

In 1879, Chopin's heart was interred in Holy Cross behind a memorial slab that bore a citation from the Book of Matthew—and one that could serve as Alice Hertz-Somner's epitaph, "Where your treasure is, there your heart will be also."

CHAPTER 6:
THE BLACK SKY (1910)

"**K**eynmol fargesn!" "Never forget!" was the rallying cry of the Warsaw Ghetto. The doomed Resistance fighters' plea was for the world to remember the systematic slaughter of Poland's Jews. Yet history should also never forget the bravery of those who fought the forces of darkness. One of these was a diminutive woman who cast a giant light.

A proverb—purportedly of Chinese origin—states, "May you live in interesting times." Although sounding like a blessing, it is meant as a curse—to live in a time of turmoil. This was all too true of Irena, the only child of Dr. Stanislaw Krzyanowski and his wife Janina. The Roman Catholic family lived in Otwock, a town not far from Warsaw, in the midst of a Jewish community. The strong sense of morality that was to define her life was instilled by her father who told her when she was seven years old, "If you see someone drowning you should jump into the water to save them, whether you can swim or not." Dr. Krzyanowski was the only physician who treated patients with typhus, a disease to which he succumbed.

Irena studied Polish literature at the University of Warsaw that

had segregated seating based on religion. When thugs attacked
her Jewish friend, she defaced her card that allowed her to sit in
the Aryan section. For the infraction, she was suspended for three
years. After reinstatement, she became a member of the Socialist
Party, married Mieczyslaw Sendler, and obtained a position as a
social worker. Her life was irrevocably altered in 1939 when the
Nazis goose-stepped into Poland. Waves of bombers, tanks, and
Wehrmacht divisions forced Poland to her knees, and the first
order of business of the Occupation was to force the Jews to wear
armbands with the Star of David and to deprive them of basic
human rights. In 1940, the German Governor Ludwig Fischer
created the Warsaw Ghetto, into which the country's Jews were
concentrated. The area, roughly the size of Central Park, was
surrounded by ten-foot high walls, topped with broken glass.
It overflowed with 450,000 unfortunate souls, and starvation,
disease, and despair ruled the streets while corpses lay on the
sidewalks covered with newspaper, makeshift shrouds. Sendler
said, "If you had seen the Ghetto, it was pure hell beyond
description." Once again, Irena decided to "sit" with the Jews. She
and her fellow social workers gathered in Irena's second floor flat.
In-between cigarettes and glasses of cordial, they decided it was
time for David to wage war against Goliath. All they needed was a
slingshot, and it appeared when typhus ravaged the Ghetto.

Fearful of the outbreak spreading to the Aryan sector, the
Germans allowed Polish medical groups to enter the arena of

contagion, and this provided a ray of light to the beleaguered. Irena had made contact with Zegota, an underground organization— financed by the Polish government in exile—to save the Jews. They issued Sendler, and her friend Irena Schultz, doctored documents stating they were nurses. In solidarity with the Jews and to blend in, they donned Star of David armbands. In addition to providing medicine, they hid under their clothing lard, meat, and money; later they were to engage in another type of smuggling.

Terror ruled the Ghetto when the handful of those who had managed to flee sent back word of camps such as Treblinka and Auschwitz, which specialized in slave labor, starvation, sickness, brutality, and medical experiments, ending with gas chambers and crematoria. The Jews, though unsure what was rumor and what was truth, became ever more desperate. Without identification cards, families who attempted escape were sitting ducks. Roving gangs of Polish youth received a stipend for capturing Jews and turned them over to the Gestapo. Zegota knew they had to take more drastic measures. Under the code name Jolanta, Irena became Zegota's most intrepid member and her role was to rescue the children. Along with approximately thirty volunteers, mostly women, they secured safe houses and found secret routes. While the connotation of "smuggling" is negative, their clandestine actions made them the 1940s conductors of an underground railroad.

The band of Resistance fighters, led by the twenty-nine-year-old, 4'10" Irena, spirited away infants and toddlers wrapped up

in packages, suitcases, and potato sacks. Sometimes the getaway
was accomplished through the sewer system beneath the city. An
ambulance driver hid infants beneath the stretchers in the back of
his van, while the barks from his dog masked any cries. Because
the Ghetto abutted the Jewish cemetery, the Resistance placed
children in coffins; to prevent their cries they taped their mouths
or used sedation. While arranging the escapes were the most
daunting aspect of her rescue missions, the most heart-rending
was separating the children from their families.

Jolanta approached parents and offered to arrange passage for
their sons and daughters. When they asked what guarantee she
could offer, she could only reply there was not even a guarantee
they could slip past the Ghetto guards. However, if they did so, the
youngsters would live out the remainder of the war in convents, in
the homes of Christian sympathizers, or Aryan orphanages. The
families were caught in a variation of a Sophie's choice: should
they trust a stranger or did they keep their loved ones together?
Sendler would be forever haunted with these meetings: sometimes
there would be deep divisions as to what they should do. Indecision
became decisions; more than once, Irena returned to the apartment
of a wavering couple only to discover they had all been taken to the
Umschlagsplatz railway siding for transport to the death camps.
Some, fearing the worst, would plant a final kiss on the little ones'
faces, take a parting hug. A mother handed over her six-month-old
baby, Elzbieta, along with a memento of a silver teaspoon with her
name and birth date.

Even post-escape, the refugees walked hand-in-hand with danger. Couriers took the displaced to temporary housing where the children acquired Christian names and received doctored baptismal certificates. The older ones learned to make the sign of the Cross and memorized Catholic prayers; those who looked Semitic had their dark hair bleached blonde. The boys not only lost their parents, their names and their religion, but their sexual identity as well. Males dressed in female clothing as the Gestapo checked for circumcision, something only Jews underwent at the time.

As dozens of countries became collapsing dominoes under the swastika, it seemed as if Hitler would never loosen his grip on Europe's throat. However, Irena believed in the ultimate victory of good over evil. With the same organizational brilliance she used to plan escapes, she devised a plan to reunite families when the madness had run its course.

Oskar Schindler was not the only one who kept a list. After each rescue mission, Irena recorded, in code, the children's Jewish and Christian names and addresses, alongside the names of their parents, on slips of paper. She placed these in glass jars which she buried under an apple tree. Edmund Burke wrote, "The only thing necessary for the triumph of evil is for good men to do nothing." This righteous Gentile, even though her life was in jeopardy, could not adopt the stance of the three proverbial monkeys.

Irena Sendler knew she was living on borrowed time, and it ran out in 1943. The owner of a laundry that had served as an underground meeting locale, under less than gentle persuasion, betrayed Jolanta. They arrested her and sent her to the dreaded Pawiak Prison, where she refused to identify the members of her organization or the whereabouts of the children. Over her three months of captivity, Irene continued her resistance to tyranny. When she worked in the prison laundry, she and her fellow prisoners made holes in the German soldiers' underwear. After their brand of sabotage was discovered, the guards lined up all the women and shot every other one. It was just one of the many times Irena cheated death. During one brutal torture session, her jailers used clubs to get her to talk, and though they shattered the bones in her legs and feet, she refused to divulge information. Even under Gestapo terror, the indefatigable Irene determined *to still rise*. In death, as in life, she would endure with dignity intact.

At the last minute, the woman who had rescued others was herself rescued. On the day she was to face a firing squad, the Zegota bribed an officer with a backpack full of dollars who allowed her to escape. En route to her rendezvous with death the guard told her, "You lousy thug, get lost," and punched her in the mouth before he threw her to the side of the road. She said of this episode, "It is beyond description to tell you what you feel when travelling to your own execution and, at the last moment, you find you have been bought out." The officials posted her name on a public bulletin board as one of those killed as a traitor to the Reich, and like her children, she went into hiding under an assumed name.

Fearful of detection, she was unable to attend her beloved mother's funeral.

During her months of convalescence, Irena could easily have descended into bitterness. Her country had been overrun, she had witnessed the worse of human depravity, and had endured imprisonment and torture. And yet she determined *to still rise*. If she had given way to hate, the butchers would have won. After she had recovered, her body permanently scarred and left with a lifelong limp, under another alias she returned to her rescue mission. During those dark days she clung to the hope of a Nazi defeat, when she could reunite the fractured families. This possibility became ever more remote after Heinrich Himmler visited the Polish town of Poznan in 1943 and told fellow SS officers of his promise to the Fuhrer: for his April 20th birthday— the liquidation of the Warsaw Ghetto.

Hitler's one thousand-year Reich ended two years later when the Red Army liberated Poland and Irena unearthed the jars and handed over her lists to the Jewish Committee. For most, there was no happy ending—the gas chambers of Treblinka had seen to that.

After the war, the Communists saw her not as a heroine, but as an agitator, and Irena Sendler fell under their radar. Her marriage ended in divorce and she married Stefan Zgrzembski, with whom she had three children. Her daughter Janka said while her mother may have been there for the children of the Ghetto, she was not there for her own family as she was committed to working with many who had survived the Ghetto. She also recalled Irena's fragile emotional state: she was petrified of thunder and fireworks, as it reminded her of shooting. One could survive the Shoah, but not its memories. Her marriage dissolved after twelve years, at which time she remarried Sendler, but they again parted ways.

Irena Sendler would have lived her life in obscurity until, in 1965, she became one of the first Righteous Gentiles to be honored by Yad Vashem, the Holocaust Remembrance Center in Jerusalem. Poland's Soviet leaders would not permit her to travel to Israel, and she was unable to collect the award until 1983.

However, her life remained essentially forgotten for sixty years until four teenage girls from Kansas discovered the story of the Angel of Warsaw—as she was dubbed—and achieved acclaim. They turned her life into a play—*Life in a Jar*—performed across America. When they discovered she was in a care facility in financial straits, they passed around a jar—symbolic of the ones used for her children—on her behalf.

Although suffering from osteoporosis and her eyesight failing, she kept abreast of politics and wrote the American girls that George W. Bush was a bastard. Her translator was shocked at the elderly saint's language. Under Solidarity she became a heroine in Poland and received her country's highest honor: the Order of the White Eagle. She was too frail to attend, and Elzbieta read her statement—one that could serve as her epitaph: "Every child saved with my help is the justification of my existence on the Earth, and not a title to glory." In a nod to her father, she had devoted her life to those who were drowning. Israel made her an honorary citizen, and Pope John Paul II wrote a letter commending her bravery.

The spotlight of international fame arrived in 2007 with the nomination of Irena Sendler for the Nobel Peace Prize. The Swedish Committee passed her over in favor of Al Gore; apparently, they felt global warning triumphed over the rescue of 2,500 children from the jaws of the Nazis.

The modern-day saint passed away at age ninety-eight, and at her deathbed was one of her rescued children. She said of her savior, "She was the brightest star in the black sky of the Occupation."

CHAPTER 7:
THIS LITTLE LIGHT OF MINE (1917)

As Susan B. Anthony lay dying, she spoke to her fellow suffragettes: "With women such as you, failure is impossible." A year after her passing, in 1920, women were allowed into the polling station, an act that had once led to Anthony's arrest. However, in the Deep South, despite the Fifteenth Amendment, Jim Crow prevented the disenfranchised from voting, determined to keep poor blacks in their place—the bottom of the social hierarchy.

Fannie Lou was the youngest of twenty children—sixteen boys and four girls—born to Jim and Lou Ella Townsend, sharecroppers on a Montgomery County plantation. When she was two, the family relocated to Sunflower County, sixty miles to the west. Despite the positive connotation of its name, life was a never-ending struggle for its African American residents. Fannie worked the fields from age six; school was only secondary, and attendance permitted only after they had picked their share of cotton. Some never attend classes so they could work full-time. The little girl, like her mother and father, and her slave ancestors, had looked on the long rows of cotton as the only future white Mississippi would afford black folks. This status quo suited the KKK and other white supremacy groups who looked with nostalgia on the antebellum South as "the good ol' days."

Jim was resourceful and hard-working, but in the Delta these virtues did not translate to a better life. He rented land and purchased mules and a cultivator. His subsequent success threatened the established social hierarchy and its proponents poisoned his livestock. However, in the segregationist state in the first half of the twentieth century, there was no legal recourse. The Townsends were obliged to return to work as sharecroppers; this entailed splitting the profits with the land-owner, but the cost for everything came from the workers, which made life a Sisyphean, never-ending economic struggle.

Fannie's formal education in the one-room schoolhouse ended at grade six. She dropped out because her parents were elderly and her mother had a bad eye, an injury she had sustained at work. An object had struck her eye as she was swinging an ax and, unable to afford medical attention, eventually went blind. Hunger stalked their home and shoes were a luxury she did not enjoy for many years. Her mother tied rags around the children's feet with string during the winter months.

As an adult, Fannie did not become one of those white-gloved, soft-spoken, Southern ladies who drank tea and sported a wide-brimmed hat. She was short and stocky, with a booming voice, and refused to "know her place."

In 1944, at age twenty-seven, she married Perry "Pap" Hamer, a young man who plowed the cotton fields, and the couple moved to Ruleville, Mississippi, where they labored as sharecroppers on the Marlow plantation. Fannie envisioned becoming a mother to a large number of children, but this collapsed after her first two pregnancies ended with stillbirths. When she went to the hospital to have a tumor removed, the doctor, a proponent of eugenics on poor blacks, performed a hysterectomy, which he said he did out of kindness. This form of sterilization was so commonplace it was known as "Mississippi appendectomy." Enraged, Hamer attended a civil rights rally at a Ruleville Baptist Church where civil rights workers from the Student Non-Violent Coordinating Committee told Hamer something she had never heard before: black people had the right to vote. They had chosen Sunflower County, as it was the epitome of Southern segregation, and felt if they could make progress there, it would send a seismic shock throughout the Delta. Mrs. Hamer had known something was rotten—and not just in the state of Denmark—but in the world she had inherited. Yet, she had never before heard of civil rights. The rebel had found her cause. She recalled, When they asked for those to raise their hands who'd go down to the courthouse the next day, I raised mine. Had it up as high as I could get it. I guess if I'd had any sense I'd a-been a little scared, but what was the point of being scared? The only thing the whites could do was kill me and it seemed like they'd been trying to do that a little bit at a time since I could remember.

She devoured the words of the speakers who said that those gathered at the church—dirt-poor sharecroppers, field hands, and domestics—could force from office the hateful politicians and sheriffs who controlled the oppressive old order.

In the evening of August 31, 1962, Fannie and seventeen others boarded a yellow, weather-beaten bus and rode the thirty miles to the county seat of Indianola. In the sobering light of the day, most of the euphoria from the meeting dissipated and they were afraid to disembark. Then Mrs. Hamer stepped off the bus while the others followed silently behind as she led the way to the registration desk in the courthouse. However, there was another hurdle to jump through—the literacy test—designed to keep the uneducated blacks from voting. Fannie was given questions concerning de facto laws of which she said, "I knowed as much about a facto law as a horse knows about Christmas Day." Another form of intimidation was the application required place of employment, a chill-inducing question. They understood there would be immediate retaliation; namely, their termination once they were branded as rabble-rousers. Just as frightening was the blank space that asked for place of residence; it was implicit that the Ku Klux Klan would have this information and they would return home to a burning cross.

On the ride back to Ruleville, a highway patrolman arrested the driver on the charge of operating a vehicle that too closely resembled a school bus. To lift flagging spirits, Fannie, in a loud voice, sang Gospel songs such as "Go Tell it on the Mountain," to which the others lent their voices.

Fannie lost her home and job but had discovered her passion. She told an infuriated Marlow, "I didn't go down there to register for you. I went down to register for myself." The first place Mrs. Hamer went was her Baptist Church, and told the congregation about her eviction. They sang freedom songs and played the piano in a bid to comfort. However, she looked at it in a positive light and said she had been set free: "It's the best thing that could have happened. Now I can work for my people." Hamer was willing to become a modern Moses, determined to lead her people to the promised land of freedom.

Fearing reprisals, Pap drove his wife and their two adopted daughters to Tallahatchie County, where they stayed with the Turners, rural relatives. The Klan left their calling card—they fired sixteen shots into their home. The act shattered everyone's nerves, but Hamer was a strong character that this tough time in history required. Nevertheless, her strong faith taught her, "Ain't no such thing as I can hate anybody and hope to see God's face."

In 1963, Fannie was returning from a meeting on voter registration in Charleston, South Carolina, when they stopped at Winona, Mississippi, and ordered food at the bus station lunch counter. Several police officers demanded they leave, despite the ordinance outlawing segregated transportation facilities.

They rounded up the offending party and herded them into patrol cars. Fannie was sitting in the bus, out of view, because her left leg, crippled from a bout of childhood polio, was sore from the strenuous week. When she saw her friends arrested, she joined them and was recognized as the hymn-singing troublemaker. The officers told her, "You, bitch, we gon' make you wish you was dead." They took her into a room where they gave two black male prisoners a blackjack and told them unless they used it on Hamer it would be used on them. It served as strong persuasion. She was forced onto her stomach and they whipped her until both men were exhausted. She was left with a permanently damaged kidney and a blood clot that formed over her eye and threatened her vision. After they took her back to her cell, she overheard them saying, "We could put them son of bitches in Big Black River, and nobody would never find them." Upon her release, she learned that the night before Medgar Evers had been gunned down in his yard in front of his wife and three children. (Mrs. Hamer—never one to be at a loss for words—would have been rendered speechless if she could have foreseen in 2009 the Unite States Postal Service would issue a commemorative stamp of her and Medgar Evers.) At this point, after a life of prejudice and poverty, it would have been understandable for Fannie Lou Hamer to return in defeat to her small home in Rulesville, but she determined *to still rise*. She lamented, "We been waitin' all our lives and still gettin' killed, still gettin' hung, still gettin' beat to death. Now we're tired of waitin'! Only God has kept the Negro sane."

The 1968 Democratic Convention, under the Chicago Seven, became a three-ring circus that left the city with a long-lasting black eye. However, four years earlier, the one in Atlantic City proved equally high theater. When Fannie and friends arrived, all were aware of the storm blowing in from Mississippi. White racists controlled the state and had openly declared themselves in favor of segregation. Fannie, as a polio survivor, had a marked limp, and this as well as her nonstandard syntax made her into an authentic image of the harshness of contemporary black life. She electrified the country with a televised appearance that revealed the demeaning discrimination that crippled the souls of her people. She spoke of the terror of living as an African American activist in Mississippi, and how this entailed sleeping with telephones taken off the hook because of nocturnal death threats. At one point, her face flaring with emotion, she asked, "Is this America? The land of the free and the home of the brave?" She told Senator Humphrey—who had described her as "that illiterate woman"—that she was going to pray for him to Jesus. The most famous line she delivered that night was, "I'm sick and tired of being sick and tired." It became the phrase heard around the country. President Lyndon B. Johnson, who would soon be campaigning and hoped to avoid controversy in the national spotlight, called a last-minute press conference to divert press coverage from Hamer's testimony, but many networks ran her speech on the late news programs. But the damage was already done; Fannie Lou Hamer had become the Rosa Parks of voting. In the 1968 convention, she was again a palpable presence and spoke out against the war in Vietnam.

Despite her national prominence, she continued to live in her three-room house in Ruleville, population 2,000, in the state immortalized in King's speech: "I have a dream that one day even the state of Mississippi, a state sweltering with the heat of injustice..." Pap and Fannie were constantly harassed by local officials. One day they received a $9,000 hydro—even though the Hamer house had no running water. She explained her reason for staying to a writer: "Why should I leave Ruleville and why should I leave Mississippi? I go to the big city and with the kind of education they give us in Mississippi, I got problems. You don't run away from problems, you just face them."

In her last years, she received dozens of honors, such as when Dr. King, in his Nobel Prize acceptance speech, thanked "the great people like the Fannie Lou Hamers whose discipline, wise restraint, and majestic courage has led them down a nonviolent course in seeking to establish a reign of justice and a rule of love across this nation of ours." She was the recipient of numerous awards, and in 1969 spoke at the White House Conference on Hunger. The indefatigable fighter passed away at age sixty from cancer in Mount Bayon Community Hospital in Mississippi. Engraved on her tombstone in Ruleville are her famous words, "I'm sick and tired of being sick and tired."

In 2015 in Washington, DC, septuagenarians from the era of the Civil Rights Movement slowly climbed the stairs of the Metropolitan Church. They had gathered for the opening of the March on Washington Film Festival that began with a documentary honoring Fannie Lou Hamer. When her celluloid image asked her famous question—What kind of country is America?—some in the audience wiped away tears. At the end, wrinkled hands clapped backs and the audience rose in the pews, wrapped their arms around one another and swayed to a joyous rendition of the gospel song Ms. Hamer had sang years ago on a too-yellow school bus: *This Little Light of Mine.*

CHAPTER 8:
PHENOMENAL WOMAN (1928)

People oftentimes view the past with nostalgia, highlighting the good times and letting dust settle on the bad. The second decade of the twentieth century—the Roaring Twenties— is remembered as a never-ending party. In contrast, under the hilarity, the Ku Klux Klan attained the highest membership in its history and Jim Crow reigned in the South.

At the bottom of the hierarchy were African American women— the mules of the world, as Zora Neale Hurston called them—and it was into this world Marguerite Ann Johnson was born in St. Louis. She was the second child of Bailey and Vivian, who divorced when her brother Bailey Jr. was four and she was three. Unable to pronounce Marguerite, he called her "mya sister;" it evolved into Maya. She attributed the "calamitous marriage" to her father, a Navy dietician. She said of her dashing, defeated father that he "was a lonely person, searching relentlessly in bottles, under women's skirts, in church work and lofty job titles for his 'personal niche.'" As single parenting was not on the table, they put their children on a train to live with their paternal grandmother, Annie Henderson, who ran the town's only black-owned store in the tiny town of Stamps, Arkansas. Their grandmother tried to make them feel safe and loved, but Maya saw herself as an ugly, tongue-tied misfit. She longed for blonde hair and pretty dresses instead of black skin and cast-off clothes. Angelou recalled "that musty little town" was so segregated that most of the black children did not even know what whites looked like. During the few interracial encounters she had, Maya had to listen to the "powhiterash" taunts. Of the landscape of her youth she wrote, "With its dust and hate and narrowness it was as South as it was possible to get." Yet the white world remained a hovering threat. On one occasion when the Klan made a night appearance, her grandmother had to hide Maya's crippled Uncle Willie in an empty vegetable bin. At graduation ceremonies a white speaker would remind the graduating class that a great future awaited them—on the athletic and cotton fields. The child had to deal with the triple demons of abandonment, poverty, and racism.

Periodically, Baxter and Maya visited their mother, who worked various jobs, such as a professional gambler. On one occasion, Vivian was living with a Mr. Freeman, who the children thought of as a "big, brown bear" who seldom acknowledged their existence. On a Saturday, when Vivian was away, he raped the eight-year-old Mayra. The defilement was recalled as "a breaking and entering when even the senses are torn apart." She confided in her brother and her molester was tried and convicted. Before the pedophile began his sentence, Maya's uncles turned vigilantes and they kicked her attacker to death in a lot behind a slaughterhouse. She was convinced because she had told on him and testified at his trial her voice had the power to kill: "Just my breath, carrying my words out, might poison people and they'd curl up and die." For the next five years—except to Baxter—she never uttered a word.

Maya and Baxter returned to Arkansas where she felt like a caged bird until she met Bertha Flowers, who she described as "the aristocrat of Black Stamps." She introduced her young charge to literature, and Maya fell under the spell of William Shakespeare ("my first white love," she said) and Charles Dickens. Flowers was pleased the emotionally-fragile child became a voracious reader but, as she told Maya one afternoon over tea and cookies, "It takes the human voice to infuse them with the shades of deeper meaning." Her efforts bore fruit; Maya regained her voice and began reciting favorite poems. Validation arrived when she graduated at the top of her eighth-grade class. In her 1969 autobiography, she explored the theme of how the love of language can help overcome the most insurmountable of obstacles, even sexual assault and racism. This was likewise the message she relayed in 1990 in the *Paris Review*: "In all my work, in the movies I write, the lyrics, the poetry, the prose, the essays. I am saying that we may encounter many defeats—maybe it's imperative that we encounter the defeats—but we are much stronger than we appear to be, and maybe much better than we allow ourselves to be."

After graduation, she and her brother rejoined their mother,

who had moved to San Francisco. She attended George
Washington High and won a scholarship to study drama and
dance at the California Labor School. To earn pocket money, she
worked as a streetcar conductor, the first African American woman
to hold the job. At age sixteen, her hard-won equanimity ended.
Concerned she might be a lesbian and wanting to prove she was
"normal" she propositioned a young man in her neighborhood.
From that one encounter she became pregnant and gave birth to
Clyde Bailey Johnson, nicknamed Guy, who she would often refer
to as her "monument in the world." Life as a single mother was a
treadmill of survival and she took a succession of jobs, such as a
dancer in a nightclub, fry cook in a hamburger joint, and worker in
a mechanic's shop, scraping the paint off cars with her bare hands.
In whatever free time she could grab, she read the Russians—
Dostoevsky, Turgenev, Chekhov. In a bid to better herself, she
tried to join the Women's Army Corps, but was rejected because
her alma mater, the California Labor School, appeared on the
House Un-American Activities Committee as having Communist
sympathies. In San Diego, she fell in love with a pimp that lead
to a stint as a prostitute and madam. In despair, she became
addicted to drugs. She was scared clean when a friend, Troubadour
Martin—a heroin addict—forced her to watch him shoot up.

In her early twenties, Maya's life was a bouillabaisse of racism,
rape, illegitimacy, drugs, and poverty. In a bid to outrun her
demons, she wed Tosh Angelos, a Greek American ex-sailor,

despite the stigma of interracial marriage. They divorced three years later, another notch on the belt of disappointments. However, in the words of her famous poem, she vowed "*still I rise.*"

Instead of adopting the victim's mentality of divorcee and once again single mother, she landed a dancing and singing gig at San Francisco's famed Purple Onion nightclub, where she shared billing with the future star Phyllis Diller, who became a close friend. At this time, she also underwent a name change: she dispensed with Marguerite in favor of Maya, and tweaked Angelos to Angelou. Her acting company embarked on a world tour—heady fare for the small town Southerner—in a production of *Porgy and Bess* in an all-black ensemble.

Angelou's acclaim garnered the attention of civil rights activists who encouraged her to join the struggle. As she had been raised in the shadow of white supremacy, and the country was inflamed with racial tensions, she embraced the movement. She became an official of the Southern Christian Leadership Conference and a friend of some of the most eminent black Americans of the mid-twentieth century, including James Baldwin, Malcolm X, and Dr. King. At last she was a rebel with a cause. During this heady period of social activism, she met Vusumzi Make, a South African freedom fighter. After hearing him deliver an anti-apartheid speech she was smitten and wrote, "Intelligence always had a pornographic effect on me." A week later, Maya had agreed to become his wife and moved with him and her son to Cairo, where she became an editor for the *Arab Observer*. The honeymoon unraveled when Maya noticed lipstick smudges that were not from her lips and the scent of perfume that did not come from her bottle. Even phenomenal women can make phenomenally bad choices. To put physical distance between them, she moved to Ghana, where she worked as a college administrator, editor, and writer. She felt she had arrived at her spiritual homeland when she found herself in a country where there was no discrimination based on skin color. However, she decided to return to America, as she felt an obligation to be a part of its struggle for equality. As she said at a conference in Utah, "Each one of us has the chance to be a rainbow in somebody's cloud." Upon her return to New York, she assisted Malcolm X in founding the Organization of Afro-American Unity, which dissolved after his assassination the following year. Three years later, she was helping Dr. King organize the Poor People's March in Memphis when the civil rights leader was slain on Angelou's fortieth birthday. In a nod to the tragic coincidence, she stopped celebrating the date, opting instead to send annual flowers to the widowed Coretta.

Maya opted to trade the East Coast for the West and she and Guy settled into a beatnik commune and lived on a houseboat in Sausalito, CA. Mother and son went barefoot, wore jeans, and embraced a free-spirited bohemian lifestyle. After a year, Maya began to yearn for a more bourgeoisie way of life, and rented a home in the Caucasian enclave of Laurel Canyon. However, after Guy faced school discipline after an incident with some white girls, they had to look for another neighborhood where "black skin was not regarded as one of nature's more unsightly mistakes." Maya was always mother lion and when Jerry, a local gang member, threatened her teenaged son, she tracked him down. She pulled a pistol from her purse and in a calm voice informed him if he harmed Guy she would find his house "and kill everything that moves, including the rats and cockroaches." Jerry, understandably intimidated by the six-foot infuriated mother wielding a luger, replied, "I understand. But for a mother, I must say you're a mean motherfucker."

Angelou's profile was cemented when she was invited to read her poem "On the Pulse of the Morning" at Bill Clinton's 1993 inauguration, making her the second poet, after Robert Frost, to be so honored. The day must have seemed otherworldly for Bill and Maya, two people born from the wrong side of the tracks in Arkansas. In her poem, she spoke of hope that the country's diverse people would find new unity after chapters in US history of oppression and division. "Lift up your eyes upon/The day breaking for you," she recited as the nation watched. "Give birth again/To the dream."

The Renaissance woman had her finger in many pies: she acted—alongside O. J. Simpson—in *Roots* as Kunte Kinte's grandmother, and made guest appearances on television shows ranging from *Oprah* to *Sesame Street*. She also served as a college professor, and in a speech to her students in Louisiana said, "See me and see yourselves. What can't you do?"

What secured her greatest niche had its genesis when she was at a dinner party with Robert Loomis, editor at Random House, who suggested she write her autobiography. Maya declined with the thought, "*A born loser had to be: from a broken family, raped at eight, unwed mother at sixteen...*" His cagey rejoinder was to remark she was probably right not to attempt such an endeavor, as writing an autobiography as literature was next to impossible. Ms. Angelou responded, "I'll start tomorrow."

She gave her 1969 book the title *I Know Why the Caged Bird Sings* after a line from Paul Lawrence Dunbar's poem "Sympathy." It was the first autobiography by an African American woman to make the nonfiction best-seller list and was translated into seventeen languages. In it she dared to enter the confessional and it shed light upon what most people would keep as their deepest buried secrets, such as her childhood rape. Of the latter she wrote, "If growing up is painful for the Southern Black girl, being aware of her displacement is the rust on the razor that threatens the throat." Its overriding message, however, was one of affirmation, of how a gifted spirit can find a way to soar over obstacles to step on the road to self-fulfillment.

She also secured her niche as the people's poet in "Still I Rise," which embodied her indomitable spirit: "You may shoot me with your words/You may cut me with your eyes/You may kill me with your hatefulness/But still, like air, I'll rise."

Although she had achieved worldwide acclaim, she still longed for a man with whom to share her life and she made a third trip to the altar with Paul du Feu, a writer and cartoonist; they lived in Berkeley, California, until their divorce several years later. She said of her failed nuptials, "I have lost good men—or men I might have been able to turn into good men—because I have no middle passage. I know I'm not the easiest person to live with." There might have been other husbands, but on the topic she was evasive. She said she would disclose how old she was, how tall she was (six feet), but not how many times she had been married. This stayed in the vault because, as she explained, she did not want to scare men off or appear frivolous.

In her later years, Maya had embraced social media, and in her last tweet she urged her readers toward reflection: "Listen to yourself and in that quietude you might hear the voice of God."

Maya Angelou's passing in 2014 was met with a worldwide outpouring of condolences. President Barack Obama said of Ms. Angelou, who he had awarded the Presidential Medal of Freedom, "Today, Michelle and I join millions around the world in remembering one of the brightest lights of our time—a brilliant writer, a fierce friend and a truly phenomenal woman." He added, "She inspired my own mother to name my sister Maya."

Maya Angelou, the indigent child who reached the White House, the mute girl whose indelible voice refused to be silent, was, to use the title of one of her poems, a phenomenal woman.

CHAPTER 9:
DANCE ALL NIGHT (1928)

C hutzpah is the Yiddish word for guts—the equivalent of the Spanish *cajones* and the English *balls*. Whatever the vernacular, it is what an octogenarian with a thick accent possesses in spades.

The therapist who is credited with taking sex out of the closet and into the world's living rooms is the diminutive Dr. Ruth (the honorific comes courtesy of her PhD in education). Despite her short stature—she is four feet seven inches and wears Cinderella size four shoes—she casts a giant shadow.

Dr. Westheimer has achieved a great deal in her eighty plus years, and one of her greatest accomplishments was surviving the nightmare landscape of her youth. In her case, *chutzpah* is another word for courage. Karola Ruth Siegel was an only child, raised in a stable and loving home, first in Wiesenfeld, then in Frankfurt. Her father, Julius, was a prosperous notions wholesaler and her mother, Irma, had met her husband when she worked as a maid in his family's home. Julius' mother also lived with them, and grandmother and granddaughter were such nonstop talkers the reticent Irma could hardly get a word in edgewise. In an Orthodox Jewish home, usually only sons attend Friday night services, but Julius always brought his daughter along and sent her to prestigious Jewish schools.

When not in the synagogue or in *cheder*, Karola was always curious—or nosy, depending on one's perspective—and managed to locate the key to a cabinet where her parents locked forbidden books. Her favorite pastime was reading, and she was frustrated that some were out of bounds. The volume that engrossed her most was *The Ideal Marriage*, by Theodor Hendrik van de Veldeone, that had pictures of people engaged in sex.

In 1938, her world was shattered by Kristallnacht (The Night of Broken Glass), which began the net of doom that descended on Europe's Jews. Seven days later, the Gestapo awakened the Siegels and wrenched Julius from his family. Ruth recalled they wore shiny, black leather boots, and her grandmother gave the Nazis money with the words, "Take good care of my son." Karola watched from the window as her father boarded a covered truck, and when he turned around he smiled and waved.

Although Irma and her mother-in-law were desperate to keep their remaining family intact, they were frantic to ensure Karola's survival. They put the ten-year-old child's name on a list of the *kindertransport*, a program designed to help Jewish children wait out the madness of World War II in a safe zone. The "orphans" in exile hoped for a happy ending that for most of them would never come.

The child took her last glimpse of her mother while her grandmother ran down the platform to keep Karola in view till the last moment. Her destination was a children's home in Switzerland; had her name been on a transport for Holland, Belgium, or France, in all likelihood she would have become a statistic of the one and a half million Jewish children who perished in the Holocaust. Karola suffered greatly as she missed her family, especially when their letters stopped arriving in 1941. In addition, the Swiss caregivers looked down on their female charges and felt with their refugee, orphan status, their best chance in life was to prepare for livelihoods as maids. They took a special dislike to Karola, who talked too much, especially about taboo subjects such as menstruation and what she had seen in the off-limits books.

The only comfort she derived was from the other children who were in the same precarious boat, and they bonded into a makeshift family. They sang the songs from their lost world and poured their hearts out into diaries. Karola endured those miserable years with the memory of her family and the knowledge they would have wanted her happiness.

As Germany had been the architect of her sorrows, and as her Swiss teachers were consigning her to a role of domestic, Karola, along with other *kindertransport* teens, made her way to the British Mandate of Palestine. She was a committed Zionist, and believed a Jewish homeland would ward off another Holocaust. When she arrived, she divested herself of both her family's Orthodox faith, and the name Karola. She replaced it with the more Hebrew sounding Ruth, but kept the initial "K" in the hope it would help her parents find her had they survived. Although she never discovered their fate, in all likelihood they perished in Auschwitz. She still retains the K to maintain ties to the past.

Ruth worked in a kibbutz (as a tomato and olive picker) until she decided she wanted a more active role in the fight for Israeli independence. She joined the *Haganah*, the Jewish underground movement, where she trained as a sniper. She recalled of those days, "As a four-foot-seven woman, I would have been turned away by any self-respecting army anywhere else in the world. But I had other qualities that made me a valuable guerrilla. For some strange reason I can put five bullets into that red thing in the middle of the target. And I knew how to assemble a Sten gun with my eyes closed."

Ironically, it was Ruth's love of books that almost proved fatal. On her twentieth birthday, the kibbutz's attack siren sounded, but she refused to go into the bomb shelter without something to read. A high explosive shell almost took off both her feet at the ankles. "I would've been even shorter," was her response. She credits Hadassah Hospital in Jerusalem for saving her from amputation, which enabled her to become a lifelong skier (she only stopped at age eighty) and to embrace her passion for dancing.

There was a third thing Ruth shucked off in Israel. Because of her diminutive stature, she believed that she would never marry, lamenting in her diary, "Nobody is ever going to want me because I'm short and ugly." Despite her fears, she had a boyfriend, nicknamed Putz, and lost her virginity on a pile of hay in the kibbutz (not to Putz.) In her recovery at the hospital, she found solace with a sexy, male nurse, with whom she began a "brief but intense love affair." In 1950, she wed the first guy who offered to marry her, fearing she would never get another chance. She described David as "handsome, well-educated and short." In her books, a plus.

When Palestine became Israel, Ruth felt it was once again time to move on; after the Nazis, she did not want to live under the threat of the Arabs. Ruth and David set off for Paris—he to train in medicine, she to study psychology at the Sorbonne. The couple were very poor and lived in a three-flight walk-up with a toilet three flights down. They went to cafes and had one cup of coffee all day long. The marriage had an expiration date of five years, and he returned to Israel. A good-looking Frenchman helped ease the breakup, and Ruth had unprotected sex because she wanted a baby. Upon receiving a restitution check from the German government for five thousand marks (approximately $1,500), Ruth and her boyfriend left Paris and sailed to her fifth country of residence, the United States. She was thrilled when she became pregnant, and the couple wed to give their child legitimacy.

A year after Miriam's birth, Ruth bid adieu to her French spouse. "Intellectually it was just not tenable," was how she summed up her split. Intelligence for her is the most erogenous of zones: "Sex is not between the waist and the knees. Sex is between the ears." In the divorce settlement she stated, "He got the car and I got the child."

At this point, Ruth could have thrown herself a huge pity party and indulged in her litany of woes: orphaned by the Nazis, twice divorced, single mother. As a bitter topping, she was now in a country where she had no money and did not speak its language. However, Ruth Westheimer is a survivor. She compares herself to a German doll that has lead in its base. When you put it flat down, it stands right back up again. She vowed, as someone who made it through Hitler's genocide, that she had to "repair the world," to make a dent to be worthy of her miraculous survival. It was the fuel which made her *still rise.*

Ruth worked as a maid at a dollar an hour but refused to let any grass grow under her size four shoes. At night she studied at Queens and LaGuardia colleges, and ultimately received her master's degree through a scholarship for victims of the Holocaust. Ruth recalls, although she was poor, she always had friends, as well as a boyfriend, Hans, who took her on a 1961 ski trip in the Catskills. However, as he was six foot, she felt their heights were not compatible. At the top of the ski slope, she met Manfred Westheimer, and told Hans that she would be skiing with the short guy. She liked his height, that they were both German Jewish refugees, and his reticence. The latter was important, as she is never quiet for long, perhaps because talking seems to be her second favorite form of intercourse. She knew right away she was going to be his wife, something he was not aware of at the time. To achieve that end, she employed her best "feminine wiles." They were married nine months later and she finally hit the marital jackpot. Fred often said of Ruth, "She was my one serious ski accident." He adopted Miriam and together they had a son, Joel. An adoring mother, she frequently *kvells*, "I have children like nobody's children."

Dr. Ruth entered the lexicon of North America in 1980 with the syndicated phone-in sex talk show *Sexually Speaking*. On it, those in need of chicken soup for the sexual soul could call for advice or information, dispensed with a thick German accent. The host describes herself, "I'm like a Jewish mother. A Jewish mother who talks explicitly." She speaks about venereal disease with ease and says "an orgasm is just a reflex, like a sneeze." Ah, *gesundheit*. *People Magazine* said of her, "She arouses only respect, the kind Golda Meir would've gotten had she been a gynecologist." As she approached her ninetieth decade, she realized that she may have to one day step out of the limelight, but she feels she has already had far more than her allotted fifteen minutes, and had found herself in more pleasurable positions than the Kama Sutra.

After losing her childhood home, she never had a place of her own; she was thrilled when they purchased a three-bedroom apartment in Washington Heights, a neighborhood with a sizable community of German, Jewish refugees. Their apartment has accents of pink that Ruth considers the hue of foreplay, and every square inch is a shrine to *tchotchkes*, as her greatest decorating fear is an empty space. One of her touches are miniature oil lamps etched with sexual positions, and innumerable photos: Bill Clinton hugging Dr. Ruth, President Obama hugging Dr. Ruth that leads to her comment, "Everyone is hugging me. It is good to be Dr. Ruth." Other photos are of her family—-including four grandchildren. Of these she says, "Hitler lost and I won."

On the train to Switzerland, Karola had left with her only toy—a doll—that she gave to a crying little girl. Ms. Westheimer seems to have spent her lifetime making up for her early lack of possessions. Vying in space with the dolls are Dr. Ruth's vast collection of turtles crafted of clay, metal, wood, stone—and one even inlaid with diamonds. They are a metaphor for their owner. "The turtle can stay in its shell and be safe. But if it wants to move forward it has to stick its neck out. That's me. If I have to mention one characteristic I have, it's *chutzpah*." One thing she has yet to do is visit the Galapagos "to see how the turtles make love. Then I can arrange *my* turtles in the right way. I don't want them to be lonely."

What stopped Ruth from being lonely for thirty-four years was her Freddy, who shared with her a commonality of background, home, and $10,000,000 fortune. (Indeed, it is good to be Dr. Ruth.) Although he did not share her loquacious nature, his humor was of a similar vein. In 1997, Diane Sawyer came to the Westheimer home to conduct an interview with the world's sexologist and asked Fred about his sex life; his response? "The shoemaker's children don't have shoes." Ruth will always mourn his 1997, passing but is still open to a fourth trip down the aisle if she could "find an interesting older gentleman who can still walk and talk—and who can dance all night."

CHAPTER 10:
CAN WE TALK? (1933)

S hakespeare's clowns were the stand-up comics of the
Elizabethan world. Their role: mock the pompous and
puncture the pretentious. Paradoxically, the fools were the wise
men of the era. As Regan observed in *King Lear*, "Jesters do oft
prove prophets." Stephen Sondheim's 1970s song that showcases
our need for humor ends, "Quick, send in the clowns/Don't
bother/They're here."

One of our contemporary clowns, who became the Grand Dame
of comedy, will be remembered as the woman who made jokes
about oral sex, terrorists, and the Holocaust, but was an insecure,
chubby girl who dreamed of rising above the ordinary. Joan
Alexandra was born in Brooklyn, *Noo Yawk,* to Meyer and Beatrice
Molinsky, Jewish immigrants from Russia. Beatrice never adapted
to life in the States or the fact she was unable to obtain the lifestyle
she had enjoyed when her wealthy family had supplied the Tsar
with furs, a run that ended with them fleeing penniless from the
Bolsheviks. Her comedic *shtick* was honed at a young age from
her doctor dad who performed impersonations of his patients to
entertain daughters Barbara and Joan. She remembered childhood

as "full of domestic tension" over money and low self-esteem. As a "fat, ugly girl," she felt she could never fulfill her parents' expectations and that she was "outshone" by Barbara. "It made me a manic overachiever. I wanted to be better, smarter and thinner than my sister at any cost," Joan stated.

Joan attended Barnard College; however, her most memorable year at university happened outside the halls of academia. In 1951, a colleague of her father hosted a dinner party and one of his guests— others were Arthur Miller, Elia Kazan, and Lee Strasberg—was Marilyn Monroe, who was so shy the host seated her next to the student. During the evening, the star passed on her wisdom: "Honey, let me tell you a secret. Men are stupid and they like big tits."

Beatrice wanted Joan to achieve her version of the American Dream—landing a rich, Jewish husband. However, Joan had an aspiration outside the Brooklyn box: she wanted to be an actress. She had fallen in love with the theater when she had performed as a kitten in her kindergarten play and had been so enchanted with her character she wore her cat ears and whiskers to bed. The bug was cemented in high school when she saw Ray Bolger perform; standing in the St. James Theater she said, "I knew then I was in the temple." After graduation, she apprenticed at the Westport County Playhouse in Connecticut, where she suffered a bout of stage fright; humiliated, she stayed in bed, in a fetal position, for days. The reviews for the production were scathing, but even more devastating was Dr. Molinsky's comment that the show was the worst piece of garbage he had ever seen and she was crazy to pursue acting. When she did not back down, he said it would not be on his dime and withdrew financial support. To survive, Joan worked as a fashion coordinator for a large chain, and in 1957 married the boss's son, Jimmy Sanger. The union was annulled after six months, lasting "six months longer than it should have."

Joan reverted to her original plan of becoming an actress, and she worked as a temporary clerk to finance her dream. But she discovered that she could earn five dollars a night as a stand-up comic at a local club—fifty cents more than she was earning at her job—and never looked back. Her agent, Tony Rivers, suggested she drop her name—so she took his. However, show business success did not come easily: "I wasn't pretty, and at that time you had to be an 8-by-10 glossy, un-retouched." Self-deprecation were the cornerstones of her act. She said, "There is not one female comic who was beautiful as a little girl," and a quintessential self-barb, "My best birth control is to leave the lights on." The funny lady made jokes about sex on the linoleum because she knew it was far better to laugh about that floor than to scrub it. Her stand-up routine closed with the punch-line, "I'm Joan Rivers, and I put out!" a shocking claim in an era when women were supposed to only surrender their virginity on their wedding night.

Rivers "endured humiliation and deprivation" for almost ten years, playing in tawdry clubs, borscht-belt hotels, and Greenwich Village cabarets before "a mercy booking" appearance in 1968 on

The Tonight Show Starring Johnny Carson. In a nod to there is no accounting for chemistry—Carson, the white-bread all-American boy from the Midwest—proved the perfect foil for Rivers' Brooklyn Jewish humor. Audiences reveled in her gags about her mother's struggle to marry her off, such as a sign she said Beatrice placed on the family lawn: Last Girl Before Freeway. When Carson asked if men ever liked her for her mind, she responded that no man ever put his hand up a woman's dress looking for her library card. Her repertoire made her a human wrecking ball and a customary target was Elizabeth Taylor, who she envied as a natural-born beauty. Indeed, she once remarked she would have traded wit for looks. Of Taylor's increasing waist-line she said, "She puts mayonnaise on aspirins;" "Mosquitoes see Liz Taylor and shout 'Buffet!'" When the host—the czar of comedy—told her on live television that she was going to be a star, it was her life-changing moment. She said, "Doors opened. Then you have to work like hell to keep them open. But they opened." In 1983, Carson made Rivers his show's first permanent guest, and she seemed the heir for his comic crown. Her signature line, "Can we talk?"

In the same year, the Brooklynite married Brit Edgar Rosenberg, and the thirty-one-year-old Ms. Rivers felt she had at last met Mr. Right. Rosenberg's family had fled Nazi Germany and had escaped with just the clothes on their backs. Four days later, they were married by a New York judge, and Joan, who had mined her personal life for her material, turned her jokes from desperate

single girl to married women gags, telling audiences she knew
nothing about sex because all her mother had told her was the man
gets on top—so she bought bunk beds. Nevertheless, Edgar and
Joan must have got it right—in 1968, they welcomed only child
Melissa. The strait-laced Edgar provided comic foil: "When the
Rabbi said, 'Do you take this man?' fourteen guys said, 'She has.'
Thank goodness my husband bought the horseback riding story."

Joan stated of her role on Carson as "career Viagra," and she
enjoyed sell-out tours in Las Vegas, commanding $200,000
for a five-night run and appeared on countless magazines. She
presided over a Beverly Hills mansion with her husband and
daughter and a flock of servants. Melissa recalled her parents tried
to keep themselves grounded amidst celebrity status by having
family dinners where her mom would start a meal by thanking
God not only for the abundance of food but for the abundance of
restaurants offering dinner within thirty minutes. It seemed as if
Joan Rivers had the last laugh on all her naysayers until even her
indefatigable sense of humor deserted.

The double-barrel bullets came when Rivers defected by
accepting her own late-night talk show for the upstart Fox
network for $15 million. This made her the first female to break
the glass-ceiling of male-hosted late-night talk shows. On the
flip side, Carson viewed her as Judas, selling out for thirty pieces
of silver, and he used his clout to make her an industry pariah.
Devastated at the loss of her mentor, Joan nevertheless joked of

the oft-married Carson, "I'm the only woman in the history of the world who left Johnny Carson and didn't ask him for money." To compound her error, Joan let Edgar serve as executive producer, where his abrasive personality sewed dissension between him and Fox owner Rupert Murdoch. She fared little better when she came to Britain for *Joan Rivers: Can We Talk?* There the assisted-blonde reinforced the British stereotype of the vulgar American and dozens of viewers called to complain about her use of the four-letter word. Rivers' offered an apology, "I'm sorry I fucking swore." Germaine Greer compared her interviewing style to "spiders copulating." The producers cancelled it after six shows, and Fox pulled the plug on her as well. The failures plunged Edgar into a deep depression; three weeks later, he took a lethal dose of Valium and alcohol. The marriage had lasted twenty-two years, and Joan's life went into a tailspin of depression and bulimia. She well knew Edgar had been the only man to truly love the clown-princess. Her career was in smoldering ruins, and at age fifty-four, believed she was beyond her expiration date. Melissa blamed her mother for her father's death, and severed what had been their wrought-iron umbilical cord. If this were not enough, with her husband's passing, she looked into her finances and discovered she was $37 million in debt because of Edgar's mismanagement.

At the Bel-Air mansion—where five telephone lines had once relentlessly buzzed—there was a resounding silence. To add to her pain was guilt over Edgar's suicide and misery at her daughter's estrangement. As her fifty-fifth birthday loomed, Joan could no longer see any reason to keep on living. She felt it impossible to dig herself out of her hole; it was hard enough for young women to succeed in show business, let alone for an aging has-been. The words of the Sondheim song proved prophetic: "Isn't it rich? Isn't it queer? Losing my timing this late in my career..." She sat on her bed, pistol in hand, when Spike, her terrier, jumped onto her lap and sat on her gun. Suddenly a terrible thoughts came to mind: if she killed herself, what would happen to Spike? The diminutive Yorkie was cute, but cantankerous, and did not like anyone other than his mistress. Moreover, he was ridiculously spoiled; his favorite food was roast beef sandwich, and who would cater to him in the manner to which he had become accustomed? There was also concern about Melissa; how would she take it having both her parents succumb to suicide? Joan had once told someone the only thing she feared was a blank diary, and she realized that the epitome of that was the oblivion of death. Rivers determined *to still rise* on her stilettoes. After all, her credo was, "Never stop believing. Never give up. Never quit. Never!"

Joan started where she had begun, and took her "merry widow tour" to tiny clubs where her gags about her husband's death met with boos—she said she had scattered Edgar's ashes around Neiman Marcus so she could visit him five times a week. But with her painted talons she clawed her way back, and in 1989 her persistence paid off with a daytime TV talk show which ran for five years and earned a nomination for an Emmy. Three years later, she also found love with Orin Lehman, a former financier who had the use of only one leg, "My Heather Mills!" which union floundered when he hobbled off with other women. Rivers' also made a financial recovery with her jewelry and clothes collection she sold on QVC, where she pulled in millions annually. In 2010, she became the star of the E! show *Fashion Police*, where she and mini-me Melissa critiqued celebrity wardrobes. In 1998, Melissa married a horse-trainer she had met in Palm Springs, and the mother of the bride shelled out $3 million for an extravaganza at the Plaza. The marriage lasted five years, but produced Joan's adored grandson Cooper. When she heard of Michael Jackson's death she quipped, "My grandson can take a walk alone again."

Rivers purchased a mini Versailles overlooking Central Park, whose former occupant J. P. Morgan had replicated from a French chateau, whose décor sported swathes of pink silk murals and acres of guilt furniture, making the Donald's Trump Tower penthouse a nod to understatement. She filled it with antiques: "If Louis XIV hasn't sat on it, I don't want it."

As an octogenarian, Joan's quips turned on her age: "The only Rivers older are the Nile and the Euphrates." Her face took on a bizarre appearance after countless plastic surgeries. She joked that her body had so much plastic that when she died she was donating it to Tupperware. Similarly, "I've undergone more reconstruction than Baghdad." Cooper called her Nana New Face.

After a twenty-six-year hiatus, Rivers returned to *The Tonight Show* where she told host Jimmy Fallon that she and a girlfriend got matching vagina rings to commemorate the milestone. "Mine is killing me, but apparently, I spoke to Bruce Jenner, and hers is fine." There was a collective cringe; it was classic Joan.

Rivers had joked funerals were a great place to meet newly minted widowers and had told Melissa she wanted her own to include Meryl Streep crying in five different accents and a wind machine so that even in her casket her hair would be blowing like Beyoncé's. The only one who could silence Rivers was the Grim Reaper himself, and she passed away in 2014 after a botched procedure on her vocal cords; the attending doctor had taken a selfie while she was unconscious. A devastated Melissa said, "I'm lost as a performer right now, but I will find my own voice. I was taught by the best."

When heaven sent for the blonde bouffant clown, one can imagine her cornering the big man himself: "Gawd, can we talk?"

CHAPTER 11:
UNDER THE BUS (1939)

A 1976 slogan coined by Laurel Thatcher Ulrich, "Well-be haved women seldom make history," stimulated the feminist G-spot. The words proliferated on T-shirts, coffee mugs, and bumper stickers. Although a docile woman may classify as Miss Congeniality, she does not leave footprints in the sands of time. In the Jim Crow South, where being female and African Americant secures a niche in the bottom of the hierarchy, one of these girls "misbehaved;" with the result, a finger was removed from a long pent-up damn.

A 1955 incident on a segregated Montgomery bus changed the racial landscape of America. The arrest of Rosa Parks set off a chain reaction: it began the bus boycott that launched the Civil Rights Movement that transformed the apartheid of the South from a local tradition to a national outrage. It also conferred a saint-like aura on the gray-haired seamstress. What has been lost in the translation of time is that Ms. Parks was not the first person to take a stand by keeping her seat.

Claudette Colvin was born in King Hill, which, despite

its name, was on the wrong side of the segregated tracks of Montgomery. Claudette remembers her neighborhood, where broken cars were permanently parked outside ramshackle houses, a section looked down upon by the middle-class blacks. There were unpaved streets and outside toilets, and nights were punctuated by alcohol and poverty-induced fights. Colvin lived at 658 Dixie Drive, where she was raised by a great aunt, who worked as a maid, and her great uncle, who worked as a gardener. They loved her as their own and she referred to them as her parents.

Besides the sword of penury that hung over Dixie Drive was the ever present bigotry. Before she even knew her ABCs she knew the societal differences between being white and being black. Not only was she victimized by Caucasians, but by African Americans with lighter skin. In the "pigmentocracy" of the South, while whites discriminated against blacks on grounds of skin color, the black community discriminated against each other in terms of skin tone. The lighter the better, as this was closer to the appearance of the prevailing power. Thus, because of her complexion, Claudette was at the bottom of the social pile.

Residents of King Hill remember her as deeply religious, a bookworm and straight-A student. Nevertheless, Claudette also sported a rebellious streak, demonstrated when she stopped straightening her hair; when her tenth grade teacher, Ms. Nesbitt, asked the class to write down what they wanted to be, her paper read: president of the United States. She said as a young teen her fantasies were to marry a baseball player and to go north to liberate her people.

During Claudette's freshman year, racism reared its head when police cars descended on Booker T. Washington High to arrest the teenaged Jeremiah Reeves for having sex with a white woman. She cried rape while he swore it was consensual. In either contingency, he was guilty of violating the South's deeply ingrained taboo on interracial sex. He was put on death row and executed four years later.

On March 2, 1955, the clever and angry Claudette boarded the Highland Avenue bus, whose stop was opposite Dr. Martin Luther King's church on Dexter Avenue. The law at that time designated seats for blacks at the rear and for whites at the front, but left the middle ones as a murky no man's land. Black people were allowed to occupy them as long as white people did not require their use.

As more white passengers got on, the driver told the African Americans in the middle to move to the back, and while three girls complied, Claudette refused. She recalls, "If it had been for an old lady, I would have got up, but it wasn't." To add to the drama, a pregnant black woman, Mrs. Hamilton, got on and sat next to Colvin. When the driver spied their defiance in his rear view mirror he shouted at them, but neither budged. They expected verbal abuse, but nothing more. However, he left the bus to summon the authorities, and the air was electrified with tension. Colvin became the target of infuriated Caucasian students, and one shouted, "You got to get up!" An African American replied, "She ain't got to do nothing but stay black and die." Passenger Gloria Hardin recalls of that, forever etched in her mind, the day that they all sat tensed, waiting for the other shoe to drop.

An officer arrived, displaying two of the characteristics for which white Southern men are renowned: gentility and racism. He did not berate the pregnant Mrs. Hamilton, and yet he could not allow the flouting of the law. He turned on the black men sitting behind her, "If any of you are not gentlemen enough to give a lady a seat, you should be put in jail yourself." Mr. Harris, a sanitation worker, stood up and exited. This left Claudette, and when she shook her head and kept saying, "No Sir," a black woman began to wail, "Oh, God." A white woman told the policeman that if he let them get away with this they would take over.

Claudette's refusal had been partly fueled by her teacher, Geraldine Nesbitt, who had just finished a unit on Black History month where she had taught about the Fourteenth Amendment. Colbert said of the decision that altered the trajectory of her life, "I felt like Sojourner Truth was pushing down on one shoulder and Harriet Tubman was pushing down on the other—saying, 'Sit down girl!' I was glued to my seat."

The policeman kicked Claudette, informed her he would take her off, followed by two more kicks. Immune to her tears, he dragged her to a patrol car accompanied by her screams, "It's my Constitutional right!" After she was forced into the back, one officer asked, "What was going on with these Niggers?" and another started guessing about her bra size. Claudette was terrified, realizing there was no telling what might transpire. She was well aware that a few months earlier, Emmett Till, a fourteen-year-old-boy, had said, "Bye, baby," to a white woman at a store in nearby Mississippi. A few days later, he was fished out of the Tallahatchie River, a bullet in his skull, an eye gouged out, and forehead crushed. The teen was filled with apprehension: "I didn't know if they were crazy, if they were going to take me to a Klan meeting. I started protecting my crotch. I was afraid they might rape me."

The police carted Claudette to City Hall, and to detach herself from the horror, she concentrated on material she had been learning at school. "I recited Edgar Allan Poe, 'Annabel Lee,' the characters in *Midsummer's Night Dream*, the 'Lord's Prayer,' and the '23rd Psalm.'" The court charged Colvin with misconduct, resisting arrest, and violating the city's segregation laws. Her pastor arrived to pick her up, and by the time she arrived at Dixie Drive, her parents, as well as everyone in King Hill, knew what had transpired. In her trial, Colvin pleaded innocent but was found guilty and released on indefinite probation. After hearing the verdict, her agonized sobs filled the courthouse.

The shock waves of the teen's bravery proved big news. Black leaders jumped at the opportunity to use her case to fight segregation laws in court. In the *Alabama Journal*, the headlines blared, "Negro Girl Found Guilty of Segregation Violation." The decision met with heated controversy. Some thought she would make a perfect figurehead given her studious, religious, and intrepid nature. Others felt she was too much of a loose cannon given her screams about Constitutional rights and hysteria. People also said Colvin was unsuitable because she was not raised by her parents, lived in a shack, was dark-skinned. Residents of King Hill felt that "it was a case of 'bourgey' blacks looking down on the working-class blacks." The heated debate abruptly ended.

The quiet fifteen-year-old was emotionally adrift when she became involved in the eye of a storm and an older, married man offered comfort that ended with her pregnancy. For Claudette, this was an equally traumatic experience: "Nowadays, you'd call it statutory rape, but back then it was just the kind of thing that happened." She refused to name the father or have anything to do with him. "When I told my mother I was pregnant, I thought she was going to have a heart attack. If I had told my father who did it, he would have killed him." Her son, Raymond, emerged light-skinned, and her community, feeling she had slept with a white man, which was not the case, ostracized her. As another kidney punch to her soul, her school kicked her out on a morality clause. The once happy teen became withdrawn and cried at every free moment. Her personal tragedy also meant the Civil Rights leaders would not consider an unwed, pregnant teenager as their figurehead.

Montgomery's black leaders determined not to abandon their cause, and cast their eyes on another person to best represent it. They settled on an elderly, soft-spoken Rosa Parks, whose act of resistance was orchestrated by an unknown twenty-six-year-old preacher, Dr. King, who made his political debut fighting her preplanned arrest. Ms. Parks went on to become one of *Time Magazine's* 100 most important people of the twentieth century, and streets and schools were named in her honor. In contrast, Claudette Colvin was regulated to a footnote of history. However, Claudette is not one to hold on to bitterness. She remembers Ms. Parks as a reserved but kindly woman who made her snacks of peanut butter on Ritz crackers and often invited her to spend the night in her apartment.

Because of their daughter's notoriety, her parents shuffled her off to Birmingham; however, eventually she returned to Montgomery to take part in the movement she had helped ignite. One year after her arrest, while her infant son slept, she became a star witness in the landmark federal lawsuit attacking segregation, *Browder v. Gayle*. The attorney in the case, Fred Gray, remembered Colvin for her bravery. He said, "I don't mean to take anything away from Mrs. Parks, but Claudette gave all of us the moral courage to do what we did."

Claudette was left in a highly vulnerable position: she was a poor, single, pregnant, black, teenage mother who had taken on the white establishment and run afoul of the black. The bleak scenario would have left most young girls bloodied and bowed, but Claudette determined that no matter what, she would *still rise*. Part of her fortitude stemmed from the responsibility of raising a child as a single parent.

Hoping to leave the injustice of the South, in 1958 Claudette and Raymond moved to the Bronx; when she first arrived, she was at a drugstore and a white man held the door open. She froze in disbelief. Ms. Colvin never married, and Raymond passed away at age thirty-seven, while a second son is an accountant in Atlanta. She loves watching television—*Who Wants to be a Millionaire* is her favorite—and she is a regular at the local diner. Ms. Colvin, who now relies on a cane to steady herself when she walks, reads two newspapers a week and chats about topics such as recent Nobel Prize winners. Less lofty subjects are Chris Rock, Alicia Keyes, and Aretha Franklin, who, she thinks, should lose a few pounds, but is impressed the singer wore a good hat to President Obama's inauguration. One thing it is best not to start her on is the topic of Sarah Palin. Colbert retired from her job as a nurse's aide in a retirement home after thirty-four years, and during that time contributed to her obscurity, never talking about how her youthful protest prompted the Montgomery Bus Boycott. The answer to "Who Wants to be Famous?" is not Claudette Colvin.

She was plucked from obscurity by Phillip Hoose's book, *Claudette Colvin: Twice Toward Justice*. Its genesis was when the author heard an urban myth that a teenager had beaten Ms. Parks to the punch in Montgomery. The retiree, with a thick Heart of Dixie drawl, grows misty when she speaks about the old days, such as when she waxes about Dr. King. "He was just an average-looking fellow—it's not like he was Kobe Bryant or anything," she revealed, accompanied by the flirtatious fluttering of her eyelashes. "But when he opened his mouth he was like Charlton Heston playing Moses." The fiery young rebel yet survives.

When asked if she is bitter that through circumstances Rosa Parks usurped her place in history, the answer is negative. She says she is content with a bigger reward: "Being dragged off that bus was worth it just to see Barack Obama become president, because so many others gave their lives and didn't get to see it, and I thank God for letting me see it." In a nod to irony, her spiritual salvation was when the black and white establishment failed to break her spirit—even when they threw her under the bus.

CHAPTER 12:
NO COLOR (1940)

Before the exchange of rings, the minister recites a quotation from the *Book of Common Prayer*: "What therefore God hath joined together, let no man put asunder." Unfortunately, to put asunder is what the state of Virginia routinely did, thereby lending an ironic overtone to its slogan, "Virginia is for lovers." And yet, through a Southern steel magnolia, Vergil's words came to pass: "Amor vincit omnia."

In 1950, a seventeen-year-old man from Central Point in Caroline County, north of Richmond, walked down a dirt pass to hear some hillbilly music, never dreaming the walk would change his life—as well as his country. Seven brothers of the Jeter family were performing that night, playing bluegrass in their farmhouse. In the audience were their two sisters, Garnet and Mildred Dolores. Although he had come for the entertainment, he was drawn to Mildred. The eleven-year-old had been nicknamed String Bean—shortened to Bean—because of her stick-thin frame. It was not love at first sight, because she initially thought he was arrogant. As it turned out he was not; rather, Richard Perry Loving was just a man of few words.

During the next several years, they spent free time together though segregation compelled their attendance in different schools and churches. Other than this, in Central Point, fraternizing between the races was not an issue; Richard's favorite pastime was drag racing in a car he co-owned with an African American friend. This was not the case, though, when they ate lunch in nearby Bowling Green, and were obliged to sit at different counters. Over the years their courtship turned romantic, but, as Lysander observed in *A Midsummer's Night Dream*, "The course of true love never did run smooth."

At age eighteen, Mildred became pregnant, and the problem was not morning sickness, but rather, societal illness. The trouble was not merely because she was an unwed teen from a poor family with a grade eleven education. The thorn was although interracial intimacy was not uncommon, legalizing it was a horse of a different color. Apartheid flourished in Cold War America as Virginia's Racial Integrity Act—instituted in 1662—prohibited marriage between the races. However, they determined to do what was elsewhere deemed the right thing to do, and decided to exchange vows. They knew it would create a tempest, but they loved each other. Mildred, who strongly identified with her Indian heritage— she had Cherokee and Rappahannock Native American roots—felt she was the 1950s Pocahontas, and the legendary princess had married a white man. Because of their honorable intentions, the couple was to have more on their plate than merely choosing the china pattern for their wedding registry.

Richard attempted to sidestep Jim Crow, and on a summer afternoon in 1958, the pair travelled to Washington, DC with Mildred's father and one of her brothers to serve as witnesses. They were saddened they could not have been married by one of their own ministers and picked a random name from a phonebook. Afterwards, they returned to Central Point, where Richard had purchased an acre of land near Mildred's family home on which he planned to build a house for his family. It was their hope that Richard's mother, a midwife, would deliver their baby, and that they would live in the bosom of relatives in a bucolic country setting. It was then that matters turned truly ugly.

Five weeks after the ceremony, the newlyweds "midsummer's night dreams" were shattered when the local sheriff, his deputy, and the county jailer (the sum total of law enforcement in Caroline County) barged into the couple's residence. They might have caught them in the act, but the Lovings were asleep. Brooks shone a flashlight in their faces and the sheriff demanded of Richard, "Who is this woman you're sleeping with?" Richard did not answer. He never spoke much to strangers, a combination of his reticent nature and embarrassment he was a bricklayer with a single year of high school. Mildred answered, "I'm his wife." "Not here you're not," the sheriff replied. In protest, Richard pointed to the framed marriage certificate on his wall from the District of Columbia, to which Sheriff Garnett Brooks growled, "That's no good here."

Virginia charged the newlyweds with unlawful cohabitation "against the peace and dignity of the Commonwealth." The officers took the newlyweds to a rat-infested jail in Bowling Green and Richard spent a night behind bars, his pregnant wife several more. It was the night the lights went out in Virginia.

Because the Lovings were indeed in violation of the law—and their court-appointed attorney did not have a high opinion of his clients and referred to Richard as a redneck—they had no choice other than to plead guilty. Judge Leon Bazile informed the defendants that "as long as you live you will be known as felons." They were sentenced to one year in prison—the maximum the judge could have imposed was five—for violating the anti-miscegenation statute. They were offered a plea bargain of a dismissal with the provision they leave the state and not return in one another's company for twenty-five years. Not surprisingly, they chose banishment. They paid the court fees of $36.29 each, and moved across the Potomac where Donald, Peggy, and Sidney were born. They secretly returned for Mildred to give birth, and were arrested once more. Their lawyer used his friendship with the judge to secure their release, but warned them there would be no further leniency.

The Lovings dearly missed their close-knit families and friends, and the concrete of their ghetto in Washington, DC was a cold contrast to the open spaces of Caroline County. For Mrs. Loving, Washington might as well have been Siberia. As her husband said, "Mildred was crying the blues all the time." For marrying the only man she had ever loved, Mrs. Loving had paid a steep price. She could have collapsed under the hammer of Jim Crow but she decided *to still rise*. She had to be strong for her husband and children. Her breaking point was when a car hit her son Donald, and she decided that sometimes when things are a crying shame there comes a time to stop crying—and start doing.

In 1963, inspired by the Civil Rights Movement and the March on Washington, Mildred wrote to Attorney General Robert F. Kennedy for help, and he put them in touch with the American Civil Liberties Union. They accepted the case pro bono, and Bernard S. Cohen and Philip J. Hirschkop served as their attorneys. Because of their religion, they may have felt a personal connection to the case—not only because they viewed Virginia as denying a basic human right—but as the case echoed Nazi Germany's Nuremberg law that forbade marriage between Gentiles and Jews. The two men paid for their part in legal history. There was cold shoulders from some disapproving bar colleagues, nasty anonymous telephone calls, disparaging references to "two Jew lawyers" in the Ku Klux Klan newspaper, and sugar poured into the gasoline tanks of family cars.

The leading attorney Cohen's first problem was that the Lovings had pled guilty and therefore had no legal right to an appeal. He asked Bazile to set aside his original verdict. The judge refused and reiterated the couple's culpability with the words, "Almighty

God created the races white, black, yellow, malay and red, and He placed them on separate continents…The fact that He separated the races shows that He did not intend for the races to mix." The attorneys saw the quagmire as the perfect leverage for a hearing in front of the Supreme Court, and though Richard disliked being used as a leverage for anything, he agreed. The private Lovings became accidental activists, cast in the roles of the unwitting righters of a historic wrong. When they were featured in *LIFE Magazine*, they were shocked to find themselves in the eye of the storm.

When the Supreme Court heard the arguments, seventeen states remained steadfast in their refusal to repeal laws banning interracial marriages. Various eyes were riveted on the trial: the Klan looked through the holes in their hoods and prayed the status quo continue; liberals hoped the bastion of prejudice would meet its demise; romantics felt the drama of a Southern love story. Cohen said there was something serendipitous about the fact that the case would be called *Loving v. the Commonwealth of Virginia*. Mildred said the only thing that mattered to her was being able to walk down the street, in view of everyone, with her husband's arm around her. Eschewing the limelight, the couple spent the trial hours at home, Mildred sewing and cooking, Richard laying bricks and mowing the lawn. Although he did not attend the hearing for which he had been instrumental, Richard sent a message to the Justices: "Mr. Cohen, tell the Court I love my wife and it is just not fair that I cannot live with her in Virginia." The Court agreed.

The 1967 decision ruled 9 to 0 that Virginia's laws were aimed at white supremacy, were unconstitutional, and a violation of the Fourteenth Amendment. Chief Justice Earl Warren—who in 1954 wrote the court's opinion in *Brown v. Board of Education*—wrote, "Marriage is one of the basic civil rights of man," and ended the proceedings with the pronouncement, "These convictions must be reversed. It is so ordered." His decree—to use the motto of Virginia—was a "sic semper tyrannis" that struck a stake through the heart of Jim Crow and eliminated one of the last vestiges of slavery. Of the ruling, Mildred later said, "I feel free now." After nine years, the Lovings were legally able to return as a family to Virginia. Richard built by hand a simple, cinder block house close to both of their parents, on Passing Road.

If the Bible Belt had been ruled by karmic justice, the second half of the Lovings' lives would have brought the serenity they had been earlier denied, but this was not the case. While laws can be changed by the stroke of a pen, attitudes sometimes cannot, particularly racial attitudes in an area that was once the capital of the Confederacy. In the years after the trial, Brooks and the Lovings never exchanged a word. The sheriff made it clear he harbored no qualms about what he did. "I was acting according to the law at the time, and I still think it should be on the books. I don't think a white person should marry a black person. I'm from the old school. The Lord made sparrows and robins, not to mix with one another." He then added, "If they'd been outstanding people, I would have thought something about it. But with the caliber of those people, it didn't matter. They were both low-class." Mildred decided to ignore the haters and lived a private, ordinary life with its ordinary pleasures—a wonderful marriage, children, and proximity to family. She attended church, cooked, smoked unfiltered Pall Malls, and drank endless cups of instant coffee with neighbors. A favorite pastime was sitting hand-in-hand with Richard on their back porch to a peaceful view of the fields they had fought to call home. However, the fates were not yet finished with Mildred Jeter Loving.

When Mildred was thirty-five, she, her sister Garnet, and Richard were driving along a highway when a drunk driver broadsided their car. Her husband died on impact, Mildred lost her left eye, and Garnet suffered minor injuries. Richard is buried in a mostly black graveyard just outside the local Baptist Church. Even in death, he refused to be bound by the confines of segregation. Mildred's widowhood was lonely, but she never considered replacing him. They had loved each other.

In the years following the ruling, the Lovings had turned down countless requests for interviews, public appearances, and honors. Mildred Loving had no affiliations beyond her church and her family, and never considered herself a hero: "It wasn't my doing, it was God's work." People had accepted they would not hear from the reclusive Mildred again, but on the fortieth anniversary of the

ruling, a gay rights group asked her to make a statement in favor
of same sex marriage, citing the parallels between their situations.
She listened with empathy, a worn bible on her end table, as the
group's founder told of his own struggles with a society that would
not permit him to marry who he loved. She agreed and issued the
statement, "I support the freedom to marry for all. That's what
Loving, and loving, are all about."

Although Mildred continued to shy away from publicity, her
legacy kept her name alive. The anniversary of the Supreme Court
decision, June 12th, is celebrated as Loving Day, a time set aside to
showcase that the right to marry lays in the hands of individuals,
not the state.

The indefatigable woman, the reluctant warrior in the Civil
rights Movement, died in her home in 2008 from pneumonia. She
left behind her two surviving children, eight grandchildren, and
eleven great-grandchildren, and was interred next to her husband.
Mildred showed that love, like water, has no color.

CHAPTER 13:
THE FEMALE DAVID (1945)

The Maid of Orleans, resplendent in white armor, for centuries held sway as the world's most fearless female fighter. In our contemporary era is a woman, far less flamboyant but equally intrepid, who has waged battle under the banner of a white star and a fighting peacock. The face of freedom in her beleaguered country belongs to a slim woman of pensionable age, possessed of a fragile beauty and a core of steel.

Shakespeare wrote, "Some are born great, some achieve greatness, and some have greatness thrust upon 'em." In a storied land, a woman was born heir to this two-edged sword and her life is so improbable it could have indeed come from the pen of the Bard. Aung San Suu Kyi was raised, along with her brothers Aug San Oo and Aung San Lin, in the once enchanted land of Burma, renamed Myanmar. Khin Kyi was a tiger mother on steroids, and the first words she taught her daughter in English were "selfish" and "waste"—and Khin Kyi tolerated neither. Suu Kyi recalled, "I was a bit of a coward when I was small. I was terribly frightened of the dark. She didn't approve of that all, because she was frightened of nothing." At the age of eleven, the child wandered in the dark,

petrified, but after a few days, she conquered her fear. An incident
that illustrates Khin Kyi's philosophy of duty above all is when
she heard of her youngest son's drowning accident in a pond at
the family's home; she stayed and finished her work. However,
the greatest influence of her life was a man she hardly knew, her
father General Aung San. He had been a revered national figure,
dedicated to wrest his homeland from the British yoke. During the
colonial era, inspired by the Buddha's call for good governance, he
led his nation's monks in resistance to their European oppressors.
The English scorned them as "political agitators in robes" and
hanged several leaders. In 1946, the General brought hope when
he delivered a fiery pro-independence speech on the steps of
the Shwedagon Pagoda. Somerset Maugham had compared the
sight of the pagoda rising above the city, glistening with gold, to
a sudden hope in the dark night of the soul. When Suu Yi was
two, political rivals assassinated Aung San, along with most of his
council. One of her memories was of her father threading flowers
in her hair, and a cherished photo is of him holding her in his
arms. She grew up wanting to be worthy of being his daughter, and
years later discovered what an all-consuming toll it would take.

The General's murder ended any hope for his country's dream
of democracy and the nation fell under the repressive dictatorship
of a military junta. To deflect from the killing, the new leader gave
the widowed Khin Kyi a position as Burma's first ambassador to
India. She instilled in her children a strong sense of her husband's

unfinished legacy; an advocate of Gandhi, the widow followed his precept, "The weak can never forgive. Forgiveness is the attribute of the strong."

After college in New Delhi, in 1964 the teenaged Suu Kyi left to England with the expectation that post-degree she would return and settle down with a Burmese man. Khin Kyi asked her old friends Sir Paul Gore-Booth and his wife, Lady Pat, to act as her daughter's guardians. With her Queen's English speech, Audrey Hepburn appearance, and omnipresent flower-bedecked hair, she charmed the couple and captured the hearts of many tweed-wearing academics. One of these was the rumpled-haired Michael Aris, a friend of the Gore-Booth's son, who introduced them at his parents' Chelsea home. Aris, a student of Tibetan language and culture, experienced his coup de foudre. Their blossoming romance was interrupted when he had to fulfill his obligation to tutor the children of the Bhutanese royal family, and she in turn obtained a position at the United Nations. During the painful months of separation, she wrote 197 letters of longing. During a visit, Michael proposed amid the snow-capped mountains of Bhutan. Before she accepted, Suu Kyi made a unique prenup stipulation; he had to agree if Burma ever needed her, he would not stand in her way. Michael, madly in love and ignoring the plea which had the improbability of a dark fairy-tale, readily acquiesced. They married in a Buddhist ceremony at the Gore-Booth's home where the Kipling poem "Mandalay" was recited:

"I've a neater, sweeter maiden in a cleaner, greener land! On the road to Mandalay." Notably absent were her mother and brother, who disapproved of Suu Kyi's marriage to a member of the hated ex-colonial power. She stated that they would eventually "get over their initial disappointment at what they probably consider my usual waywardness." Khin Kyi did come around with the birth of sons Alexander and Kim (the latter named after the eponymous character in Rudyard Kipling's novel).

Suu Kyi settled into the undistinguishable role of scholar's spouse, content to be the perfect homemaker. She sewed curtains and clothes, decorated with Bhutanese rugs, and ironed everything, including her husband's socks. In the kitchen she prepared exquisite meals for dinner parties with Oxford intellectuals, and orchestrated picture-perfect birthday parties. A friend said she brought out the best in you, straightened your back. The first fifteen years of marriage were all about her family of men until the Burmese Suu Kyi was confronted with a variation of the Polish Sophie's choice.

The serene life of the Aris family came with an expiration date; in 1988, as the couple were reading on their sofa, a phone call informed them Khin Kyi had suffered a stroke. Suu Yi took her farewell and they said goodbye in the belief she would return in time for Christmas, and life in their Victorian home would return to its well-appointed rounds.

Shortly after Suu Yi's arrival in Rangoon, the 8888 Uprising erupted and the city was in the middle of an anti-dictatorship riot, under the control of General Than Shwe, characterized as a psychopath in the great tradition of Idi Amin and Kim Jong-il. An admirer of Burma's ancient kings, at his daughter's wedding supplicants bowed before her; his regime has created its own version of Brownshirts. Her mother's hospital flooded with injured protestors; since public meetings were forbidden under martial law, it had become the epicenter of the leaderless revolution. Word that the great General's daughter had returned spread like wildfire. The demure Oxford housewife inadvertently had become a beacon of hope for millions. It was her father's name that drew the crowds when she delivered a speech, in defiance on the brutal regime's edict against public assembly. Over half a million turned up in front of the Shwedagon Pagoda, in the symbolic shadow of where Aung San had held sway against the colonial oppressors. The microphone broadcast her words, "I could not as my father's daughter remain indifferent to all that is going on." She went on to proclaim that moral force would prevail over military force, and to adhere to the Buddhist principle of nonviolent protest. The smitten crowd embraced her as the embodiment of their prayers.

Soon after, a delegation asked Suu Kyi to spearhead the liberation movement, the National League for Democracy, which had its symbol a fighting peacock and a white star, dedicated to oust the barbaric regime of General Than Shwe. She agreed in the belief that once it proved victorious, she would be free to return to her sons and husband. Back in Oxford, Michael nervously watched the news as his wife toured her homeland, accosted by the military that harassed her and tortured her followers. Ever present was the fear she would meet the same fate as her father. When her party secured more than 80 percent of parliamentary seats, the junta summarily dismissed the results.

It was at this juncture Suu Kyi was confronted with an agonizing moral quandary: stay in Burma and become the mother to millions or return to Oxford and remain a mother to Alexander and Kim. In direct opposition to E. M. Forester's sentiment of choosing friendship over country, she made the heart-rending decision to remain in her homeland. She felt as the daughter of Aung San she could walk no other path. For Michael, the prenuptial promise had taken on a terrifying reality.

A year after Suu Yi cast her lot with Burma, she had her first close encounter with death when a column of soldiers assembled to fire on her and her followers. While her companions ducked for cover, she walked into the middle of the road, directly in the line of danger. She explained in an interview, "It seemed so much simpler to provide them with a single target." A senior officer revoked the death sentence at the last moment. She survived a second rendezvous with the Grim Reaper in 2003, in which seventy of her followers perished. News quickly spread how the petite, unarmed woman with the flower in her hair had emasculated the regime's soldiers and her legend blossomed. General Than Shwe was faced with King Richard's own plea: can no one rid me of this accursed priest? However, as he felt an assassination would only increase her stature as a martyr, he ordered her house arrest in her ancestral lakeside home. He dictated her name not be mentioned and so the Burmese took to calling her Lady.

During the years of detention, Suu Yi had to endure isolation from family, friends, and followers. Rather than accept food from her captors, her guards sold her furniture to buy provisions. Her hair fell out from lack of nourishment and her diminutive frame grew skeletal. She spent the monsoon months moving buckets to catch the leaks from the decaying roof. San Oo could have helped with repairs; however, having cast his lot with the dictator, abandoned his sister.

Suu Kyi had traversed the path from an enviable life to one most unenviable. Despite all she had to endure, her back, always ramrod straight, refused to bend, even when locked in her home turned prison without access to a telephone, television, or computer. She adopted the same sentiment as Richard Lovelace in his poem, "To Althea, From Prison:" "Stone walls do not a prison make/Nor iron bars a cage." What gave Suu Kyi the sustenance to survive was her faith. Her daily ritual was to rise at six, feed the crows as an act of Buddhist tenet, and eat a breakfast of noodles. This was followed by an hour of meditation, the practice that fed her fortitude during two interminable decades. She also battled crippling ennui by playing the piano, reading, and listening to Bach and Mozart. She spent several hours a day listening to BBC on her radio, which is how she discovered she had won the Nobel Peace Prize in 1991, one her son accepted in her name. For Michael, bereft of communication, it was only the report from those who heard her piano that brought solace. When it fell into disrepair, even that fragile scrap of comfort was lost. Suu Kyi voraciously studied the words of Mandela, imprisoned on Robben Island in South Africa. She shared with him the bond that they were the world's two most famous political prisoners. The difference is she could have walked free any time. However, she knew if she were to leave Burma, it would mean permanent exile.

In 1997, Michael was diagnosed with terminal prostate cancer. Than Shwe would not grant him a visa to enter Myanmar, despite the appeals of the Pope and President Clinton—and the only way to be with him as he lay dying would be to return to Oxford. After Suu Kyi realized she would never see her husband again, she put on her dress of his favorite color, fastened a rose in her hair, and through the British embassy, recorded a farewell film in which she told him that his love for her had been her mainstay and to forgive her waywardness. The film arrived in Oxford two days after Michael's passing. She was distraught at not being by her husband's side and for leaving her sons virtual orphans, trading her role as doting mother to global force for justice. Alexander— especially after the passing of his father—was angered by his mother's choice, while Kim took the stance he had to follow in the steps of his grandfather. She refuses to discuss the subject, except to admit that her darkest hours were when "I feared the boys might be needing me." A pang of remorse stemmed from the fact her sons had not been part of the pact she had made with their father. Undergoing a tsunami of guilt, after dozens of years of house arrest, Aung San Suu Kyi could have succumbed to despair, but the Lady knew the only choice was *still to rise*. Rather than aggrandizing herself as the incarnation of the Asian Nelson Mandela, she deflects her role as Burma's Great Lady: "I don't think I have achieved anything that I can really be proud of. When we've achieved democracy, I'll tell you."

In a nod to how good ultimately triumphs over evil, in 2010 Suu Kyi was finally released, after spending fifteen of twenty-one years under house arrest. Kim flew to see his mother after a ten-year separation. He wore a T-shirt emblazoned with one of the monsters from the childhood classic *Where the Wild Things Are*; on his arm was a tattoo of a fighting peacock. Aung San Suu Kyi now serves as Myanmar's de facto president, a contemporary parable of the female David who defeated General Goliath.

CHAPTER 14:
A MIRACLE WORKER (1946)

The term stage-mother carries negative connotations: those who wanted a star to be born—at any cost. Ethel Gumm initiated Judy's Garland lifelong addiction by supplying her with diet pills, uppers, and downers. Her constant pushing led her daughter to brand her "the real Wicked Witch of the West." Marie Gurdin refused to let Natalie Wood wear a cast on her broken arm, fearing it would hinder auditions—the bone never properly set. Terri Shields made Brooke infamous at age twelve by letting her appear nude in *Pretty Baby*. Then there was that blue jean ad of the pubescent Brooke with its caption, "Nothing comes between me and my Calvins." Terri's mothering was even criticized in her obituary in the *New York Times*. Currently, we have "momagers" Kris Jenner and Mamma June Shannon. Another child actress had even more reason to cry, "Mama mia!"

A 1962 *LIFE Magazine* carried a glossy pictorial on the making of *The Miracle Worker*, and one depicted an aged Helen Keller and a young Patty Duke, who played her as a girl both on the Broadway stage and on the big screen. It seemed as if the two were worlds apart: the blind, deaf octogenarian and the beautiful star. The connection: they both were gifted with a miracle worker.

Anna Marie Duke, the youngest of three children, was born in Queens, New York, into a threadbare existence, both in terms of family and finances. Her father, John Patrick, a taxi driver, spent his off hours drinking, and mother Frances—who had become an orphan at age five—suffered from debilitating depression and recurrent hospitalizations. She became a cashier when her husband deserted the family and, a devout Catholic, was devastated at the breakdown of her marriage. On one occasion, Frances decided to kill herself and her three children. "We're all going together," she announced as she turned on the gas. Fortunately, she had neglected to close the windows.

Her older brother Ray attended a local boy's club and was acting in plays when the husband and wife theatrical agents, John and Ethel Ross, became his managers. Frances was delighted when Ray started bringing in desperately needed income and was grateful when they offered to represent the seven-year-old Anna Marie as well. They saw something in the little girl with the heavy Queen's accent. She was not classically beautiful with her gap-toothed grin, but they sensed she had something—something that had the makings of a golden goose. And she had something else: the desire to please. Maybe if she was perfect, her mother wouldn't be crazy, her father would come home. The Rosses were able to convince Frances that the best thing for her daughter would be for Anna Marie to live with them; Mrs. Duke tearfully agreed and accepted a salary to help ease the family amputation. Anna Marie was devastated; she had already lost one parent and now she was losing the other, as well as her siblings. And soon she was to lose something else. The Rosses decided her name did not have the right ring to it and told her, "Anna Marie is dead. You're Patty now." Ms. Duke later said that line was to launch a thousand hours of therapy. They had chosen Patty after the beautiful child actress Patty McCormack, star of *The Bad Seed*. The adult Patty said of this bleak period, "I was stripped of my parents, I was stripped of my name, I was eventually stripped of my religion, and they had a blank slate to do with as they wished." The Svengalis couple erased her Queens accent, dressed her like a miniature Grace Kelly, and life revolved around auditions, rehearsals, and performances, all under the thumb of her brow-beating managers—her surrogate parents. The dynamics succeeded professionally: she worked with Sir Laurence Olivier in *The Power and the Glory,* with Richard Burton in *Wuthering Heights.*

When Patty was thirteen, they began to ply her with Percodan—happy pills—and booze. Years later, watching a program on incest, she remembered a repressed sexual episode. Once, both Rosses got into bed and fondled her; that served as an introduction to sex. At other times, just John. The first incident was after a day of sun-bathing and drinking banana daiquiris. Patty says she still cannot bear the smell of Sea n' Ski tanning lotion. Yet her public persona remained Perky Patty, the polite child star. Her life resembled a script by Dickens, musical score by Freud.

For eighteen months, before the audition for the Broadway play of *The Miracle Worker*, the Rosses spent time each day treating their protégée as if she were deaf and blind, banging pots and pans behind her until she no longer flinched at the sound and made her perform household chores blindfolded. She garnered the role of Helen alongside Anne Bancroft, who played teacher Anne Sullivan. The theater production proved so successful it became a 1962 Hollywood film adaptation; Ms. Duke won the Academy Award for Best Supporting Actress, at age sixteen the youngest person in history to receive the honor. As the world watched the beautiful teen accept her Oscar, they felt oh, lucky girl.

Patty found TV fame by playing a scientific impossibility known as identical cousins on *The Patty Duke Show* that ran from 1963 to 1966. Although critics viewed it as going from a sublime role to a ridiculous one, the public ate it up, along with its blitz of merchandising. Female baby boomers delighted in the antics of the prim Scottish Cathy Lane and her perky all-American first coz Patty Lane. Its theme song yet reverberates, "Where Cathy adores a minuet/The Ballets Russes, and crepes suzette/ Our Patty loves to rock 'n' roll/ a hot dog makes her lose control..." But it was not hot dogs that made the real Patty lose control.

Deliverance came at age eighteen when Ethel's mother told her just before she died to break away—the Rosses were crazy. "It was like the last words from a guru before the spirit leaves the body. She was the one authority figure who told me that I wasn't hallucinating, I wasn't nuts." Her means of escape was marriage to the former assistant director of her hit TV show, thirty-two-year-old Harry Falk. Shortly afterwards, she discovered that the Rosses had spent most of her almost million dollar earnings to support their very lavish lifestyle, leaving her with $84,000 in savings bonds.

At this juncture, her appendix ruptured and the medication triggered her first manic episode. She did not eat or sleep and spent enormous sums, followed by crushing lows. While Falk had ostensibly married the acclaimed Patty Duke, he found himself the husband of the emotionally fragile Anna Marie. She sank into a depression so acute that she could not go to a supermarket without suffering an anxiety attack. During this time she made the first of several suicide attempts and was a patient in various mental hospitals. As Falk was a producer, not a saint, their union ended in divorce. The same year, she co-starred in the film of Jacqueline Suzann's *Valley of the Dolls*, along with Sharon Tate, victim of the Manson family. It was a bid to distance herself from the two adorable teen cousins. Her role was the pill-popping, boozing, sex-crazed Neely O'Hara, whose signature line was, "Sparkle, Neely, Sparkle!" Many people suspected it was a case of type-casting.

At age twenty-four, Duke began a widely publicized affair with the seventeen-year-old Desi Arnaz Jr. The tabloids dubbed them the kiddie version of Elizabeth Taylor and Eddie Fisher. While everyone might have loved Lucy, Patty did not, as the red-headed mama was no way going to accept the twice divorced, mentally unstable older woman for her only son. Nevertheless, Desi accompanied her to the Emmy Awards that year for her nomination in *Sweet Charlie*. The impression she made for the TV play did not compare with the one she made at the awards ceremony. She wore an evening dress topped by a long crocheted sweater tied around the waist with red yarn. She rambled on, incoherently. The episode ended with a three-day stay at a psychiatric hospital. "The truth of the matter is that my condition had nothing to do with drugs or alcohol. I was having a serious emotional breakdown. Unlike most people in trouble who fall apart in the privacy of their bedrooms, I fell apart on network television," she stated. In rebound from Desi, Ms. Duke took her vows for a second time with Michael Tell, who she met when he sublet her apartment. It ended after thirteen days. She also became pregnant, though she was not sure if paternity belonged to Desi, Michael, or the married John Astin, who played Uncle Gomez, the head of the macabre Addams family. He became her third husband and adopted Sean. However, marriage did not signify a happier time, though it did produce son Mackenzie. Part of the problem was the household consisted of Astin's three teenage sons, and five boys proved too much for the unraveling mother. It resulted in divorce number three. She admitted she was not marriage material.

At critical mass, Patty locked herself in the bathroom, determined to take her life. The manic episodes were getting worse, her third marriage was crumbling; she just could not carry on any longer. However, what made her *still rise* was Sean and Mackenzie banging on the door, begging her to come out. She realized she could not abandon them; her mother had done so and it had led to her ruination.

Patty turned to psychiatrists, praying they could provide the remedy that her self-medicating substance abuse had not. Helen's breakthrough moment was when she felt the cold water from the pump and associating it with an early memory had her epiphany, "Waa! Waa!" In 1982, Patty had hers when she was finally diagnosed as suffering from manic depression—now known as bipolar disorder. "It's not a giant thrill to hear someone give you the label manic-depressive but to me I was so relieved. What I was suffering from had a name and could be treated," she said. The magic bullet to battle her soul-crushing illness was lithium, which evened out the mood swings. While many of those so afflicted reject the medication in an act of self-sabotaging denial, Patty took hers religiously. The demons started to crumble.

It was not enough for Patty to embark on the road to recovery; it became her mission to help fellow pilgrims in psychological pain. She broke celebrity ground by making public her diagnosis: "It's like being a scientist and finding something new in the universe. I had to go out and tell people that they weren't the only ones."

This was courageous, as it was a different time: while people would fall over themselves in empathy if someone suffered from an illness that carried physical manifestations, an individual who exhibited signs of mental illness was labeled as nuts and was sanctimoniously shunned. This made mental disorders all the worse, as the victim would take pains to hide their symptoms and would not seek help, an admission of instability. While now we are used to the darker side of fame—we've experienced actors spill their substance abuse beans to Ellen and Oprah—Duke suffered at a time when there was a lid on our dark secrets, and she risked her career to perform an emotional strip-tease. She spoke candidly of her drugs, drinking, anorexia, promiscuity, and binge-spending. Patty Duke further helped take bipolar out of the closet with her 1987 memoir, *A Brilliant Madness: Living with Manic Depressive Illness*.

Patty finally became marriage material when she wed ex-Army sergeant Michael Pearce, who she met while filming the television movie *A Time to Triumph*, with who she adopted son Kevin, and lived on a seventy-acre Idaho farm. It was a sanctuary where she found refuge from the clutter, noise, and turmoil of the big cities and from her tumultuous past. She referred to Michael's dog tags that she wore as a necklace and asked, "What do people do who don't have you in their lives?" On a more serious note, she added, "This marriage is the best thing for me...I don't even have to think about it anymore—this thing called security. For the first time in my adult life, I really am just being me, whatever that me is at that moment. Mike can criticize me and not have to worry that I'm going to run into the bathroom and swallow the neighbor's Valium." Anna Marie Pearce, the name she went by, became a grandmother, and son Sean followed in her footsteps, most notably in *The Goonies* and as the hobbit Sam in *The Lord of the Rings* trilogy. Patty renewed her television career and garnered three Emmys, served as the president of the Screen Actors Guild, and remained a tireless advocate for mental health.

One afternoon, while strolling along the Hollywood Walk of Fame, she told her grandson there was a rumor she would be getting her own special star—which she did in 2004. He replied, "Oh, Nana, people will remember you!" However, even without the Hollywood memorial, because of her on and off stage work, Patty would live on.

In her autobiography, entitled *Call Me Anna*, the last sentence is, "I've survived. I've beaten my own bad system and some days, on most days that feels like a miracle." Like Helen's teacher, Ann Sullivan, in salvaging her own life, proved herself a miracle worker.

CHAPTER 15:
MY MOTHER'S DAUGHTER (1952)

In the *Battle Hymn of the Tiger,* Mother-author Amy Chua wrote a blueprint on how to raise certifiably Grade A children: thou shalt not have any play dates; though shalt not receive any score lower than A+; thou shalt not attend any university devoid of ivy. Another Chinese mother raised her daughter with similar expectations; however, this tiger mama threatened to kill her cub with a meat cleaver as murder weapon.

The generation gap leads to family tensions and the problem is exacerbated in immigrant households. Born in Oakland, California to John and Daisy, Amy (Enmei, "blessing from America") Tan, along with brothers John Jr. and Peter, grew up in an environment light-years away from China. John became the minister of a Chinese Baptist Church in Fresno—rather than work as an engineer—that led his wife to complain he had consigned them to a life of poverty. John preached the ghost of God was always present, while Daisy's ghosts crouched in the shadows.

As a child, Amy fantasied about plastic surgery to make her look less ethnic and felt humiliated by her mother's accent. While

American parents cautioned their children not to run into the street, a Daisyism was, "You don't look, you get smash flat like sand crab." She also experienced a sense of rootlessness from constant moves around the San Francisco Bay Area. Amy later wrote her childhood was shadowed by a sense of double jeopardy, realizing that her mother could both help and hurt her in the best and worst ways possible.

When Amy began to date, her mother offered her variation of the birds and the bees: "Don't ever let boy kiss you. You do, you can't stop. Then you have baby. You put baby in garbage can. Police find you, put you in jail, then you life over, better just kill yourself." In truth, it was Daisy who threatened to kill herself, "sometimes weekly, sometimes daily, whenever she was displeased with me or my father or my brothers, whenever she felt slighted by her friends, whenever the milk spilled or the rice burned."

In 1968, the calamity Daisy dreaded came to call: Peter died of a brain tumor and six months later Mr. Tan passed away from the same affliction. Amy, dad's darling, began to act out. While author Amy Chua's daughter rebelled by insisting on violin lessons instead of piano, Amy was in open revolt. On one occasion, when Amy angered her mother, she began to hit her daughter and offered a glimpse of her life in China: "Why did I have you? I have other daughters who are good; they speak Chinese and they love to obey me." In despair, the new widow turned to her Ouija board: "Amy treat me so bad...What I should do—send her Taiwan, school for bad girls?" She ended up sending her to a community church elder for grief counseling who sexually molested the teen. Daisy, who believed in ancestral spirits and malign imbalances, felt the house and its inhabitants were cursed and relocated once more, this time to Europe. Their first stop, in 1968, was Holland, because Daisy had used a product—Old Dutch Cleanser—and interpreted it as the country was clean. After a Volkswagen odyssey through the Netherlands looking for a furnished house, an American school, and a place free from evil spirits, the trio settled in Montreux, Switzerland.

In New Haven, Amy Chua threatened her daughter's stuffed animals with destruction when met with defiance; in Switzerland, at age sixteen, Amy thought she was going to be murdered by her own mother—a Chinese Medea. Despite Daisy's earlier dating mantra, Amy had begun sneaking out and Daisy hired a private investigator. He reported Amy was in a relationship with a German army deserter drug-dealer who had escaped from a mental hospital. Daisy was unimpressed, for more reasons than her daughter had not found a nice, Chinese-Baptist boy in pre-med, and a violent stand-off ensued. "I saw the flash of a meat cleaver just before she pushed me to the wall and brought the blade's edge to within an inch of my throat. Her eyes were like a wild animal's, shiny, fixated on the kill...She pressed the blade closer and I could feel her breath gusting," Amy said. This lasted for twenty minutes, with Amy pleading, "I want to live. I want to live. I want to live."

Daisy, alienated in Europe, returned to San Francisco, where she could commiserate with other Chinese mothers who rued their wayward American daughters. And indeed she had fresh material. She had expected her daughter to be a neurosurgeon by profession and a concert pianist as a hobby. Instead, Amy abandoned pre-med studies at Linfield College, a Baptist school in Oregon, one of two her mother had chosen. Ms. Tan left to follow her Italian-American boyfriend, Louis De Mattei, to San Jose State University, where she enrolled as an English major. Although Daisy did not follow—meat cleaver in tow—the two stopped speaking for six months. Eventually they reconciled, and Daisy invited her and Lou to dinner, where Daisy, in the kitchen, was throwing pots and pans while Lou remained mostly quiet, but enjoyed the food, two things of which her mother approved. At age twenty-two, the couple wed—he became a tax attorney, and once proved a charm. Although Tan's literary theme is mothers and daughters, she decided against having a child of her own, fearful of passing on her instability and feeling her books are her offspring. Another reason could well have been a vision of Daisy as Tiger grandmother.

Wedded bliss, however, did not keep the demons at bay. Burglars broke into her best friend Peter's apartment; Amy had to identify his body and witnessed the carnage. As the murder occurred on her birthday, she always associated the date with the traumatic event. Devastated, she gave up on her PhD in linguistics at Berkeley and worked with disabled children, Peter's vocation, and for therapy began writing. Incredibly, Tan did not initially think to write about her own family dynamics:

When I started writing fiction I thought I had to make it all up because my life never would have been interesting enough. That I grew up in a suburb and my parents had friends who came over to play mah-jongg, and eat Chinese food—who would want to read that? And I was trying to distance myself from all that anyway.

It was on a holiday in Hawaii when Amy received the news her mother had suffered a heart attack. It turned out to be a false alarm: Daisy had gotten into a row with a fishmonger and had undergone palpitations. The incident served as a wake-up call: she had to get to know her mother before it was too late, and also decided to make good on an earlier promise to take Daisy to China. In the country of her birth, Daisy was extremely proud to be able to translate to her daughter after all the times Amy had done the same for her. Unsurprisingly, Daisy got into as many arguments with shopkeepers as she did in America. The most emotional moment was the reunion with her three daughters, who Daisy had not seen in thirty years. The trip was bonding, and their relationship was further strengthened after Daisy was diagnosed with a benign brain tumor. Faced with her mortality, she asked her daughter, "If I die, what will you remember?"

Daisy's grandmother had been raped by a wealthy businessman and became pregnant with his child. To save face, she joined his family as a concubine. Trapped and mistreated, her means of escape was to kill herself by swallowing raw opium buried in rice cakes, a suicide enacted in front of the nine-year-old Li Bingzi, the Americanized Daisy. In turn, Daisy was forced into a feudal marriage to an abusive man, and eventually ran away after blaming him for the deaths of two of their five children. Leaving her husband without a divorce was a crime, and Daisy found herself behind bars. Her trial became fodder for the Shanghai tabloids, made all the more salacious as she had fallen in love with John Tan, an electrical engineer and Baptist minister who had fled from Beijing to America. Daisy managed to escape days before the Communists took over and joined her lover; her plans to send for her three daughters ended with the descending of the Bamboo Curtain. Amy had the fabric for her 1989 novel, *The Joy Luck Club*, set mainly in San Francisco's Chinatown; it interweaves the past and present lives of four migrant women who gather to ostensibly play mah-jongg, but in reality to discuss their troubled relationships with their Coca-Cola swilling daughters.

Ms. Tan said that throughout her life she has been a magnet for extraordinary events and near disasters: "I accumulated, as others might Hummel figurines, a variety of accidents, assaults and acts of God." Apparently, Tan never lacked for high drama. Besides the passing of her father and brother, the attempted attack on her life by her mother, and the murder of her best friend, she survived two serious car crashes, robbery at gun point, getting beaten up in a bar by a drunk. Joy luck indeed. She said, "I have survivor skills. But what makes people resilient is the ability to find humor and irony in situations that would otherwise overpower you."

Amy enjoyed literary success that brought fame and fortune, had finally made peace with her mother, and had a rock solid marriage. Some perks of her celebrity status: she visited the White House and shared New Year's Eve dinner with the Clintons. She also had the thrill of sneaking her two tiny Yorkshire terriers, Lilli and Bubba, in a mesh bag past the guards at the Supreme Court Building for a meeting with Chief Justice William Rehnquist. She spends leisure time jamming with the Rock Bottom Remainders, a musical group composed of such best-selling writers as Stephen King, Mitch Albom, Maya Angelou, James McBride, and Matt Groening, among others, who perform charity concerts. Her trademark song—that she performs in dominatrix gear—is a version of Nancy Sinatra's *These Boots are Made for Walking*.

In 1993, the Tans hosted a gala film premiere of *The Joy Luck Club*, where Annette Benning introduced the screening in Amy's elegant eight-room home overlooking the Golden Gate Bridge—her neighbor is Columbian writer Isabelle Allende—and a proud Lou and Daisy were in attendance. All the ingredients were present for over-the-moon happiness, but Amy had cried all day and felt like jumping off the roof. Why, she wondered, should she possibly be this way? The answer was a crippling depression that made her believe she could not go on. What stopped her from acting on her suicidal impulses—from making the exit from the roof—was her will *to still rise*. After all, Daisy had endured; she could not add another litany to her woes. She had already lost three children. With reflection, she realized it might have been caused by all that had happened to her, but, whatever the reason, decided she had to soldier on. She reluctantly began taking antidepressants, and it made the world of difference. She said, "What a different childhood I might have had had my mother taken antidepressants." Of course, a happy life does not make for a fertile writer, and perhaps this was the price she had to pay to birth *The Joy Luck Club*. Unfortunately, the ghosts were not yet finished with Ms. Tan.

Amy grew alarmed when she had a hallucination about a naked man by her bed. She initially assumed it was her husband, but it was the dead of the night and he was not speaking. She sprang up and found the flesh-and-blood Lou calmly watching TV. What Amy later discovered was the apparition had been caused by Lyme disease from a deer tick that had attached itself to her shin when she had attended a wedding in upstate New York. The symptoms were devastating: memory lapse, vertigo, and epileptic-like seizures that prevents her from driving. The only silver lining was Daisy had passed away and was not witness to this horror.

In Daisy's later years, she exhibited signs of encroaching Alzheimer's, and it was a double-edged sword—she was finally able to forget the things she had so desperately not wanted to remember. Haunted by the memory of the meat cleaver, she told

Amy, "Amy, know I did something to hurt you...But now I can't remember what...And I just want to tell you...I hope you can forget, just as I've forgotten." Tan said of the confession, "How wonderful to hear her say what was never true, yet now would be forever so."

Daisy's words dredged up her earlier question of many years ago: "If I die what will you remember?" The dedication in *The Joy Luck Club* provides Amy's answer: *You asked me once what I would remember. This, and much more.*

Despite Amy's dual diagnosis of depression and Lyme disease, as well as the heavy baggage of memory, she is determined to squeeze every drop from the orange of life—something she jokes she plans to do if she can break free of her addiction. She stated, "I have a terrible addiction that has destroyed a lot of my writing time. It's called eBay. I buy everything on eBay. I buy wineglasses. I don't want to worry about breaking crystal wineglasses, so I buy them off eBay for a dollar. When they break, who cares?" This statement gives pause. Tan is extremely rich. Why would she worry about breaking crystal wineglasses? "I am," Tan says, conjuring a lifetime of joys and sadness, "my mother's daughter."

CHAPTER 16:
MY BELOVED WORLD (1954)

It is a common belief that those born on the wrong side of the tracks usually end up in the same place; that environment is destiny. But as one woman proved, it is possible to travel far afield from humble roots, especially when equipped with the mindset that dreams do not just have to be for sleeping.

The Supremes—not a reference to Diana Ross and her back-up singers—is a nod to nine of the most powerful people in the United States. In 1954, they ruled segregation in schools is unconstitutional; in 1973, they ruled women have a right to abortion; in 2015, they ruled on the legality of same-sex marriage. Traditionally, the justices have been white, Protestant males from comfortable backgrounds; this changed with the admission of an African American and a female. The color of the bench was also altered when it admitted its first Latina, a woman born into challenging circumstances, a woman whose mantra was *always to rise.*

Sonia Sotomayor, reflecting on her past, described herself as a child with dreams. It is testimony to her indefatigable spirit that they did not shrivel up under the harsh reality of her youth. The greatest influence on her life was her mother, Celina, who had left her orphanage in Puerto Rico at age seventeen in order to sign up for the Women's Army Corps, her contribution to the war effort. After her discharge, she married Juan, a fellow islander, and they settled in a tenement in the East Bronx. While her husband worked at a tool-and-die factory, Celina obtained a position as a telephone operator at Prospect Hospital, and later became a nurse. Her increased paycheck was especially important after the birth of Juan and Sonia. The projects were not the place to raise children, as it was populated with gangs carving up the neighborhood; stairwells needed to be avoided because of muggers and addicts shooting up. However, Celina drilled into her son and daughter that though they were living in a bad neighborhood, they could still make the right choice: be the flower that grows in the crack of a sidewalk. She also believed that education was the key to success in America, and she purchased the entire set of Encyclopedia Britannica, a novelty in the tenement.

To add to this unsavory cocktail were problems at home, chiefly caused by Juan's alcoholism. Because of his losing battle with the bottle, angry shouting matches ensued and Celina started to work nights and weekends to avoid being in his presence. When eight-year-old Sonia started wetting her bed, she was taken to the doctor and admitted to the hospital with a diagnosis of diabetes. Her disease furthered the stress as Celina, who worked nights, was not able to administer the insulin needle, and, because of alcoholic tremors, Juan was incapable of performing the procedure. Infuriated that she could not rely on her husband, the tension escalated until Sonia displayed the fortitude that would sustain her through the struggles that lay ahead. In her memoir she recounted, "The last thing I wanted was for them to fight about me. It then dawned on me: If I needed to have these shots every day for the rest of my life, the only way I'd survive was to do it myself." She learned to inject herself by practicing on an orange. Her mother showed her how to light a burner on the stove with a match, fill a pot with water to cover the syringe and needle, and wait till they were sterilized. Her family referred to her affliction as "a deadly curse." However, a positive effect of this was she learned self-reliance at an early age. In addition, because the 1960s was the era when a diagnosis of Type I diabetes came with a dramatically shortened life expectancy, it ignited a desire to do more with her allotted time.

And yet the valleys of the Sotomayors came with peaks as well. They spent summers in Puerto Rico where Sonia enjoyed eating her fill of mangoes (always keeping an eye on her blood sugar level). Another safe harbor from the chaos of her home was her *abuelita* (grandmother) Mercedes' South Bronx apartment, a place of music, poetry, and the homey smell of her comfort foods of Puerto Rican delicacies: pigs' feet with beans and pigs' tongues and ears. She also delighted in the presence of her best friend, her cousin Nelson, and the two were as inseparable as twins. Sonia says that it was the love of her grandmother that allowed her "to imagine the most improbable of possibilities for my life." From her and her great-aunt, Aurora, she learned how to be diplomatic among her many relatives and the numerous confrontations that ensued. The biggest source of contention was between Celina and Mercedes, who blamed her daughter-in-law for Juan's drinking that turned the man into a monster. Sonia later writes of him drinking at parties: "I saw my father receding from us, disappearing behind that twisted mask. It was like being trapped in a horror film, complete with his lumbering Frankenstein walk as he made his exit and the looming certainty that there would be screaming when we got home."

When Sonia was nine, her mother delivered the news:"Dios se lo Llevo," ("God took him"), when her father suddenly died from a combination of heart condition and alcoholism. Later, Sonia heard the liquor bottles clank in the trash bags that were removed from under his deathbed where they had been stashed. Because it meant an end to the battles at home, Sonia felt, "maybe it would be easier this way." However, Celina, for all her animosity against her husband, went into a state of protracted mourning. She shut herself in her dark bedroom and slid into a cocoon of depression.

Juan and Sonia, reeling from the dual onslaught of their father's loss and their mother's emotional abandonment, were left to their own devices. Sonia retreated into the world of books, especially the *Nancy Drew* mysteries, and yearned for a career as a police detective. When she confided her aspiration to her doctor, he said because of her diabetes, she would not be incapable of such a job. She also spent hours watching *Perry Mason* on her plastic-covered couch, and from the courtroom drama she realized that the most important person in the room was the man in the black robe who delivered the ruling. She had decided on her next career aspiration.

Finally, after months of reading and evenings spent sitting quietly with Juan watching television, Sonia literally hurled herself at her mother's closed door and screamed at her not to die, too. This roused Celina, and she returned to the land of the living; she began to work six days a week to support her children on a single income.

Her mother's emphasis about the importance of education had struck a respondent note, and Sonia excelled academically at the Cardinal Spellman High School, the Roman Catholic school Celina had enrolled her in as the public ones in her neighborhood were rife with trouble. When she graduated as valedictorian in 1972, her friend told her about the Ivy League—something she had never heard of—and urged her to apply to Princeton. He cautioned her of the pitfalls she would face as a Puerto Rican female from a modest background. There would be students with Roman numerals after their names who came from families that had been Princeton alumni for many generations, those who would boast of ancestors who had landed on Plymouth Rock. However, well-versed in adversary, she put in her application. She stated, "Qualifying for financial aid was the easiest part. There were no assets to report."

In fact, her parents never had a bank account.

When she enrolled in the Ivy League university—on a full scholarship—she was one of the only Latinos on campus, and this also was the case with professors. Princeton women were sharply numbered as well; the first ones had been admitted only a few years before. Because of the strikes against her, Ms. Sotomayer was too intimidated to ask questions. She also felt insecure that she could "barely write," and on her first essay received a C. She was ignorant of the classics her fellow students had studied at prestigious private schools. To help even the playing field, she immersed herself in the library; however, she was not a complete bookworm, and in her free time smoked, drank beer, and danced a mean salsa. She eventually gave up her three-and-a half packs of cigarettes a day when her young niece held a pencil between her fingers and blew imaginary smoke rings. She was able to quit cold turkey after five days in a residential program. She also married her high school sweetheart, Kevin Noonan. During this time a source of pain were the regular letters to the *Daily Princeton* complaining that students like her—those who had been helped by Affirmative Action—were displacing worthier applicants. Her mantra was her mother's own: "A surplus of effort can overcome a deficit of confidence." She graduated summa cum laude; unfamiliar with the Latin, she had to look up its translation.

She continued her studies at Yale Law School—shades of Perry Mason. In 1979, the Manhattan District attorney hired Ms.

Sotomayor as a prosecutor in a city struggling with a drug-related crime wave, and she joined a unit that handled everything from misdemeanors to homicides. However, what distilled her joy at her accomplishments were two heartaches. Her marriage ended in divorce partly because of the demands of her career and her husband's belief she did not really need him. She had decided to remain childless in fear of passing on her diabetes and did not adopt in fear she would die at an early age. Another tragedy was when her cousin Nelson asked her to drive him to what she later learned was a drug den in the Bronx, where he left to shoot heroin. He contracted AIDS from a contaminated needle that culminated in his death.

A few years later, she left to join a private law firm in Manhattan. If the firm had a tip from the United States Customs Office about a suspicious shipment, Sonia would often be involved in the risky business of going to the warehouse to have the merchandise seized. One occasion in Chinatown, where the criminals ran away, Ms. Sotomayor jumped on a motorcycle and gave chase.

Her youthful aspiration came to fruition when the first President George Bush nominated her to be a federal judge. On her first day her knees were literally knocking together as she began addressing the courtroom. However, just as Stella found her groove, so did Sotomayor, and the minute she jumped in with a question for the litigants, the panic passed. Later she told her friend of her newfound confidence, "I think this fish has found her pond."

She struck down as unconstitutional a White Plains law that prohibited the displaying of a menorah in a park. The following year she ordered New York prison officials to allow inmates to wear beads of the Santeria religion under their belts, even though the jail staff argued they were gang symbols. Another notable case included a ruling in which she mandated the government make public a photocopy of a torn-up note found in the briefcase of a former White House counsel, Vincent Foster, who later committed suicide. Her most celebrated case was when she ended a baseball strike by ruling against the team owners in favor of the ballplayers, and she was touted as the savior of the sport. She said of her position, "Each day on the bench I learn something new about the judicial process and about being a professional Latina woman in a world that sometimes looks at me with suspicion." One of the fruits of her labors was her purchasing a condominium in Greenwich Village—both a subway ride and a world away from the housing projects where she grew up. A second president, Bill Clinton, nominated her as a judge in the Court of Appeals. To be recognized by two Chief Executives was heady fare for the ethnic girl from the projects—but the best was yet to come.

It was a day for the history books; the occasion that marked the transition from the Bronx to the Bench. In 2009, President Barack Obama nominated Judge Sotomayor to the highest court in the land, making her its third woman and its first Hispanic. He pointed out that Sonia's life story was an extraordinary journey and the embodiment of the American Dream. Her up-by-the-bootstraps tale mirrored the President's own life and achievement as the only African American Chief Executive. Sonia stated, "It is our nation's faith in a more perfect union that allows a Puerto Rican girl from the Bronx to stand here now. I am struck again by the wonder of my own life and the life we in America are so privileged to lead."

Sonia Sotomayor's biography can be divided into two halves (though they are intricately interwoven): her pre- and post-judgment days. If one wants to understand the political woman, one need read her rulings. However, if one desires to gain a glimpse of what lies under the black robes, it can be found in her memoir; the title is her encapsulated emotional biography, *My Beloved World*.

CHAPTER 17:
THE FORCE (1956)

The Grimm Brothers and Walt Disney led to generations of girls' wish-upon-a-star-dream to be a princess. The caveat: they had to be damsels in distress, saved by a prince, before riding into the happily ever after. Cinderella endured domestic servitude, Snow White apple lodged in trachea, Sleeping Beauty eternal slumber. In contrast, another princess refused to wait helplessly by—she slew her own demon, in her case an alien slug. Her story had its genesis not once upon a time, but a long time ago—in a galaxy far, far away.

Carrie Frances Fisher's life began with the same flashbulbs that would forever shadow her days. She was the daughter of Hollywood royalty: "America's sweethearts" actress Debbie Reynolds of *Singin' in the Rain* fame and crooner Eddie Fisher— what Carrie called inbreeding. Their son Todd was named after Eddie's best friend, Elizabeth Taylor's husband, Mike Todd, who died in a plane crash. Eddie rushed to the grieving widow's bedside—both literally and figuratively. The affair became the major Hollywood scandal of its day, with Taylor—the Angelina Jolie in their threesome, minus the tattoos—and Eddie, who became her next Jewish husband. In her memoir *Wishful Drinking*, Carrie wrote, "He rushed to her side, gradually moving to her front. He consoled her with flowers and, ultimately, he consoled her with his penis." They were married till Taylor met Burton on the set of Cleopatra—and the rest is history. So was Eddie. Carrie said of her famous stepmother that she regarded men more as donors of jewels than as sexual partners. Eddie went on to marry three more times and had so many facelifts Carrie said he looked Chinese. She referred to him as "Puff Daddy" because of the number of joints he smoked a day, and, on one occasion, ate his hearing aids, mistaken for pills. He was mostly AWOL; if his children wanted to see him they turned on the television.

After he died, Carrie eulogized him by saying, "There hadn't been a note he couldn't hit, a girl he couldn't hit on, an audience he couldn't charm." Debbie took for next husband shoe store magnet Harry Karl, who spent his wife's fortune on gambling and prostitutes. Debbie raised her children in a house with eight pink refrigerators, three swimming pools, and a "Shrine of Wigs." A youthful memory was watching Mom enter one end of a room-sized closet—"the Church of the Latter Day Debbie"—and exit the other, powdered and perfumed. Her manse included a pair of Dorothy's original red slippers on the mantelpiece. When Carrie was fifteen, Ms. Reynolds gave her daughter a vibrator for Christmas, and another to her own mother, who declined its usage for fear it would short out her pacemaker. Years later, in a nod to further inbreeding, she suggested Carrie have children with Richard Hamlett,

Ms. Reynold's last husband, because it would have nice eyes. "It hadn't occurred to her this might be odd. I think she just thought, you know, my womb was free and we're family." As a consequence of her upbringing, Ms. Fisher said, "I find that I don't have what could be considered a conventional sense of reality." It did not require a crystal ball to predict that Carrie would grow up with an abundance of issues, and these might lead to a life involving alcohol and drugs, detox and rehab. Indeed, as a teenager she dropped so much acid her parents called in the greatest LSD expert they knew: Cary Grant. Carrie wrote of her obsession with cocaine, LSD, and painkillers, "You know how they say that religion is the opiate of the masses? Well I took masses of opiates religiously."

In Debbie's household entertainment ruled, and from ages thirteen to sixteen Carrie performed as a back-up singer in her mother's stage show, dropping out of high school to pursue a stage career. At seventeen, she went to London to train at the Central School of Speech and Drama, and enjoyed "the only unexamined time of my life, where I was just a student among students." For a time there were no light bulb flashes.

In a sense, Carrie Fisher's career peaked in 1977 at age nineteen. She explained *Star Wars* was meant to be a "cool little off-the-radar movie directed by a bearded guy from Modesto" that unexpectedly became a worldwide box office sensation. Its merchandising bonanza splashed her likeness on everything from action figures to PEZ dispensers, and she found herself in a seesaw of fame. George Lucas had sealed her destiny when he chose her for the role of Princess Leia; others who competed for the part were Jodie Foster, Sissy Spacek, and Amy Irving. Lucas said he picked Carrie as he was looking for an actress who could hold her own against her male co-stars—like Wonder Woman, the only girl in the gang. Leia cast a long shadow that was to follow throughout her life, making her a cinematic icon and a pinup girl for generations of geeky adolescents who had the poster in their bedrooms of the teen: coiled bagel hair and gold metal bikini, chained to a giant slug. There was even an episode of *Friends* in which Ross asked Rachel to role-play in a gold bikini to fulfill his childhood fantasy—and she did, side-buns and all. The infamous bathing suit is currently in the possession of an anonymous buyer who purchased the slave-costume in a "Profiles of History" online auction in 2015 for $96,000. Her other trademark outfit was a long white shift, sans bra. The director boycotted any undergarment with the rationale that there is no underwear in space, and according to Lucasian physics, if you were to wear a bra in a weightless environment, it would strangle you. "No breasts bounce in space, no jiggling in the Empire," Carrie stated. In celluloid, she faced down the villainy of the dreaded Darth Vader, took none of Han Solo's *mishegas*; however, off-screen, she succumbed to the sexual advances of the thirty-three-year-old, married co-star Harrison Ford. In another memoir, *The Princess Diarist*, she revealed he seduced her in the back of a taxi when she was seriously drunk.

In *Wishful Drinking*, Carrie explained her reliance on men:

while her mother was under anesthetic delivering her, her father fainted and the nurses were so starstruck, "I was virtually unattended! And I have been trying to make up for that fact ever since." There was an affair with, among many others, Senator Christopher J. Doo of Connecticut, who said of their relationship, "It was a long time ago, in a galaxy far, far away," a remark that Ms. Fisher thinks probably doomed his bid for the presidency. Another love interest was Dan Aykroyd, who proposed after she choked on a Brussels sprout and he saved her by performing the Heimlich maneuver. At twenty-six, she married Paul Simon: "My father was a short Jewish man. My husband Paul was a short Jewish man. Go figure." Carrie admitted, "It was a fantastic wedding but a bad marriage." The two tried to mend their differences by visiting a spiritual healer in the Amazon, where Fisher took psychedelic tea to cleanse her spirits. Simon allegedly wrote the song *She Moves On* about their painful parting. She took an accidental overdose (not planning to kill herself, just to numb the pain) and stayed in the first of many rehabilitations. She took so much cocaine that even world class partyer John Belushi warned her to put on the brake.

In *Wishful Drinking*, Carrie admitted two of her three main problems was drug use and the fact that a good friend passed away beside her after taking painkillers. In 2005, a night of debauchery ended with Republican lobbyist R. Gregory Stevens dying of an overdose in her bed. She says people often ask her whether she was naked at the time, "I haven't been naked in fifteen years! I haven't even gone sleeveless in twenty!" This had not been a sexual encounter—the friend who died was gay, like so many of her friends. She thinks she has some supernatural power to turn men gay. It happened to Bryan Lourd, her ex-husband and father of her only child, daughter Billie. She said he had been an attentive lover for two years and then went off with a man. Her mother had remarked, "You know, dear, we've had every sort of man in our family—we've had horse thieves and alcoholics and one-man bands—but this is our *first* homosexual!"

Life post-Leia was a two-edged sword: Carrie partied with the Rolling Stones and had a many-splendored bank account, but an aging former sci-fi sex goddess is never an easy path to tread. Food was one of her many addictions, and she suffered from weight problems. She winced as she remembered her bloated days when she had "Sequoia-sized thighs." Once she did the epitome of masochism and Googled herself: "Whatever happened to Carrie Fisher? She used to be so hot. Now she looks like Elton John." Carrie sums up the bittersweetness of once being an era's It-girl: "What I didn't realize, back when I was a pin-up for geeks in that me myself and iconic metal bikini, was that I had signed an invisible contract to stay looking the exact same way for the next thirty to forty years. Well, clearly I've broken that contract."

Her third problem, and the underlying reason for her drug use, was for self-medicating; as she explained, nothing felt worse than what she was feeling. Although Eddie did not leave a will when he died in 2010—"True to form, my father continued to neglect his parental duties in death as he did in life"—he left his daughter with a lingering legacy: bipolar disorder. Often one of the symptoms is uncontrollable spending, and Eddie once returned home from a trip to Hong Kong with 180 silk suits.

But unlike most people who struggled with mental health and addiction in the '70s and '80s, Fisher shared her story in several memoirs; she even joked about being named Bipolar Woman of the Year. Fisher took mental illness out of the closet when the female lead of the most iconic movie of its time let the public peek behind the addict's curtain. She said of her public confessional, "We're only as sick as our secrets." Her modus operandi was not self-pity; rather, it mimicked Dorothy Parker's art of self-deprecation: she gave her dueling dispositions the nicknames Roy ("the wild ride of a mood") and Pam ("who stands on the shore and sobs"). She explains the importance of finding humor in our life stories, the way to find peace. She explained, "Resentment is like drinking poison and waiting for the other person to die." Her memoirs are self-help books to navigate pain and deserve as much recognition as do a certain princess.

As Carrie admits, in 2013 she "went off the rails" aboard a gay-patron cruise ship, the Holland America Eurodam, where she plunged into the grip of a severe manic state bordering on psychosis. Alarmed passengers attributed it to alcohol; however, she had attended onboard AA meetings and was sober. She said there had been warning signs that presaged a breakdown, such as scribbling on everything in sight; her medicine was not working and her inability to sleep contributed to a perfect storm. In *Star Wars* Leia said, "Help me, Obi-Wan Kenobi, you're my only hope." Carrie knew her only salvation lay not with the Jedi master, but rather the one who stared back in the mirror. She vowed *to still rise*.

Carrie desperately wanted to tread the road to wellness, both for herself and her loved ones—especially her mother and daughter. She said, "The most painful thing about returning to this dark planet is seeing the look of disappointment and hurt that these forays invariably put in the eyes of your loved ones." She had grown up with Debbie's mantra, "The show must go on," and it was a line she took to heart. Although Reynolds may have fallen short in Carrie's formative years, she proved an anchor to her adult daughter. Carrie said in tribute, "If anything, my mother taught me how to sur-thrive. That's my word for it. She would go through these amazingly difficult things, and the message was clear: Doing the impossible is possible. She should be put on that thing with the four presidents—Mount Rushmore. Right after Teddy Roosevelt, but have the eyes looking down at her cleavage."

As 2016 drew to a close, the indefatigable Carrie Fisher moved on; she suffered a heart attack on a flight from London to Los Angeles. A flood of grief poured in from across the galaxy, proving she was truly the people's princess, and her obituaries gave her top billing. This was not just because of her youthful role as Leia, but because of all the souls she had touched, the stigma of addiction she had battled. In the end, she was not remembered because of her famous parents—Debbie Reynolds passed away the day after her daughter—or a gold bikini, but because of her integrity, smarts, talent, wit, and kindness. She exuded forgiveness, both for herself and others, and did her best to reassure those with mental illness, "You can lead a normal life, whatever that is." Hers was an extraordinary one. Earlier in 2016, after Kenny Baker—the actor who played the droid R2-D2—passed away, the president of LucasFilm wrote, "There is no Star Wars without R2-D2, and Kenny defined who R2-D2 was and is." The same could be said of Princess Leia and Carrie Fischer. Her funeral was attended by a firmament of stars; Meryl Streep sang Carrie's favorite song, "Happy Days are Here Again." Todd was also there to say farewell to his mother and sister and carried Carrie's ashes in an urn shaped like a giant Prozac pill, a nod to her trademark humor.

After Lucas had banned undergarments in space, Carrie had jokingly offered her own epitaph, "However I go I want it reported that I drowned in moonlight, strangled by my own bra." Of the innumerable tributes, perhaps the most touching was on Hollywood's Walk of Fame, surrounded by mementoes of light sabers, flowers, and messages of love. Fan Jason Thomas decorated a blank one. "Our princess didn't have a star, so I gave her one. Now she lies among them," he said. On it he wrote, *Carrie Fisher May the Force Be With You Always. Hope.*

CHAPTER 18:
THE BOOMERANG (1959)

Many of the greatest stories are of the motherless—Oliver Twist, Mary Lennox, Harry Potter. Yet, in the case of one British author, it would have been preferable to have been an orphan than subjected to Mummy Dearest.

Most writers mine their childhoods for material, and this was the case with Jeanette, the adopted daughter of John and Constance Winterson. The couple lived in the north English town of Lancashire and their lives were dominated by their Evangelist Pentecostal faith. Her father's wages as a laborer were so low that the family was dependent on the vegetables they grew for subsistence. Jeanette later provided a snapshot of life mired in poverty:

> Thursday nights were always boiled onions or potatoes. Dad got paid Fridays and by Thursday there was no money left. In winter, the gas and electricity meters ran out on Thursdays too, and so the onions and potatoes weren't quite boiled enough and we ate them in the dark of the paraffin lamp. We had no car, no phone and no central heating. In winter the windows froze on the inside.

But at least hardship was shared with those around her. What made her circumstance worse was Mrs. Winterson—a name rich in symbolic value—and how Jeanette would refer to her in both her memoirs. John was described as "poor Dad," an adjective referring to his marital mishap more than his dire finances.

Many adopted children are reassured by their parents that they are special because they were chosen. Constance's version was she had been promised Paul, a baby boy, and had already picked out clothes when the birth mother backed out. Her oft-repeated aphorism: "The Devil had led her to the wrong crib." When Jeanette was older, she wanted to offer the rejoinder that it was doubtful that Satan would have taken "time off from the Cold War and McCarthyism to visit Manchester in 1960." It was less than reassuring that the five-foot-ten-inch 280 pound monolithic mama kept a revolver in a drawer and bullets in a tin of Pledge. Mrs. Winterson also stayed up all night—not from insomnia—but to avoid sleeping with her husband, as sex, even marital relations, was another Original Sin.

Mrs. Winterson loved Jesus, but he brought her no joy, and mainly looked forward to the Apocalypse that would destroy her bothersome neighbors and deliver her to the exalted status she deserved for her piety. She liberally shared her belief that the universe was a cosmic dustbin with the lid on. Her favorite song, "God Has Blotted Them Out," was meant to be about sinners, but in her case referred to anyone who had ever annoyed her, which was everyone. She did not merely instill the fear of God in her daughter, but a fear of just about everything. In the outdoor lavatory she hung a sign: "HE SHALL MELT THY BOWELS LIKE WAX." Other than praying, she smoked (in secret) and had two sets of false teeth, matte for everyday and pearl for occasions. Every day involved church, and all day on Sundays, that entailed a three mile walk round trip. The only time Constance dared dip her finger in happiness was Christmas, the holiday when she felt the world more than a vale of tears. The household was indeed grim and matters were made worse as Jeanette proved recalcitrant. As punishment, Constance routinely locked her daughter out all night in a coal hole. Optimistic by nature, though definitely not by nurture, Jeanette later said the bright side of this punishment was that "it prompted reflection," though for most it would have prompted thoughts of matricide. She said that in that dark, freezing, claustrophobic space, she made up stories so that she was transported from blackness to anyplace she wanted to be. She would be left there till morning and, in an act of rebellion, when the milkman came, she would guzzle both pints. Jeanette was determined that her mother would never see the hurt, to deprive her of that satisfaction. There were also beatings, where her mother would instruct her father to hit her, specifying with which instrument and how many times. "It wasn't pleasant," Jeanette explained in a nod to understatement.

School should have offered an avenue of escape to a child with

a high IQ, but Jeanette was too emotionally damaged to thrive.
Forbidden to play with the other children, they turned on the misfit
in their midst. Her outsider status was not helped by the message
Constance had embroidered on her daughter's gym bag: The
Summer is Ended and We Are Not Yet Saved. Social status did not
improve when, at age twelve, she was obliged to preach the words of
the Lord on the street corners of her 1970s industrial town.

One refuge from misery were books. In the printed page Jeanette
was offered a magic carpet that transported her from family
dysfunction and its ambience of brimstone; they held the promise
there was a world beyond her cage, and she became each character
in every story. Of course, the dominate one in the Winterson
home was their dog-eared bible. Another book was *Jane Eyre*;
however, when Constance read it to her daughter, she altered
the ending— instead of marrying Mr. Rochester, Jane became a
missionary. Mrs. Winterson was wont to remark, "The trouble
with a book is that you never know what's in it until it's too late."
Psychological salvation came when Constance gave her daughter
a library card so Jeanette could check out murder mysteries for
her mother, her guilty pleasure. It was in the Accrington Public
Library that Jeanette formulated her goal of reading her way
through the classics of English literature, in alphabetical order.
The printed word offered a way out from the coal hole and into the
light, an oasis in her desert. Books became her support system—
she literally slept on them as a teen when she hid them under her

mattress. Even this reprieve was denied when her mother noticed her ascending mattress that held her stash and burned them; by way of explanation, she said that fiction was the realm of the Devil. Winterson foraged through the scraps and consigned the words to memory.

If Mrs. Winterson were upset over Jeanette's love of literature, she became far more apoplectic when she discovered Jeanette's physical attraction to her own sex. News of her daughter's lesbianism literally caused Constance to burst a blood vessel in her varicose veins. Jeanette later recalled how it hit the ceiling, leaving behind a crimson souvenir: "I was running around in a panic with cloths trying to staunch the flow; I had a tourniquet of tea towels. And she was looking up and all she said was, 'We've just had that ceiling decorated.'" The blood spatters proved a variation of Rorschach ink blots testifying to images of horror. Furious, Mrs. Winterson—along with the church elders—arranged a brutal three-day exorcism.

The ritual failed to convert Jeanette's sexual orientation, and at age sixteen her mother delivered an ultimatum: stop seeing Janey or she would be kicked out of the house. For Mrs. Winterson, homosexuality was on par with bestiality. Jeanette explained her girlfriend made her happy; Constance's embittered rejoinder, "Why be happy when you could be normal?" This question became the title of Jeanette's second memoir. Her words illustrate the nightmarish *Alice in Wonderland* dynamic of this family cauldron, a topsy-turvy universe where values are so twisted that happiness is unattainable and misery the norm.

Fortunately, Jeanette did not share Constance's generous proportions, as her new home was a borrowed Mini, parked in a street. Determined and desperate, she applied "to read English at Oxford because it was the most impossible thing" she could think of. This was an audacious act, as Winterson knew no one who had been to university, and it was not conceivable that a girl from a working class mill town would be accepted. After a two year hiatus, Jeanette returned to Lancashire for Christmas; the mother and child reunion was not a joyous one. She brought along Vicky, a black friend from St. Lucia, and Jeanette's words of warnings of Winterson World were brushed off as exaggeration. Trying to mend fences, Constance tried to be nice, and figuring a girl from the Island loved pineapple, she endlessly offered her cheese on toast with pineapple, pineapple upside down cake, and pineapple fritters, until Vicky confessed she did not care for the fruit. Mrs. W. reacted like a punctured balloon. That night, Vicky found her pillow removed and the pillowcase stuffed with warning leaflets about the Apocalypse. It was the last time Jeanette and Constance saw one another. Jeanette had published *Oranges Are Not the Only Fruit*, a coming-of-age, coming out novel. Its title was an allusion to the memory of when Jeanette was sad, her mother had always offered her an orange; her book's theme was heterosexuality is not the only kind of love. Jeanette felt betrayed at her mother's rejection of her debut novel—that she ordered under an assumed name—and Constance felt it was wrong of her to air the Winterson dirty laundry in public. Jeanette said, "If she had been able to say, 'Well, I don't like it, but I'm proud of you,' or if there had been a bridge, a rope slung across space...it would have made a difference. But there was nothing." Constance died during the BBC production of the book, at age sixty-eight. She had an enlarged heart and a thyroid condition, but Jeanette believes she passed away from unhappiness. She had happily learned the truth that the trouble with motherhood is that you never know what's in it until it's too late.

In 2006, Winterson was named an Officer of the Order of the British Empire for her services to literature; at least she was able to side-step the perennial reader question, "Where do you get your ideas?" She was a lesbian icon, financially secure, and owned a home wallpapered with books, estimated at one thousand volumes. She acknowledged she has a Kindle, but feels its uses are limited: "Great for travel, but no substitute for the real thing. A bit like phone sex." Despite all practical appearances, content proved elusive. The source of her misery was that her demons returned to haunt her, triggered by the demise of her six-year relationship with theater director Deborah Warner. She often found herself alone in the fields near her Cotswolds home where she would sit for twelve to fourteen hours at a time, oblivious to rain. She recalled, "I had to go to the very bottom. There was no further to go: That. Was.

The. Bottom." Her subsequent nervous breakdown—in F. Scott Fitzgerald's words, a crack-up—proved a rapid descent, and she was unable to cope. One day she curled up into a fetal position, muttering, "Mummy, Mummy." Jeanette felt like Humpty Dumpy and would never be able—even with the help of all the king's horsemen—to put herself together again. In the belief death was the only escape from unbearable mental pain, she locked herself in her garage and turned on the engine of her old Porsche 911. She felt like it was her only choice. Jeanette's suicide attempt was aborted when she discovered her cat had followed her, and not willing to bet on his other eight lives, *decided to still rise.* She had not survived Lancashire to succumb to defeat.

Jeanette decided to perform a psychological journey to the past to help deal with the darkness. Her first step was to search for "bio ma," though Constance had assured her she was dead. She wrote of those who were adopted that it feels like "reading a book with the first few pages missing. It's like arriving after curtain up. The feeling that something is missing never, ever leaves you—and it can't, and it shouldn't, because something is missing." Eventually, she tracked down Anne, still living in Manchester, who explained she had given her up because she was seventeen, not married, and had felt it better for her little girl to have two parents. Not always. The reunion of mother and daughter was moving—only a Mrs. Winterson would remain detached—but it did not slay her dragons.

Jeanette knew in order to divest herself of the hole at her core she would have to make peace with yesterday—with the memory of her mother—and in the process learned under the searing resentment ran an undercurrent of love. She also understood to know all is to forgive all. She acknowledged that Constance was also a victim, trapped in a life of no hope, no money, no possibility. Although Constance was contemptuous of *Oranges Are Not the Only Fruit*, the copy Jeanette had sent her with a signed dedication had not been consigned to the flames. And for the woman who could never express her feelings, that spoke volumes. Another crack in her protective armor appeared when Anne made a scathing comment about Constance, to which Jeanette replied, "She was a monster but she was my monster." Finally Jeanette was able to see the silver lining of her singular upbringing: "It has rather made me appreciate Mrs. Winterson and her lunacy. I'm now convinced that the worst life for a child is to have an empty head. At least I got everything stuffed in there. Wintersonworld was bonkers, but it made me. I am Jeanette Winterson because of Wintersonworld!" She had transcended the cards she had been dealt, the fantastically bad luck of landing in the clutches of a woman who understood motherhood as an arm-wrestle with the Devil over her child's soul. What had begun as exorcism of the monster mother ended with a moving acceptance. Mrs. Winterson had believed in Christ's miracles. Her tragedy was she had not been able to see the miraculous girl under her roof.

The biblical adage, "The truth shall you free," proved prescient, and Jeanette was able to shoulder on, although the damage was done and the scar will always remain. But that is OK; it is the mark of a survivor. Hungry for a partner who would become both lover and surrogate family, besides Deborah, there was a romance with Pat Kavanagh, the late literary agent and wife of novelist Julian Barnes. There were also several male lovers because, as Jeanette explains, she believes that being a lesbian is not in the genes, but is rather an emotional choice. However, her coup de foudre arrived when she met the writer and psychotherapist Susie Orbach, author of *Fat is a Feminist Issue*, the one-time therapist to Princess Di. However, Jeanette did not believe a romance would develop "because Susie was heterosexual and I have given up missionary work with homosexual women. But something was going on... Susie talked to her daughter Lianna who said, 'Just kiss her, Mummy.' So we did." Although both are intellectual writers, there are differences between the British Pentecostal Jeanette and the American Jewish Susie. They ended up tying the knot in a London ceremony in a flower-filled garden on Valentine's Day in 2013.

One day they want to move to Italy and live together until the end. Jeanette said, "I've found happiness after a life of despair." Perhaps armed with love, the past can no longer be a boomerang and become an arrow.

CHAPTER EIGHTEEN *The Boomerang*

CHAPTER 19:
THE GLASS CASTLE (1960)

In *Anna Karenina*, Tolstoy wrote, "All happy families are alike; each unhappy family is unhappy in its own way." The latter proved the case—in spades—for a woman whose dysfunctional parents made them the antithesis of Dr. Spock. Through a steely determination, she survived a childhood that entailed self-immolation and the battle cry, "Skedaddle!" Her hardscrabble youth could have come from the pages of *The Grapes of Wrath*—if Ma Joad had been bipolar, if Pa Joad had been an alcoholic.

If you were in a taxi on the way to a society party and saw your mother scavenging through a dumpster, would you: a) pray for spontaneous combustion, b) slither to the floor. or c) rush to her side? This was the conundrum faced by a gossip columnist, a woman who dished dirt while hiding her own.

Most children grow up with parental issues: getting stuck with the imitation Barbie, helicopter parenting, scrimping on affection, or preferring a sibling. However, in the case of Jeannette Walls, her formative years were so traumatic it is miraculous she survived.

Jeannette, along with Lori, Maureen, and Brian, were born in Phoenix, to parents who were not cut from the same cloth as Ozzie and Harriet. Her father Rex was her North Star and was charismatic and affectionate, especially with Jeannette, who he nicknamed Mountain Goat. He fueled her imagination with mesmerizing bedtime stories and showed affection in a unique fashion. One of her most cherished memories occurred when she was five, and, as Rex had lost his job, there was no money even for modest Christmas gifts to place under the tree; he had salvaged off a street. The family always celebrated the Yuletide a few weeks late in order to take advantage of holiday discards. (On another occasion, he set a tree on fire with the explanation it was a pagan symbol.) Usually he explained the lack of gifts by saying Santa was a fraud, but one year Rex took each of his kids into the Mojave Desert to pick out a star, telling them that years from now, when all the plastic junk the other kids got was no more, they would still have their stars. To this day, when Jeannette sees her Venus, the effect is magical.

Unfortunately, dad was also a paranoid alcoholic, ranting conspiracy theories, hurtling obscenities at his wife, and disappearing for intervals to go on a bender. Even when sober, he was a meager provider. Instead of gainful employment, he busied himself with get-rich-quick schemes—like the Prospector—a gold detecting gizmo. He sometimes lowered himself to work odd jobs, but they came with understandably brief expiration dates. The family frequently had to leave town in the middle of the night so that they could escape his latest trouble-doing, what he called "the skedaddle:" getting out of town pretty darn quick. Sometimes it was caused by skipping out on rent, or fear the FBI was on his heels. Not surprisingly, the Walls had twenty-seven addresses in the first five years of their marriage. On one of these getaways, Dad felt compelled to toss Jeannette's cat out the car window. Nevertheless, Jeannette looked at him much as Scout did Atticus, and as a little girl felt he was perfect, though he had what his wife called a "drinking situation."

Rose Mary, while not Mother Dearest, was not exactly Mrs. Cunningham from *Happy Days*. She set their self-esteem: Lori, the smart one; Maureen, the pretty one; Brian, the brave one; Jeannette, the hard worker. Never a doting mother, her mantra was, "Suffering when you're young is good for you." Despite being qualified as a teacher, she did not care to pursue her profession, as she felt it boring and she was, above all, an "excitement addict." "I'm a grown woman. Why can't I do what I want?" she'd say. In the selfishness department, it is hard to choose between the two parents. Rose Mary once indulged in a Hershey Chocolate bar while her four children rooted through garbage bins for scraps. When the youngsters chanced upon a two-carat diamond ring, rather than sell it for shelter, she would not consider that option: "At times like these, self-esteem is even more vital than food." She was also not a fan of glasses—Lori squinted until age twelve.

When she first put them on, she cried for all that she had missed. In the midst of the mayhem, the children underwent their version of homeschooling. Rose Mary taught them how to read and the health advantages of drinking unpurified ditchwater. Rex taught them how to shoot with empty beer cans as targets, something that would come in handy when the feds arrived.

One of the events that stand out in sharp relief was the time Jeannette caught on fire. Rose Mary declined to cook, rationalizing, "Why should I cook a meal that will be gone in an hour when I can do a painting that will last forever?' At age three, as Jeannette boiled hotdogs, she watched in terror as flames consumed her pink dress. Rose Mary remained oblivious, too caught up in her painting to notice, and a woman from a neighboring trailer, hearing screams, took the child to the hospital as the Walls did not own wheels at that time. When asked by the nurses while she was boiling water, she responded her mother said she was mature enough to do so; her third-degree burns indicated otherwise. Six weeks later, Rex collected his daughter before her recovery to skip out on the bill and his dislike of the uppity doctors. When she returned home, she once again boiled hotdogs, to which Rose Mary said, "Good for you. You've got to get right back in the saddle." She then resumed painting; her parenting role model seems to have been Nero. Another near death calamity occurred at age five when Jeanette hurtled from the family station wagon onto a railroad embankment while her father was at the wheel—

smoking and drinking beer. Jeannette waited in the desert sun until her folks realized she was missing; her father picked out glass fragments with a tweezer. The parents in *Home Alone* had nothing on Mr. and Mrs. Walls.

To sweeten the mix, Rex and Rose Mary also had a volatile relationship. After an argument, as the children looked on, he dangled Rose Mary from an upstairs window. One way in which the couple made their nomadic lifestyle appealing to their children was by telling them their lives were an exciting adventure—a nod to what the father did in the film *Life is Beautiful* to help his son endure the concentration camp. They believed this until their teens, when the rose-colored glasses came off. After years of roaming the Southwest, out of options and out of money, Rex threw himself on the slim mercy of his family in Welch, West Virginia. Rex's Appalachian hometown made the desert seem like the good old days. It was a vile hamlet along a river distinguished by having, as her father explained, "The highest level of bacteria of any river in North America." The cold in their unheated home chilled, and miserable at returning in defeat, Rex sunk further into alcoholism and Mary Rose descended further into bipolar disorder. The children suffered physical and sexual abuse at the hands of their paternal grandmother and ostracism from the community, who viewed them as the bottom spectrum of white trash. Meals sometimes consisted of cat food, and the family used a yellow bucket as a makeshift toilet. Jeannette and Lori were devastated when their father, in order to buy booze, stole their piggy bank, where they had kept the proceeds from babysitting and odd jobs. Another less than father-daughter bonding moment was when Rex used her as sexual bait to distract a man he hustled at pool. Many teens undergoing such an existence would have turned to self-medicating through drugs, alcohol, cutting, or suicide. Yet Jeannette decided to *still rise* because, whatever she had lacked from her father, he had always provided unconditional love. This was made manifest when Rex promised to build her a glass castle once he found his fortune. He carried around the blueprints— never forgetting them even in the chaos of "skedaddle!"

Desperate for a better life, at age seventeen, Jeannette followed Lori, whose getaway was New York City. The sisters, eventually joined by Brian and Maureen, rented a small Bronx apartment in a run-down area, but to the girls it was hog's heaven. They marveled at its heat, hot water, and electricity, paid for by service jobs. Jeannette, who had been an avid visitor to the library—as they had owned no television—graduated from Columbia's Barnard College. (Rex's contribution to tuition was a mink coat he had won at poker.) The Walls children had successfully executed their own version of "Skedaddle!"

Although it would appear Rex had done little to equip his children to survive, this was not the case. He had given Jeannette the gift of Venus and the promise of a glass castle, the former a symbol of love, the latter a metaphor for hope. And there was also the lesson he taught when she was seven: "If you don't want to sink, you better figure out how to swim," and, by way of explanation, threw her into a pool of deep water.

Jeannette married Eric Goldberg, a Jewish man who had grown up on Park Avenue and, marvel of marvel, still lived there. They had a big reception at the Harvard Club; her parents were not invited. It was not because she did not love them, but she did not want the society guests to know the bride's past. In addition, with the open bar, her father would have descended into a drunken orgy. Her mother had caused a scene at her brother's—a police officer—Long Island wedding by showing up in a stained, tattered dress, having angrily refused an offer of a new one. To have done so would have been painfully bourgeois.

Not one to lounge at home—even at a Park Avenue address— Jeannette obtained a position as a gossip columnist at *New York Magazine*. In a nod to irony, one off her coworkers once lashed out at her, "You Barnard bitches don't know what it's like for the rest of us. You had everything handed to you." Mum was the word.

The fly in the ointment was Rex and Mary Rose, those old agents of chaos, whose final "Skedaddle!" was to follow their children to New York, where they became squatters in an abandoned tenement. When she introduced Rex to Eric, neither was impressed; after Jeannette explained her husband was her anchor, her dad replied, "Problem with an anchor, is when you got one attached to you, it's damned hard to fly." Rex passed away soon after, and his daughter realized he had been right; she cut loose the husband who had weighed her down. He had not dangled her from their Park Avenue apartment, but she realized she did not love him and she had enough lies to juggle.

During Jeannette's years at *New York Magazine*, she befriended—and later married—John Taylor, a diplomat's son. On a stroll through Central Park, when, like the good journalist he is, he mentioned there was something about her that didn't add up, she revealed her story, warts and all. His response was her life would make an incredible book, one that would illustrate how one needs not to be flatlined by one's childhood. To further nudge her in that endeavor, Walls had published an inflammatory column concerning Scientology, only to discover, in a retaliatory move, the church had launched an investigation into her past.

In a nod to "if these walls could talk," they did in Jeannette's 2005 memoir, *The Glass Castle*, which sold for six figures, spent several years on the *New York Times* best seller list, and is currently in development for a film. Charles Dickens' classic novel, *A Tale of Two Cities*, lends its title to the two distinct lives of Jeannette, and its opening line is also apropos: "It was the best of times, it was the worst of times." For Walls, penning the memoir was both lucrative and liberating. As she said, "Secrets are like vampires. Once you expose them to the light, they lose their power over you."

In a version of an Appalachian fairytale, John and Jeannette purchased a 205-acre farm in Virginia and a nineteenth century dream home, replete with sweeping views of the Blue Ridge Mountains. The kitchen's rustic floors are from nearby Montpelier, once home to President John James Madison. Rose Mary came to live with her daughter by default: Lori and Bryan could not deal with her, and Maureen had once stabbed her mother in the back. The youngest Wall currently lives in California, in a life that sadly mimics the mother with who she no longer has contact. The eighty-year-old lives in a cottage on the spacious grounds, her home in marked contrast to her daughter's impeccable abode. Her favorite outfit is a soiled blue coat, and as soon as she opens her door, there is an overwhelming odor of cat urine. The cottage is an ode to a hoarder; dominating the clutter are her paintings, including a portrait of her late husband.

Jeannette, based on her roller coaster odyssey, reflected, "We all have our baggage, and I think the trick is not resisting it but accepting it, understanding that the worst experience has a valuable gift wrapped inside if you're willing to receive it." She added, "So, O.K., Mom kept the chocolate bar. But she gave me a lot of good material." One element noticeably absent from Jeannette's memoir is bitterness. She explains this is because her parents loved her the best way they knew how, and in the end, that is what matters. After all, she now has not only Venus, but her prince, to share her glass castle.

CHAPTER 20:
THE LIGHT (1965)

No one feels sorry for Joanne Rowling, the beautiful British billionaire. She is the most staggering successful author in the world, with a fan base of hundreds of millions clamoring for her every written word. Yet her true wizardry was not turning a bespectacled boy into a literary phenomenon. The hallmark of her greatness is that she discovered an alchemist's stone which enabled her to rise from the rubble of shattered self-esteem.

Before the novels, before the films, before the millions of pounds, there was a little girl (Jo) who liked to play—not as a princess and prince—but as a witch and wizard. The life of the author began with the meeting of two strangers in 1964. Pete Rowling was an eighteen-year- old soldier when he met Ann Volant, on the train from King's Cross. The tedium of the ride, coupled with pheromones, led to an introduction, followed by kisses under hanging duffel coats. By the time they disembarked in Scotland, they were a confirmed couple. When Ann became pregnant with Joanne, it led to marriage and a home outside Bristol. Two years later the family welcomed second daughter Dianne (Di).

The advent of childhood measles segued to a love of books as her father read to his bed-bound little girl from the Edinburgh-born author of *The Wind in the Willows*. Books were crammed into every nook and cranny, and Joanne was inspired to write her first story, *Rabbit*, at age six; her first reader, Dianne. She proved a captive audience—literally—as her sister sat on her to force her to listen. In 1974, the Rowlings purchased an old stone cottage in Tutshill, on the Welsh border, close to Dean Forest, which served as a blueprint for Harry Potter's Forbidden Forest. The idyllic Church Cottage was a mere goblin's throw from the local graveyard, and its surrounding countryside provided the stage for the sisters' magical adventures. Sometimes they were joined by a neighboring fellow-thespian who bore the surname Potter. In contrast to these carefree hours was Tutshill Church of England School, where Mrs. Morgan believed terrorizing went hand-in-hand with tutoring. She would serve as the role model for the less than sympathetic masters at Hogwarts.

When Joanne entered Wyedean, her stay-at-home mother secured a position at her daughter's high school as a lab technician. At this point, home was a happy place, with Peter working as an executive engineer at a Rolls Royce plant, Anne content with a job she enjoyed, and sisters, despite sibling rivalry, devoted friends. One of their favorite games involved the stairs, which they used to enact cliffside dramas. Joanne would dangle from the top stair, holding Dianne's hand, imploring her not to let go. However, this golden time came with an expiration date. As Joanne later recalled, "Home was a difficult place to be."

The first specter of Anne's illness became manifest in 1978 when her hand shook uncontrollably as she poured tea. When Joanne was fifteen, her mother was diagnosed with multiple sclerosis, and her loved ones watched helplessly as she was reduced to crawling upstairs. A blanket of depression settled over Church Cottage, and Joanne later voiced her view that the teenage years are "a dreadful time of life." Her character Hermoine is loosely based on her days during this bleak period. To add to the gathering gloom, Joanne's relationship with her father was no longer the idyll of an earlier time. The avenue of escape was her friend Sean Harris, who whisked her away in his blue Ford Anglia to the bars and concerts of Bristol. His car would be reincarnated as Ron Weasley's family vehicle and he would be remembered in the dedication to *Harry Potter and the Chamber of Secrets* as "getaway driver and foul-weather friend." A more steady form of escape was when she departed for the University of Exeter. Anne attended her daughter's graduation filled with pride, but watched the ceremony from the confines of a wheelchair.

After university, Joanne moved to London, where she worked as a secretary at Amnesty International in the day and wrote at night. Heartbreakingly, her two novels never saw the light of publication. It was at this juncture that the defining moment of her life occurred. In the summer of 1990, Rowling's boyfriend moved to Manchester, and she was returning home after they had spent the weekend searching for a flat. Just as Joanne had been born as a result of a train, the same held true of Harry Potter, whose image inexplicably popped into her head on the journey home, when the one heading for King's Cross Station was at a standstill for four hours. The plot that had taken shape during the delay was of a boy who learned, at age eleven, that he is a wizard. Her fantasy world became as real as her actual one, and she was fired with turning him into a protagonist. However, the best laid plans of witches and warlocks was derailed six months later when Anne passed away. It was her mother's death that inspired the image of the Mirror of Erised. The name spelled backwards is "Desire," and when Harry looked into it he saw his lost loved ones. Joanne spiraled into a black hole of depression. This led to the end of her relationship and her break with a pain laden past.

In lieu of a blue Ford Anglia, Joanne answered an ad in the *Guardian* for Teachers of English as a Second Language in Portugal, which offered the lure of a fresh start coupled with adventure. She relocated to Porto, and after work went to Swing, a nightclub, in search of another adventure—this time of the romantic variety. Her close friend recalled she was "desperate for love." She believed she had found it with Jorge Arantes, a television journalist student who she met at another bar, Mela Cava. Jorge was smitten with her blue eyes, while she was drawn by his profession—he was a Jane Austen fan. Feeling this was sufficient glue, they embarked on an affair. Joanne shared her paycheck while Jorge looked for work, an elusive endeavor. A miscarriage brought them closer together, and when Jorge proposed, Joanne accepted. She ignored a premarital wake-up call: they were drinking coffee in a cafe when an argument erupted. In anger, Jorge violently pushed his fiancée. She burst into tears and onlookers called the police. Remorseful, he called out "Joanne, forgive me! I love you." Joanne echoed his words.

While common sense dictated Rowling should make like the gingerbread man and "run, run, as fast as you can," the couple wed in a Porto registry office. The bride wore black and held red flowers. In attendance was Dianne and her boyfriend; conspicuously absent was Peter. In Gertrude fashion, he had married his secretary soon after the death of his wife, and the rift between him and Joanne had widened. The Arantes' marriage lasted one year and a day. While Harry Potter and Joanne shared the same birthday, in *Harry Potter and The Prisoner of Azkaban*, Professor Trelawney told a pupil the thing he most feared would occur on October 16th, the date of her ill-fated wedding.

Two months after the nuptials, Joanne became pregnant, but once again home was not a happy place to be. In 1993, she gave birth to Jessica—so named after author Jessica Mitford—and despite the exhortations of her friends to escape her abusive relationship, she fought for the preservation of family. This ceased to be an option when her husband slapped her after a five in the

morning spat and physically threw her out of their home. She
returned the next day, accompanied by a policeman, and Jorge
relinquished Jessica. For the next two weeks, mother and baby went
into hiding until they could board the freedom express to Britain. On
her flight, she took only her daughter and the first three chapters of
her novel. Post-publication, Arantes claimed to have had a hand in
the book, of which claim Rowling remarked, "He had as much input
into *Harry Potter* as I had in *A Tale of Two Cities*." Later Joanne
mined her personal pain when she observed that humans have a
knack for choosing precisely the things that are worst for them.
Robert Frost in *The Death of the Hired Hand* observed, "Home
is the place where, when you have to go there, they have to take
you in." In the winter of 1993, a train carried mother and daughter
towards Dianne's Edinburg home. Metaphorically, they were back
on the stairs of their childhood home, with Joanne begging her sister
to save her. Although Dianne welcomed sister and niece with open
arms, Joanne knew it could only be a visit with a short expiration
date. Her sister was a newlywed, and a death-knell to marital bliss
was the sudden arrival of a relative in the throes of deep depression,
along with a baby. Joanne swallowed the last remnant of pride and
through social services obtained her own flat and a small monthly
stipend. To add to the ambience of the cold-water apartment, she
constantly played the soundtrack of *Everybody Hurts*. Matters
further deteriorated with the sudden appearance of her estranged
husband, who in the interim had succumbed to drugs. She applied
for both a restraining order and a divorce.

During the nadir years, she was beset by the degradation of poverty, lack of self-worth, and maternal shame. She contrasted the lives of her friends' children, replete with nuclear family and well-appointed nurseries, with her own fatherless infant whose few toys could comfortably fit into a shoebox. She later recalled of the blunder years, "There was a point where I really felt I had 'penniless divorcee lone parent' tattooed on my head." The fact that she had become immersed in such a dire situation despite the advantage of an Ivy League education served as another nail in her emotional coffin. It was during this low ebb life dictated it was sink or swim, *and like dust she determined to rise.* Through counselling she was able to wrestle her suicidal thoughts. She decided against obtaining a teaching job in order to birth Harry. In light of her former literary rejections, she knew it was a gamble, but she held fast to the belief, "Everything's possible if you've got enough nerve.'"

Writing became her emotional life-preserver, providing her with a purpose, with hope. Once again, Dianne was her first reader, and this time she did not have to be sat on to listen. As her flat was too cold, she often wrote in her brother-in-law's restaurant, Nicolson's. She made the pilgrimage even though it was situated at the top of twenty stairs, a navigational feat when undertaken with a stroller. From this bleak period she incorporated the soul-sucking *dementors* into her story-line. She stated of the overwhelming depression which smothered her, "It's so difficult to describe to someone who has never been there, because it's not sadness. I know sadness. Sadness is to cry and to feel. But it is that cold absence of feeling that really hollowed out feeling. That's what *dementors* are."

In true muggles and magic fashion, it was an eight-year-old named Alice who rescued Rowling. After receiving enough rejection slips to wallpaper her miniscule flat (the publishers who rejected her must be subjecting themselves to the torments of Hades), agent Christopher Little submitted her manuscript to the small *Bloomsbury Press*. Its owner had decided to champion it when his daughter, Alice, had read the first chapter and begged for more. Based on her enthusiasm, he decided to give the unknown author a chance along with a paltry check. A caveat was the name on the book spine was to be gender ambiguous initials—J after Joanne and K after grandmother Kathleen—to disguise its author was a female, as the anticipated readers would be adolescent boys. Its dedication page read, FOR JESSICA, WHO LOVES STORIES, FOR ANNE, WHO LOVED THEM TOO; AND FOR DI, WHO HEARD THIS ONE FIRST. The acceptance turned out to be the most prescient move in publishing history, and the alchemist's stone made multi-millionaires of everyone involved. Rowling was to add as many new words and images to childhood as Walt Disney. Rowling remembers after hearing the news of a publishing contract, she screamed so loud she startled Jessica. She stated, "The purest most unalloyed joy was when I finally knew it was going to be a book, a real book you could see sitting on the shelf *of* a bookshop." Within weeks of *Harry Potter and the Sorcerer's Stone*'s publication, sales exploded as the British wizard, a German Pied Piper, cast a spell on youngsters the world over. She no longer would ever have the worry of whether Jessica would outgrow a pair of shoes before she could find the money for the next pair.

Ms. Rowling not only achieved success beyond her wildest dreams, she also entered Hogwart's Heaven with second marriage to Scottish physician Neil Murray. They married in one of Joanne's mansions, the thirty-one-room, seventeenth century Killiechassie House. The low-key affair included bridesmaids Jessica and Dianne and her foul-weather friends, who knew her when. The couple have two children together, David and McKenzie. Unlike Jessica, whose toys had fit into a shoebox, they get to play in magical forty-foot tree houses that cost upwards of $100,000. Anne, who loved stories, would have loved her daughter's most of all. Perhaps the secret to regaining the land of lost content can be summed up in Joanne's own words: "Happiness can be found, even in the darkest of times, if one only remembers to turn on the light."

CHAPTER 21:
UNBROKEN (1967)

In Coleridge's poem, the Ancient Mariner lamented, "Instead of the cross/the albatross about my neck was hung." His reprieve from purgatory was relaying his grisly tale. The old seafarer is a metaphor for a contemporary woman whose story involves a deceased horse, a velveteen rabbit, and a relentless albatross.

The association of the word "fatigue" is cramming all night on a last-minute report, hiking to the mountaintop, receiving a kidney punch to the soul. Yet one is buoyed by the knowledge this too shall pass. But what happens when fatigue is chronic?

Laura Hillenbrand's grew up in Bethesda, Maryland, in a stately, white colonial home where she played in its backyard and dreamed of horses and of becoming a great writer. It was at the Edgemoor Club where her interest in language was whetted. During a rainstorm, her swim team sat indoors while a man entertained with *The Tale of the Ancient Mariner*; it made Laura realize the power of words and their ability to transport one to another world. What she did not realize was the story was to prove an ominous foreshadowing of her life.

Laura was the youngest of four children of Bernard, a World War II veteran, scarred by the trench warfare in Hurtgen Forest; his position as a lobbyist often kept him from home. Her mother, Elizabeth, had been a reporter for *The Washington Post,* but later became a psychologist. When Laura was in elementary school— where she always wore riding boots—her parents drifted apart. As home became unhappy, Laura took refuge at their country farm, situated on the banks of the Potomac River, where centuries of history lay shrouded in the surrounding hills. The stone cottage had once served as a hospital during the Battle of Antietam. At age eight, her parents separated, and by high school Laura was the only child still at home, which she shared with a depressed mother. The ticket on the Midnight Express came when she entered Kenyon College in Ohio. An avid tennis player, she arranged to live in proximity to the courts. The campus was like her extended country home, one filled with friends, and soon it became the setting of romance.

Laura was in the campus deli, run by Craig, who wore fluorescent-yellow sunglasses. She had on a yellow dress that showed off her tan from her summer vacation in France, when in walked Borden Flanagan, a twenty-year-old senior from Seattle. He wore a white T-shirt with The Smiths on it and, a fan of the British rock band, she asked him to join her. In truth, she said he was so cute that had he come in with a T-shirt of the Monkees, she still would have struck up a conversation. Laura had it all: beauty, brains, boyfriend—but then came the albatross.

Six months later Borden, Laura, and her best friend Linc
were returning from Spring Break, a rose from her lover on lap.
She was aglow from her vacation and anticipating her junior
year abroad at the University of Edinburg. Suddenly, she was
in the grips of intense nausea, and by the time they arrived at
the campus, she was in agony. Too ill to attend classes, she was
forced to move back to her mother's house. Rumors abounded:
she was pregnant, had contracted AIDS, suffered a nervous
breakdown. Her friends slipped away with the exception of Linc
and Borden—the latter sent postcards and she responded with
dirty limericks. Laura plunged into a combination of physical and
emotional distress. A string of doctors tried to convince her she
had an eating disorder—an assumption based on her twenty-two
pound weight loss. A walk to the mailbox left her so exhausted she
had to lie down. Laura's misery was increased when her family
only offered a collective shrug. Her world was confined to her bed
and window; unable to shower, her hair appeared soaking wet;
her period stopped. She was bedridden for months at a time, her
body so emaciated she could not sleep on her side because her
bones dug into her flesh. She said, "I could tell you a lot about the
weave of my carpet because I spent hours staring at it, unable to
leave my room." Finally, a physician at John Hopkins diagnosed
her with chronic fatigue syndrome, likely caused by eating tainted
chicken that had weakened her immune system. He added the
chilling pronouncement: there was no cure. At that time, CFS
was trivialized as a yuppie flu rather than a debilitating medical

condition. Laura takes exception to the term: "The illness is to fatigue what a nuclear bomb is to a match." Bereft of friends and health, she became mired in a bottomless depression. In the dark night of the soul, she took her mother's bottle of Valium and poured the pills onto the bed. She decided that she had *to still rise* for the love of Borden.

In the fall of 1988, Flanagan began graduate school at the University of Chicago and Laura felt well enough to join him in his one-bedroom apartment where the bathtub—compliments of the former tenants—was filled with kitty litter. An ancient hamburger sat on the stove, and an army of cockroaches was indulging. As the apartment was four flights up, with no elevator, Laura had to spend all her time in its crumbling walls, listening to her neighbor hurl things at her husband. Two years later, she felt strong enough to chance a road trip to Sarasota to visit its racetrack. Although the ten hour drive was risky, she was tired of living in confinement, and so was Borden. She became so ill they had to detour to a friend's home in New Jersey. As she lay sliding in and out of delirium, all she could repeat to Borden through chattering teeth was, "I love you. I love you. I love you." She returned to Bethesda, sicker than ever, burdened with the thought she was destroying Borden's life. When she voiced her fears, before he left to university, he gave her a silver ring engraved with the words "Vous et nul autre" (You and no other). Laura joked she wanted Brandon to propose while dressed up as a pirate or a matador.

He remarked, "The theme was definitely tights." Although they considered themselves partners for life, they made no plans to marry. She quipped it was futile to plan a wedding when the bride was not certain she would be able to show up. Flanagan says that even at her sickest, Hillenbrand retained her sense of humor: "One time she had this awful fever, going up and up. It was 104 and she said, "When I hit 107, sell."

Desperate not to be known as Laura the invalid, but as Laura the author, she researched the story she had read as a young girl who had dreamt of becoming a jockey. She still had her dog-eared copy she had purchased at the Bethesda Elementary School Fair. As an adult, she focused on Seabiscuit's half-blind, crippled rider, Red Pollard, who overcame his injuries by sheer willpower. She placed the picture of his thin, battered face above her desk.

Unable to visit libraries, Laura bought vintage newspapers on eBay, and the disadvantage proved propitious. Rather than just reading the pertinent articles, she became engrossed in the trivia of the period through its ads and gossip pages. She learned that the number one book at the time was *Gone with the Wind*, the Hindenburg flew over Manhattan emblazoned with a swastika, and Roosevelt vowed America would never become involved in foreign wars. The book, *Seabiscuit: An American Legend*, revolved around the horse who had triumphed over astounding odds to become a racetrack legend and an icon in Depression-era America. The gimpy horse that could became such an inspiration to a weary nation was mentioned in more newspapers in 1938—the year he beat the Goliath of the track, War Admiral—than either Franklin Delano Roosevelt or Adolph Hitler. The trick for her was to pretend that she and her characters inhabited the same world—a sort of parallel reality in which their struggles were her own. It took her four years to finish, often writing from bed. While it is always daunting to write a book, it is even more so when one is suffering from constant vertigo, an off-shoot of her disease. Laura likens its effects to riding on the deck of a pitching ship. Earning one million dollars for the movie and more from the sale of millions of copies—translated into fifteen languages—assured her financial future. When it shot to the top of the *New York Times* bestsellers list, Borden threw open a window and shouted the news to the neighborhood. Laura said that it felt good "being able to be something other than Flanagan's invalid girlfriend." Unable to leave her house, *Good Morning America* and NBC interviewed her from her home. She joked that her fichus has been in so many media appearances that it "is going to get its own publicist." With her book's breakaway success she said, "Seabiscuit is to me what he was to people in the Depression. He is possibility."

In 2003, Hillenbrand was in the White House where she had been invited to a special screening of *Seabiscuit*. Unable to watch a bright screen, as the film played in the forty-seat family theater to an audience that included George W. and Laura Bush, , Steven Spielberg, and Toby Maguire—among other luminaries—the author sat gazing out a window that overlooked the Rose Garden.

In 2008, during a good spell, Laura and Borden decided to tie
the knot and wed on the rooftop deck of the Hay-Adams Hotel. The
couple recited vows that they wrote in front of sixty friends and
relatives, and a guest read from the *Velveteen Rabbit*—the story of
a stuffed animal that came to life through love. Laura had to remain
seated throughout the ceremony and was not well enough to stay for
the reception. Both bride and groom agreed it had been a lovely affair.

It was during her research on Seabiscuit that Hillenbrand
noticed another preoccupation of the 1930s sports pages: Louis
Zamperini, who had been the most famous racing mammal aside
from Seabiscuit, which is how Laura stumbled on his story in the
vintage newspaper. After his juvenile delinquent teens, Louis had
found redemption through running and had raced in the Berlin
Olympics and survived internment in a Japanese prison of war
camp. When Laura reached out to him, he was an eighty-seven-
year-old living in California. As with Pollard and his horse, she
developed a kinship with Zamperini and his fellow POWs. All off
them—like the author herself—were indomitable characters facing
incredible long shots. She said,

I can't compare my situation to theirs, but something I do
understand is being in a situation of ultimate desperation,
or suffering to the last point of our ability to tolerate it. I can
understand how bad it felt, and I can draw strength from the
fact that they got through those things. What you feel more than
anything else in these situations of great extremity is an experience

of terrible aloneness, when you get truly desperate and hopeless, and it's reassuring to see that other people have gone to those places and come back.

By writing, she gained both courage and escapism from her own stark reality. Although his age and her infirmity prevented them from meeting, they shared hundreds of phone calls. Laura explained this was not a handicap, as "there is intimacy in distance." Zamperini had not understood why their relationship was long-distance until he learned about her illness through one of her interviews. Afterwards, he sent her one of his Purple Hearts. He said she deserved it more than him.

Another unintended result of her research on the runner was a personal connection. Her father had returned from Europe with a rebuilt hand and physical scars, but he was never able to discuss the emotional impact of the war. Through Zamperini, Hillenbrand found another way to understand her distant parent.

Zamperini's biography debuted in 2010 and dominated the *New York Times* best-seller list and became the subject of a film. What tarnished her happiness was that after twenty years, she separated from her husband. Her new home has the feeling of a furnished house, but one not lived in, except for a few personal touches: a statue of a show horse in the foyer and a huge photograph of Zamperini. Journalists have pointed out the irony of Hillenbrand's two blockbusters: a woman for whom walking around the block constitutes a marathon writes about the finest specimens of physical endurance. Laura's response: "It's not irony, it's escape. I'm looking for a way out of here. I can't have it physically, so I'm going to have it intellectually. It was a *beautiful* thing to ride Seabiscuit in my imagination. And it's just *fantastic* to be there alongside Louis as he's breaking the mile record. People at these vigorous moments in their lives-it's my way of living vicariously."

Laura is feeling better than she has for years, and that may be because of the new love in her life. She felt well enough to move to Oregon to be with her boyfriend, where she finds solace in car trips with views of the resplendent Mount Hood. The new couple journeyed in their RV for a month-long trip crossing the country, and she relished every drop of rain, every stretch of highway, every blade of grass, because she was not in bed. Laura understood the risk, but felt she had to try—she could not continue to live locked in a room. While Seabiscuit serves as a metaphor for Laura—a horse that brought hope to a despairing nation—the title of her second book is her encapsulated biography: *Unbroken: A Story of Survival, Resilience and Redemption.*

CHAPTER 22:
HOOAH! (1968)

In a Salinger short story, Esme, an upper class British schoolgirl, tells a forlorn American soldier, "I hope you return from the war with all your faculties intact." Her words are not prophetic; after witnessing atrocities, he suffers a nervous breakdown. In another war, a nonfictional woman also goes through unmitigated hell; her indomitable spirit exemplifies the human spirit's ability to soar—against all odds.

Ladda Tammy had a singular upbringing. She and her younger brother Tommy were born in Bangkok, to mother Lamai Sompornpairin, a Thai of Chinese descent, and a Marine father from Virginia, Franklin Duckworth, a World War II, Korean, and Vietnam vet. His job in the United Nations entailed the family's relocations to Thailand, Indonesia, Singapore, and Cambodia. Her itinerant childhood meant always pulling up roots, but it left her trilingual—Thai, Indonesian, and English—and made her emotionally resilient. The Duckworths lived in Cambodia until two weeks before the Khmer Rouge takeover. She recalls devastating sights that made an indelible impression.

When Tammy was sixteen, the family moved to Hawaii, but her years were anything but a tropical idyll. Franklin had been reduced to financial dire straits by a late-in-life layoff and the Duckworths descended from middle class into poverty. No one would hire him because they said he was overqualified. She explained this comment, "Those are code words for 'you're too old.'" At low ebb, the family of four was down to their last ten dollars. They were forced to live in a pay-by-the-week motel and Tammy recalled, "We'd use the food stamps for baloney and white bread, praying it would last the week." At McKinley High School, a teacher gave them money for Taco Bell. Tammy bought two tacos for ninety-nine cents, and would offer her father one, pretending she was full. Despite her difficult home situation, partially due to her Tiger Mother Lamai, Tammy graduated with honors.

In 1990, Tammy enrolled in the master's program in international affairs at George Washington University with the aspiration to become an ambassador. She joined the ROTC and recalled, "I fell in love with the military. I even loved the drill sergeants yelling at me." It was how she met her husband, Bryan Bowlsbey. When they were cadets, he made a comment that she felt was derogatory about the role of women in the Army. Contrite, he apologized and helped clean her M16. The couple married three years later.

Duckworth enrolled in a political science PhD program at Northern Illinois University and concurrently became a member of the National Guard. In 2004 she trained as a Black Hawk pilot, as it was one of the few jobs with combat potential for women. She said she "got a lot of shit" as the first female platoon leader of her unit. When she made her team cocoa before training exercises, the pilots called her "mommy platoon leader." In 2004, she was deployed in Operation Iraqi Freedom.

On November 12, she was copiloting a Black Hawk with Daniel Milberg when insurgents lurking along the Tigris River launched a rocket-propelled grenade at their cockpit. She tried to control the helicopter and wondered why the pedals did not respond. It did not occur to her that she no longer had any feet with which to press them. She recalled with a lightness of tone that belied the horror, "I did not realize my legs were already gone. I mean, how many times a day do you ever look down to check if you still have your legs?" Duckworth had also lost half her blood and her right arm was barely attached. Milberg—who risked his life to save hers—described the rescue as straight out of *Saving Private Ryan*. Surgeons in Baghdad amputated the remains of her right leg just below the hip and her left leg below the knee. They stabilized her arm and she eventually arrived in the Walter Reed Army Medical Center in Washington, DC, where specialists and her husband awaited. Her stay—in the facility she called "the amputee petting zoo"—was of thirteen months duration. Duckworth had the dubious distinction of being the first female double amputee of the war. She was virtually helpless, with only one usable limb. In agony she battled the pain by looking at a clock and counting to sixty as each minute ticked by. At first she recited, "One dead Iraqi, two dead Iraqis, three dead Iraqis." However, she soon stopped herself from giving into hate and determined she was not going to be defined by "some guy who got lucky with a grenade decide how I live my life." Instead, she repeated the Soldier's Creed: "I'm an American soldier. …I will never accept defeat. I will never quit."

Bowlsbey had just returned from his brother's wedding rehearsal dinner when he received the devastating news. He flew to the hospital to be there when Tammy regained consciousness, and did not leave her side to shower or sleep. He said breaking the tragedy of her injuries was one of the most difficult things he had ever done, but she took it "with poise and stoicism." After she listened to his rundown of all the things amputees were capable of doing, she replied. "I love you, but you stink. Go shower."

During the months of convalescence, when the psychological and physical pain was so great, and the future as a potential three limb amputee was so bleak, she could easily have succumbed to despair. But the spirit of defeat was not the stuff Tammy Duckworth was made of. She persevered—*to still rise*—even if physically doing so entailed prosthetic limbs. These became state-of-the art titanium; one bore a camouflage pattern, the other an American flag.

The patients at Walter Reed helped dispel the gloom with their own brand of dark humor. They would joke about the doctors ruining their tattoos when performing surgery and Tammy got into the spirit with her T-shirt: *Lucky for me, he's an ass man.*

The staff also helped through the long road to recovery when they encouraged their patients to set goals, and hers ranged from the practical to the daring. First, she wanted to regain enough mobility in her right arm so she could wear a ponytail without assistance. Bryan's was well-meaning, but proved clumsy in this endeavor. She also wanted to fly once again with the National Guard.

When Forest carried Lt. Dan from the jungle of Vietnam, the officer railed against Gump, shouting he had cheated him of his destiny. He had lost his legs in the sniper attack and would have preferred to die with honor than live as a cripple. Tammy Duckworth never felt this way. She marks the November 12th ambush with her Alive Day, a tradition that arose in Vietnam as wounded American soldiers struggled to cope with the physical and emotional scars left by their injuries. The anniversary marks a bittersweet moment. She said, "It could be a horrible day, but I choose to celebrate it. I know it's the day I lost my legs, but it is also the day that I survived." Duckworth says the celebration is not about her, but rather a tribute to those who aided in her recovery. Many guests attended, of whom Tammy said, "When you have all these people behind you, you don't want to let them down. That's where my strength comes from. If I gave up, it would be disrespectful to them." As Milberg said of the woman he refused to leave for dead, she hosts no pity parties. On the first of these occasions, she put on her pink T-shirt that reads *Life is good* before she headed off to the banquet hall. Her tops are emblematic of her character. Another reads, *Dude, where's my leg?* Another, *Wanna touch it?* When asked about her sense of humor regarding her amputations, she explained, "You can choose to cry about it, and you can choose to be depressed for the rest of your life about it, but at the end of the day, I earned my injuries in defense of my nation." She added to honor those who saved her was to maintain her sense of humor and to show that her life is actually quite normal. She continued, "My husband and I have fights all the time. We don't fight because I don't have legs. We have fights because he leaves the toilet seat up. And it annoys me."

Lt. Dan re-embraced life when he let his bitterness go, and Tammy is endlessly grateful to have survived. She stated, "Every day is a payback for me. I measure each one on how effective I am. I don't ever want to be sad about my life." Then, as if to prove her point, she suddenly moved her chair and revealed flirty, flashy shoes. They were pointy, zebra-striped with silver buckles strapped onto her two shiny titanium carbon fiber legs. She continued, "One of the good things about losing your feet is I can wear all the pointy shoes I want and it doesn't hurt anymore. I can wear shoes just for fashion now." She chuckled, though it camouflaged sadness.

Post-release, she realized one of the many items on her bucket list, when she piloted a single engine Piper-Cherokee, her left prosthetic manipulating the pedals, making for a daunting feat at two thousand feet. For Tammy, flying equals freedom, even if it is not the adrenaline-pumping combat duty but sailing over Virginia's forests. She completed the Chicago Marathon in the wheelchair division, and relearned how to scuba dive. However, in her more vulnerable moments, she admits she is not bionic, her emotions not bullet-proof. She shuns her flesh-colored prosthetics since they serve as a reminder that she will never be able to put on "sexy heels and a sexy dress" for a date with her husband. Some days all she can do is battle fatigue; on other days it's a fight against "phantom limb pain." She also is saddened she did not regain the full use of her dominant right hand, an irritation because her salute is no longer crisp.

Tammy also achieved her goal of again giving back to the country she loves when she entered the arena of politics—even though it placed her in another line of fire. Not surprisingly, Ms. Duckworth did not prove to be a straitlaced politician. On one occasion, she joined fellow Democrats in the House to sit on the floor to demand a vote on gun control legislation. Members had taken to tweeting photos and livestreaming the motley crew, singing "We Shall Overcome" on Facebook—a blatant violation of the decorous rules of the chamber. To forestall the Capitol Police confiscating her phone, Tammy slipped it into the hollow of her prosthetic. When asked what else she had hidden there, she replied her secret vice—Sour Patch Kids.

By this time, Duckworth's trials and her joie de vivre made

her a darling on the talk show circuit, and she earned praise in magazines such as *Glamor*. A commentator extolled her virtues and mentioned if Tammy ran as a Republican, she would have his vote. Duckworth declared her first candidacy for Congress in 2005 as a Fighting Dem. She lost by two points and admitted she sat in her bathtub and cried for three days. Tammy attempted a second run in 2012 against Senator Mark Kirk, and if biographies alone won elections, Duckworth would have been a shoe-in. In her speech she stated, "My family has served this nation in uniform, going back to the Revolution. I've bled for this nation." The already contentious Illinois Senate reached a new low when Kirk insulted his mixed race opponent: "I forgot that your parents came all the way from Thailand to serve George Washington." Ms. Duckworth did not answer, and the audience dissolved into a stunned silence. Both parties agreed Kirk had crossed the line by attacking a lieutenant colonel, the recipient of a Purple Heart, who had given her legs for America. It flew in the face of the fact the Illinois chapter of the Daughters of the American Revolution had erected a statue of her standing next to the War of Independence hero Molly Pitcher. He offered his "sincere apology" via Twitter. However, Tammy took the comment in stride. As she said, "These legs are titanium. They don't buckle. Go ahead, take a shot at me. There's nothing you can do to me now that will ever be as bad as that day in Iraq. I'm tough enough for it. I am." In 2012, Senator Tammy Duckworth became the first disabled female veteran and the first female Asian American woman to serve in the House of Representatives.

As with many survivors, Tammy questioned why her life had been spared, and one of the many reasons became manifest with her pregnancy. This was no easy feat, as she was forty-six and had to conceive through reproductive technology. Carrying a baby was further complicated, as this made walking on her prosthetics more difficult as they had been calibrated to her height and weight and the added pounds played havoc with their electronics.

Bryan and Tammy toyed with calling their daughter Piper after their plane; however, they settled on Abigail O'kalani Bowlsbey, when a former senator from Hawaii bestowed a traditional island name. Her regret from retiring from the National Guard was Abigail would never get to see her serving in its ranks. Although it will be a challenge to raise a child without legs, the full use of her dominant hand, a career as a senator and a husband who can be deployed, there is no cause for worry for the woman who is as tough as titanium.

An expression in the US military that is a shout-out to the affirmative is one Tammy Duckworth, survivor extraordinaire, deserves: Hooah!

CHAPTER 23:
A BUTTERFLY (1981)

The setting of horror films are as memorable as their characters and plots, and deliver collective shivers. In *Psycho*, the Bates Motel housed a mother—preserved through taxidermy—and a shower that makes audiences seek another method of hygiene. In *The Shining*, the Overlook Hotel elevator oozed blood, a ghost resided in room 237, and a door displayed "REDRUM." In *Carrie*, Bates High is the venue for cinema's worst ever prom that involved pig's blood and flames that transformed the school into an inferno. A non-celluloid setting on Seymour Avenue became a nonfictional house of horror.

Michelle Knight was born with the opposite of a silver spoon in Cleveland, an industrial center pockmarked by crime-ridden neighborhoods, one of America's ten most dangerous zip codes. A male family member started molesting her when she was five years old, and Michelle recalled of the violation, "It's like I was buried six feet under and screaming and nobody can hear a thing." She and her younger twin brothers, Eddie and Freddie, spent a year living in a brown station wagon, and when the Knights moved into a house, it was in a neighborhood populated by prostitutes, pimps, and drug dealers. She had a contentious relationship with mother Barbara, and in their household, soap and toothpaste were luxuries; Pop-Tarts and SpaghettiOs were as nutritious as things got. At age fifteen, she ran away and lived under a bridge in a blue garbage can with wheels, where, in Oscar the Grouch fashion, she made her home. She recalled, "I had my own little room. If I wanted to sing, I didn't have to listen to my mother, 'You're a horrible singer, shut up.'" Michelle fell in with a marijuana dealer who provided a room in exchange for work as a drug runner.

Her teen years were angst-ridden, and she was miserable at James Ford Rhodes High School, blighted by overcrowded classrooms and poor facilities. Michelle, nicknamed by the other students as Shorty because of her four-foot-seven-inch height, struggled. At age seventeen, two boys gang-raped her at school, traumatizing her. She dropped out before graduation. As a result of the attack, she became pregnant with son Joey. However, the baby became the one shining light in her life, and she determined for his sake to complete her education so she could obtain a career. Her mother's boyfriend shattered that dream; he broke the toddler's leg. Social workers removed Joey from the home, an act that unleashed an event that was to make her a character in a Hitchcock horror.

In 2002, Michelle walked into a Family Dollar Store, exhausted, sweaty, and desperate. The twenty-one-year-old had spent the past few hours searching for the location of social services for a hearing to reclaim Joey. After asking the cashier for directions, a man overheard her and offered to give her a lift. Michelle recognized Ariel Castro as the father of Emily, a former classmate, and gratefully explained why it was imperative to make it to the court on time. In his orange Chevy, she noticed discarded wrappers from McDonalds and Chinese food containers; however, even if she had wanted to leave, the door had no handle. When Castro began to head in the wrong direction, he explained he was just popping into his house so she could choose from a litter of puppies as a welcome home gift for Joey. Inside the dilapidated home, the air smelled of stale beer, urine, and rotten beans, and the windows were boarded with planks of wood. The twenty-one-year-old Michelle Knight was going to become Rapunzel locked in a tower, except her hair was shaved and her tower a filthy, dilapidated hovel.

The details of her imprisonment hurt like body blows just to hear about them, let alone endure. Castro led her to an upstairs bedroom to retrieve a phantom puppy, and as soon as she entered, the door slammed shut. He hogtied her, unzipped his pants, and ejaculated over her body. Castro stuffed a dirty sock in her mouth, blasted the radio, and left. "The first thing that came to my head was, 'Holy shit, I'm gonna die here. I'm not gonna be able to say to Joey I love him. I'm gonna miss every moment of his life.'" Knight had to fight those same fears, day after day, for the next eleven years. During this time, she was repeatedly raped, made to sit for hours with a motorcycle helmet on her head, and forced to relieve herself in a plastic bucket. Castro gave her napkins in lieu of tampons, and during one stage, left her naked in a freezing room on a soiled mattress for months. In a nod to the Lord giveth and the Lord taketh away, Ariel gave Michelle a puppy she named Lobo; when he went to rape her, the dog attacked, and in retaliation Castro broke his neck. The dungeon-master discovered Michelle's allergy to mustard and forced her to eat a hot dog coated in the condiment. Her face puffed up and she could not breathe. Michelle became pregnant on five occasions and Castro beat her on her belly until she miscarried. He put the placenta in the fridge as a memento. Despite her surname, Michelle harbored no illusion a knight in white armor would come to her rescue. Despite every reason to give up, Michelle swore *to still rise*—she felt in her heart she would be reunited with Joey, and this—as well as her staunch Christian faith—gave her resilience to endure the unendurable.

Eventually, Castro permitted the luxury of a radio and a small television that became Michelle's lifeline to the world from which she had been amputated: Michael Jackson suspended his baby over a balcony! Kelly Clarkson became the first winner on American Idol! Elizabeth Smart found alive! A year after her own abduction, Knight was watching the news when she heard about a missing local girl, sixteen-year-old Amanda Berry. Icy fingers clutched her throat when she had the hunch—that proved prescient— that Castro had another victim trapped in Seymour Avenue. A third became the fourteen-year-old Gina Dejesus, who ended up sharing Michelle's room. Sometimes Castro would rape one of them while the other lay there, helpless. Michelle, as the older woman and the most inured, would often volunteer for the sexual assault to spare Gina.

On Christmas Day in 2006, Castro took a fourth captive: his daughter Jocelyn, who, like the child in Emma Donoghue's novel *Room*, was born into captivity. Amanda had given birth in a plastic kiddie pool and Michelle had acted as midwife. Ariel had inexplicably wanted this child and had told Knight if the baby died he would kill her in retaliation. Jocelyn became the darling of the house—and a reason for the three prisoners to survive. When she became a toddler and asked about the "bracelets," Castro removed them.

In 2013, Gina and Michelle were in their room when they heard pounding and kicking noises at the front door, followed by shouts, "Police!" Castro had accidentally left the door open and Amanda and Jocelyn had escaped and alerted a neighbor, who called 911. After four thousand days, the first thing Michelle did when she stepped outside was to kiss the ground and to thank God. Residents of Seymour Avenue lined the streets and applauded as emergency vehicles whisked the women away.

However, while Gina and Amanda had homes to return to and families ecstatic at their release, after a hospital stay Michelle lived in a shelter. Her first order of business was to rebuild her life, and boy was there a lot of rebuilding. Her first steps on the road to wellness was physical healing. After over a decade of darkness, her eyes were extremely sensitive, and the first moment she left her prison she felt they were being fried like eggs. Later, when asked if her sight was improving, she shook her head and replied, "I still got hope." Her stomach is permanently damaged from a combination of untreated infections and the five forced miscarriages that may have rendered her infertile. Knight's jaw was severely damaged from the number of times Castro had punched her, sometimes with barbells. Emaciated, the scale hovered in the eighties.

The diminutive Michelle proved herself an emotional giant when she declared she would nevermore be defined by "the dude" (she explained he doesn't deserve a name) and changed her own to Lilly Rose Lee—the latter is Joey's middle name. "It's about making a brand new start. I didn't want people to know me as *that* girl. I want people to know me as *this* girl," she said. She is also celebrating her newfound freedom with an array of tattoos, each deeply symbolic, that has made her body a visual diary. One displays a face, part skeleton and part flesh: "My heart is not chained to my situation;" two guns: "Know me as a victor not a victim;" and five large roses, covered in droplets of blood—for each of the babies lost in Seymour Avenue, "Too beautiful for this world." The largest of the tattoos are on her back and shoulders, a pair of wings: "Freedom to Fly."

Because of donations that poured in from well-wishers,

and with the advance of her memoir of misery, *Finding Me: A Decade of Darkness, A Life Reclaimed*, Michelle lives in her own home—a source of wonder to the girl who spent a year living in a car, months surviving in a garbage bin, and a decade existing in a dungeon—where the blinds are always open: "It's to see the beautiful sky that I never saw for years, to watch the clouds go by." She shares her digs with Sky, her puppy. She said the main reason for writing her book was to tell people they can overcome anything.

In a bid to make up for lost time, Michelle exemplifies the idiom "going concern." She recorded a song entitled "Survivor," attends boxing class, and enrolled in cooking school. She also took up skydiving to overcome her fear of heights and, because, "I'm adventurous." And yet she must avoid triggers: paper napkins, used to clean herself after rape and menstruating, and rammed down her throat; nothing with chains, including decorative ones; and no mirrors, as these were used so Castro "could watch." But any bitterness is sublimated by Michelle's indomitable spirit: "Our life is a painted canvass, painted by everything you do. Make it a beautiful one. I look at the world and I see all the beauty I missed."

The fifty-three-year-old Ariel Castro pleaded guilty to hundreds of charges, and Michelle finally had her day in court—the two other victims were not present. Mustering every ounce of steel her petite frame could muster, she stated, "I look inside my heart and I see my son and I cried every night. Christmas was a most traumatic day because I could not spend it with my son. Writing this statement gave me the strength to be a stronger woman and to know that there is more good than evil."

Behind her sat the prisoner, dressed in an orange jumpsuit, his legs manacled, now the one to eat the food, wear the clothes, and follow the rules of his jailer. Ms. Knight continued, "I spent eleven years in hell and now your hell is just beginning. I will overcome all this that happened, but you will face hell for all eternity." The dude received life in prison, plus one thousand years with no possibility of parole. He had pled guilty to 937 charges, including aggravated murder, rape, and kidnapping.

In 1937, Dr. Seuss wrote about a boy who imagines a fantastic parade in his hometown: "And that's a story that cannot be beat/ And to think that it happened on Mulberry Street." In contrast, Seymour Avenue held nothing but horror, and Michelle Knight was one of the many—Gina and Amanda were not present—who stood by and cheered its demolition. She thanked her neighbors for their support, never blaming them for not questioning—after the disappearance of three women not far from Seymour Avenue— why the house had all its windows covered. She understood the code of the mean streets, "Snitches have stitches." She passed out yellow balloons as symbols of freeing the world's missing children. She also thanked the Cleveland police and wrote them for saving her: "Life is tough, but I'm tougher." Castro hung himself in his cell a month later, not able to take the captivity to which he had subjected his victims.

Rapunzel enjoyed a happily ever after when the prince rescued her from her tower, but Michelle had no happily ever after. Because the Knights made no effort to reclaim Joey from social services, a family adopted him and never revealed biological details. Although she could have fought for visitation—as she had never relinquished parental rights—she refrained, as she did not want to cause her son emotional trauma. However, she takes comfort in the photographs of the teen, and though she made the heart-wrenching decision not to see him, "I still got hope."

Michelle refers to her tattoos as her "therapeutic art." She had only one before her abduction, inked by a friend at age fourteen. It is an image that she feels is a metaphor for her life—a metamorphosis from a larvae that blossoms into a kaleidoscope of color. As Ms. Lillian Rose Lee stated, "Just when the caterpillar thought the world was over, she became a butterfly."

CHAPTER 24:
SIN AND SALVATION (1982)

I n *Exodus*, Moses lamented, "I have been a stranger in a strange land." The pain echoes throughout the ages, yet even more heart-rending is alienation in the land of one's birth. This was what a contemporary woman faced: an outcast from her world, a misfit beyond its gate.

Isroel Miller was a respected rabbi in his Squirrel Hill, Pittsburg Yeshivas congregation—a religion unchanged since the biblical Abraham—where he and wife Deborah raised eleven children, the fifth daughter Leah. The reason for the large brood was their subset of Hasidim takes literally the biblical injunction "be fruitful and multiply." The Miller girls were born into a world that taught them to worship messiahs, men, and modesty. The family's three-story home was in such close proximity to the synagogue that throughout her childhood she could hear daily ancient Jewish prayers float through the bathroom window. It was the air she breathed; she knew no other. In the rigid household, love was not a word bandied about; Leah later wrote of her youth, "My parents were not literate in the language of human emotion." Rather, love was limited to the feeling one had toward God. In the context of this world, being a woman followed a formula: marry after high school and produce a baby each year as motherhood was their greatest purpose. Females were indoctrinated in the belief that any questioning of their faith would lead to drug addiction, prostitution, or death. Leah explained of her ordained role, "It's like asking a penguin, 'How do you feel about growing up to be a penguin?' It's like, 'I'm a penguin. This is my calling.'"

It was not until her teens Leah realized that she might not be a penguin: she had expressed an interest in attending college and Deborah had threatened to have her locked up in a psychiatric hospital. Alarmed at her rebelliousness, at fifteen her parents sent her to Manchester, England, to finish her education in an even more religious setting. Away from family, Leah wrote a G-rated letter to her best friend's older brother where she revealed her interest in him and, just as scandalous, questioned her ultra-Orthodox faith. Her aunt discovered it and promptly informed Deborah, who called Leah and launched into a diatribe of how such transgressions diminished her prospects of finding a respectable Yeshivish husband. In the hope of salvaging their daughter's reputation, Leah's parents arranged for her to live with her sister in Israel and attend a seminary to study Jewish law.

However, the Holy Land did not make for a pleasing roadmap. Looking at her sister was like peering into the telescope of her own future: crooked wig, ever-pregnant belly, demanding husband. If Leah had been permitted to listen to pop culture music, she could have heard Peggy Lee's lament, "*Is that all there is to it*?" Leah questioned her pre-ordained destiny: "Was this, I wondered, the gorgeous, idealized union I had longed for all of my life?"

The day before Yom Kippur, Leah went window shopping in Jerusalem, where she spotted a mannequin sheathed in a charcoal-gray sweater, decorated with lace collar. Although it covered collarbone and elbows, it was fitted and showed off her adolescent curves. Aware she was flirting with danger, she bought the forbidden garment. It led to her mother's second angered phone call after hearing about the slutty sweater from her other daughter: "Your behavior has become unacceptable. We give you chance after chance, and you keep on disappointing people. You think you're so grown up? Let's see how grown up you are. You'll have to figure out how to get by on your own." Her parents united against her both for the shame she had brought on them and in fear the bad seed sister would taint her sibling's marital prospects.

The Millers, after Leah bringing "shame" on the family in Pittsburg, Manchester, and Jerusalem, banished her to a dreary, basement studio apartment in a Yeshivish section of Brooklyn and found her a job as a secretary for minimum wage. They paid the first month's rent of $450.00, and told her after that she was on her own—in every sense. Rabbi and Deborah Miller did to their teenage daughter what the Eskimos did to their elderly—set her adrift on an ice floe. It was the start of a heartbreaking and terrifying odyssey, one that consisted of so much pain and sorrow she felt she could not endure.

Money was her most immediate pressing concern, as she did not earn enough to afford both food and rent. She mostly subsisted on a slice of bread, a bottle of ketchup, and a few slices of American cheese, but even worse was a lack of social nourishment. In her former cloistered world, she had always been surrounded by immediate and extended family, friends, and her tight-knit congregation; however, now she was in a Ziploc bag of solitude. With no previous access to television, secular music, and other popular media, and dressed in long, dark skirts, she was considered odd at work and members of the Yeshivish viewed her as a pariah. Her voice was often hoarse in the morning because she had not spoken to anyone since she had left the office the day before. Her alienation was the self—same as the Ancient Mariner's adrift at sea, "So lonely 'twas that God himself/Scarce seemed there to be." Not surprisingly, Leah went looking for love—and money—in all the wrong places.

On her way to and from work, she walked by a basketball court and began watching the men from a bench, desperate for attention. However, the Yeshivish girl in her modest clothes did not exactly make her a sexual magnet. Finally one approached her, and began to flirt, calling her princess, a painful reminder of her father's nickname, "Leahchke." Leah prayed he would be her savior, but he was not savior material. Other than basketball, the man's chief pursuits was taking and selling drugs. She agreed to go back to his place, and when she refused to go beyond a make-out session, became a victim of rape. A few months later, she was hospitalized for untreated chlamydia that had turned to green slime. The doctors told her it might have rendered her infertile.

Alone in her basement, Leah used razor blades to cut her arms and body. In a suicide attempt, she overdosed on painkillers and was committed to a psychiatric hospital for ten days. In her memoir, *Cut Me Loose*, a double entendre on her desire for freedom and her self-mutilation, she wrote of her nadir, "I was a crazy, broken-down slut, weighed down by history that tormented me in my nightmares." Desperate, she reached out to her parents, who ignored her pleas and told her siblings she just wanted attention.

It was everything the Yeshivish had warned would happen if she strayed. Leah figured if they considered her a whore, she might as well start acting like one, and envisioned herself leading a glamorous, badass life. She posted an ad on Craigslist, seeking a "mutually beneficial relationship." She figured as a call girl she would make a $1,000 a night, with no income tax. This time, she got plenty of attention, and she chose a lawyer from the Upper East Side. Although she had been in Manhattan for four years, she was still naïve. She never quoted a fee and invited him to her place with visions of herself walking out of Saks loaded down with bags. Before he arrived, she placed Band-Aids and stuck them over the patch of crusty scars on her arms. Mr. Attorney was not a fan of condoms, and as he thrust into her, demanded she say she loved him. During the nightmare Leah reverted to her old prayer, *HaShem. HaShem.* However, as she lay pinned down, she did not think God would hear a prayer from a rabbi's daughter impaled beneath a sweaty stranger. He paid her only after their second sexual rendezvous: $60.00. When the door shut, Leah lay on the soiled sheets, cupping her burning crotch, and cried, "Poor stupid little baby." Mired in abject misery, she yet found the inner resource *to still rise.* Upset she was just as much a failure at being bad as she had been in being good, she ended her foray into prostitution.

Leah, still burdened with the notion that affirmation could only be achieved through a male, began a series of sexual encounters. There was her neighbor Tim, the long-haired hipster who complimented her backside, and after they spent the night, only greeted her with grunts, Josh, the Star Wars fanatic who called her Princess Leia, and a string of others who did Houdini vanishing acts.

Redemption arrived in an epiphany: the mainstay of Leah's misery was her family had cut her loose. However, on a rare occasion when she was invited home—for her sister's engagement—she sat at the table eating off a paper plate with disposable cutlery. This was not because Deborah felt her non-prodigal daughter carried a host of secular diseases—she was probably oblivious to this phenomena—but because she did not want Leah to sully her *Shabbos* china. Suddenly Leah realized she had misunderstood her longing for her family, for her desire to return home. Her epiphany was she was not homesick for this "family of foreigners, their religiosity and gender divisions," rendering them incapable of giving love. Leah stated this time she was leaving in every sense of the word. Her mother shrugged; her father gave a cold stare. There is a price to be paid when, in the name of religion, people forgo humanity.

Armed with newfound confidence, Leah started classes at Brooklyn College on a scholarship and earned straight A's, even while continuing her full-time job. Another step to casting off her emotional chains came via an affair with a married professor— forty-two years her senior, a father-surrogacy relationship—who she called "Pupa." He encouraged her to voice her opinions, something she had never dared to do. His less than impressed wife eventually found out and made her husband end his extracurricular adultery; however, through her newly-acquired confidence, she applied to graduate school at Harvard. When she was accepted—again on a full scholarship—she packed her childhood suitcase that she had lugged to Manchester, Jerusalem, and Brooklyn. Back then, she had crossed out her sister's name and written her own; before leaving for graduate studies, she crossed out her surname and wrote one of her own creation: Leah Vincent, a woman without a history. Leah assumed the surname Vincent in her twenties when she was briefly married to a roommate in need of a green card. He got to stay in the United

States and she got to forge a new identity, one separate from the upbringing from which she desired escape.

Post-graduation, she returned to New York and became active in Footsteps, a nonprofit organization devoted to helping former Orthodox Jews adapt to their new lives. There she met Zeke, who had left his Hasidic upbringing, and she felt they were twins in mind and spirit. A few weeks later, she told a friend she could see herself spending her life with him. When they decided to get married, the question was in what type of ceremony. She imagined herself in a little strapless dress kissing her groom after they had exchanged vows, barefoot, on a beach. Zeke was in accord, and suggested a potluck dinner of sushi and strawberry smoothies and readings from their favorite books. It was to be all about kisses, cake, and Gandhi quotes. The problem was their families would not recognize such a wedding. As both sides were Orthodox, it would only be valid if Zeke and Leah stood chastely side-by-side under a *chuppah,* blessed by elderly rabbis and wedded through a traditional contract, a ring, and a broken glass. Her dress would have to be high necked and long sleeved; it would have to be celebrated with men with long side curls and women with wigs segregated by a long wall, whirling in traditional dances on either side. The problem with pleasing their relatives was the couple did not want to begin their new lives with the weight of a faith they had relinquished. At the end, they decided to go with an Orthodox ceremony, as it was the venue to show forgiveness to a community that had shunned them. Unfortunately, her father did not share her view on reconciliation: shortly before giving birth to her daughter, she wrote her father and never received a reply. Leah refers to herself as a "zombie orphan," one where your parents are alive but are dead to their offspring.

Their second wedding was one after their own hearts: they went off to a remote part of Africa and expressed their love on a blanket on a rocky river band, celebrating their commitment with Zulu women who shared their traditional dance, songs, and food.

In her new life, Ms. Vincent does not often think of the teachings that had shaped her youth. However, she does remember a Hebrew teaching of Hillel the Elder: "If I am not for myself, who will be for me?" Through her long road of self-discovery, Leah realized she would have to be for herself. On her suitcase, though she had written a "woman without a history" because of her phenomenal persistence, she is a woman with a future. The subtitle of Vincent's memoir can serve as the bookmarks of her two separate lives: *Sin and Salvation*.

CHAPTER 25:
THE BEST REVENGE (1989)

The Internet can be an unkind place, a fertile stomping-ground for trolls. The most vulnerable victims are teens whose cell phones are their windows to the virtual—and often vicious—world. All too often we are confronted with young lives cut short, unable to withstand the scourge of bullying. In contrast, one girl used cyberspace as a crusade for a cause.

Lizzie's upbeat nature was severely tested when the seventeen-year-old went on a search for online music—purely homework procrastination—never dreaming this mundane act would change her life. She had stumbled on a YouTube video entitled "The World's Ugliest Woman." What she saw was heart-wrenching, because what she saw was herself. It was an eight-second clip of an interview Velasquez had given to a local news station and had been viewed over four million times. Devastated, she nonetheless read the hundreds of cruel comments that made her stomach sink: *Why didn't her parents just abort her? You're gross. I just threw up all over my keyboard. Kill it with fire.* Another post stated people would go blind if they saw her on the street, another called her the modern Medusa. She read each and every one, not in a nod to masochism, but because she hoped to find someone in her corner. No such luck. The footage ripped to shreds the fragile self-confidence that had taken years to build. She cried herself to sleep for many nights; although she could not remember ever being free from cruel comments, this was on a whole other level. Lizzie felt like Humpty Dumpty, and believed she would never be able to put herself together again.

Elizabeth—Lizzie—fought herself into the world, four weeks premature, and weighed two pounds ten ounces; the only clothes that fit were from the doll section at Toys R Us. Her misshapen appearance was so shocking nurses used a photograph to introduce her to her mother and father. They told her parents (father Lupe is a public school principal and mother Rita is a church receptionist) in all probability Lizzie would never walk or talk and her life expectancy would be of a short duration. The baby was a question mark to the medical community—understandable, as only two other people in the world share this genetic abnormality. It carries in its wake a host of physical afflictions, such as facial deformity and extreme emancipation. The doctors offered little hope, but hope is to what the new father and mother clung. Filled with love for their newborn, Rita and Lupe never thought, "Why is this happening to us?" They just wanted to take their daughter home.

Raised in a family filled with love—that grew to include brother Chris and sister Marina—she had no inkling she was different. This changed when she stared kindergarten, her first memory of being bullied. She arrived at Galindo Elementary School in Austin, excited to make friends, but the other children were far from thrilled with what they feared was the bogey-girl. She endured name-calling, finger-pointing, and stares; being innately kind, she was at a loss to understand their cruelty, as she felt she was an awesome kid. Whenever asked what she wanted to be when she grew up, her answer was a waitress. Her dream was to be able to serve people and bring whatever was needed. Unable to shield her from a hostile world, all her parents could do was assure her she was the same as the other kids, just smaller. Unfortunately, although her family saw her as being no different than everyone else, the world did not. She remembers going to amusement parks and feeling like an attraction; even adults would stop mid-conversation to gawk.

With Lizzie's unfailing kindness and bubbly enthusiasm, she eventually won over her classmates. And yet her cross was a heavy one. She recalls that every birthday wish, every candle lit at church, every prayer before bed, "God, please take this all away from me. Please make me normal." When Lizzie entered Crockett High, she decided not to sit on the sidelines and became a cheerleader, and, of course, because of her extreme emaciation, was the girl thrown up in the air. When she fell during practice, her teammates panicked, but she just picked herself back up: "I'm little but I'm tough. Let's try it again." Lizzie admits she tried out mostly for the cute uniform; however, it was something deeper that drew her to the uniform. She said whenever she wore it she felt like it was her superhero cape. She felt by dressing like the other girls, subconsciously she could look like them as well. Her hard-won equanimity ended when she came across the YouTube video in which she was the unwitting star.

When Lizzie confided to her parents what had happened, Lupe told her that sometimes to know all is to forgive all. He explained that she was not aware of what was going on in those people's lives that had driven them to post such hateful—such hurtful—things. He added that bullies are often damaged people, as sorely in need of help as their victims. At the time she thought he was insane for suggesting such a thing, but eventually came to the same conclusion. She was also aided by her Roman Catholicism: "It's been my rock through everything, just having the time to be alone and pray and talk to God and know that He's there for me." She never underwent a crisis of faith, never turned on God for her affliction. She had trust He had a plan which had not yet become manifest.

The teen decided to turn a vehicle of hate into an instrument of love and to fight fire with fire. Rather than letting the video define or destroy her, she seized the same method of communication and used it to spread positivity and empowerment. She felt by telling her story, she would be able to turn people's view of her around and in the process help both the bullied and the bullies. Velasquez became a motivational speaker, and turned into a web sensation after her TED Talk, "How Do You Define Yourself?" viewed more than nine million times. Dressed to the hilt, she owned the stage. In it, she reveals the person "Behind the World's Ugliest Woman" video and spreads her message: "We can either decide to feel sorry for ourselves and throw the biggest pity party in the world—or there's this whole other side with everything that we *do* have in our lives." Her promise was the light at the end of the tunnel is indescribable. She gained tens of thousands of faithful followers on Facebook and Twitter. In its wake, she garnered guest appearances on *The Today Show, Dr. Drew,* and *The View,* where her interviewers were Barbara Walters and Whoopi Goldberg. The latter introduced her by saying true beauty shines from within, and no one shines brighter than Lizzie; she praised her for triumphing over the truly ugly.

The indefatigable young woman earned a bachelor's degree in communication from Texas State University and created her own YouTube channel that garnered seventy million views, filming herself, her family, and friends. Lizzie expressed her pleasure that the community that has built up around her online presence has been amazing, and people who have been victimized are posting comments expressing she has made them feel able to stand up to their tormentors rather than internalize their pain.

Lizzie also used writing as a salve as well as a medium for reaching out with her message of acceptance, a lesson she learned from her ever nurturing parents and siblings. From the YouTube video, she discovered words can hurt more than physical abuse—but also came to realize they have the power to heal. Her first work, co-authored with Rita, was her autobiography, released in English and Spanish: *Lizzie Beautiful: The Lizzie Velazquez Story.* It includes journal entries her mother wrote to her as a child that told her never to lose heart even in the face of heartlessness, to never use the word "can't" in regard to her aspirations. Lizzie wrote two additional books for teens that offer encouragement to those undergoing hardship. *Be Beautiful: Be You* shares her journey "to discover what truly makes us beautiful and teaches readers to recognize their unique gifts and blessings." Her third work, *Choosing Happiness,* deals with the seemingly insurmountable obstacles Lizzie faces and how she "learned the importance of choosing to be happy when it's all too easy to give up." In it she shared the scourges of her disease, not as a way to mire in self-pity, but to show resilience is always possible, no matter the circumstances.

Velasquez has zero body fat and is medically unable to gain weight, an offshoot of her rare disorder. At 5'2", she has never surpassed sixty-four pounds despite her consumption of 5,000 to 8,000 daily calories and snacks up to sixty times a day. She has a recurring problem with her right foot which easily fractures due to the lack of fat on her sole. In addition, she is blind in her right eye, which began to cloud over when she was a toddler, and is vision impaired in her other. The young lady has undergone more medical procedures than she can count on two hands. Her heart has to be carefully monitored to prevent aortic rupture. It was only when she was an adult that the question mark of Lizzie's disease was revealed: a hen's tooth rare combination of Marfan syndrome and lipodystrophy. Despite her litany of physical woes, she has committed herself to the mantra of *still I rise* and to help fellow pilgrims in pain.

Lizzie turned political activist when she teamed up with Tina Meier, whose daughter Megan hung herself shortly before her fourteenth birthday in 2006 after suffering cyber cruelty. The two women are campaigning the US Representatives of Congress to vote for the first federal anti-bullying bill that would mandate how educational facilities deal with the scourge of bullying. (To date, it still has not passed.) On the day Lizzie had scheduled to visit members of Congress, she fell ill—either with either nerves or a physical ailment—but powered through with her usual aplomb.

In 1995, *Braveheart* showcased Mel Gibson as Sir William Wallace, the war-paint on his face the same cornflower blue as his eyes, rocking a kilt, locks flowing like Fabio. Twenty years later, a documentary debuted with a similar name, *A Brave Heart: The Lizzie Velazquez Story*. People of all ages, from all walks of life and sixteen countries, contributed to its $421,000 Kickstarter campaign. Directed by Sara Bordo, it won acclaim at nine film festivals and aired on Lifetime. In one scene, she has an awkward meeting with Hillary Clinton—who appeared not to have been versed who Lizzie was—but nevertheless the encounter left

Ms. Velazquez giddy. It narrates Lizzie's one-of-a-kind biography, and she proves such a charismatic subject, with a smile as wide as her native Texas; at its conclusion, viewers are firmly members of Camp Lizzie. Its conclusion has Ms. Velasquez stepping onto a stage to a standing ovation before a crowd of ten thousand in Mexico City. Just prior to this, she had received another vitriolic message. It's a searing scene that makes the audience want to rush to her aid. Yet, she reacted with her characteristic turn-the-other-cheek, that showed the dauntless lady is in no need of succor. The overriding theme of *A Brave Heart,* as well as her videos and books, is that she turns the spotlight off herself to make her story not about her, but rather a universal one for all of society's underdogs.

A Brave Heart also serves as a litmus test for how society—despite its flaws—is inching forward. The 1980 movie, *The Elephant Man*, explored the pain-filled life of the nineteenth century Joseph Carey Merrick, whose physical deformities forced him to earn his livelihood as an exhibit in a sideshow attraction. In its most harrowing scene, he turns on his tormentors and cries, "I am not an animal! I am a human being!" In a letter he included a poem by the hymnist Isaac Watts that concluded, "Tis true my form is something odd/But blaming me is blaming God."

Ironically, the girl who was never expected to talk or walk now does both professionally. Velazquez still chuckles about her unlikely role as a movie star. "I definitely never thought anybody would make a movie about me. The best way to describe how it feels is to say it's very, very surreal." She said after the exciting but grueling promotion of her film, she intends to write a fourth book and "then find a nice tropical island on which to relax for a while."

Truly great people forgive their tormentors, and that is something Lizzie has magnanimously done. She has received apologies from a number of people who had written the scathing comments on YouTube. Her response was she applauds their bravery and their courage for owning up for what they did. Her heart is too big—too brave—for hate.

In her younger years, Lizzie would have done anything to have been born in a different skin; however, the adult Ms. Velazquez now embraces who she is. She stated, "Instead of just taking shelter in my tears, I chose to be happy and realize this syndrome is not a problem but a blessing that allows me to improve myself and inspire other people." God has finally revealed her purpose, and that is why she has no interest in a cure. "No, there's no way, I wouldn't even consider it. I've come such a long way to be able to accept who I am and own who I am that, if I changed anything about me I wouldn't be Lizzie, I wouldn't be true to myself," she explained.

If ever there was a poster child for the adage that living well is the best revenge, it would be Lizzie Velasquez, one of the world's most beautiful of women.

EPILOGUE

In my four books, I researched famous people and pivotal times in history; in *Still I Rise*, I learned about emotional resilience. From the example of those who climbed to the mountaintop from the valley of despair, it made me realize no matter how great the problem, failure to succumb often leads to a kidney-punch to one's nemesis.

The chapters that resonated the most with me are those dealing with bipolar disorder—Patty Duke and Carrie Fisher—because that illness plagued my mother's life and carried with it residual collateral damage. Traditionally, society has been empathetic with physical afflictions, but not so with mental disorders. What Patty and Carrie had the courage to do was take bipolar out of the closet, which both encouraged public acceptance and made those so afflicted seek treatment.

I also felt a personal connection with Alice Herz-Sommer, a victim of the Holocaust. I grew up in a Jewish neighborhood in Toronto that had a large concentration of survivors. Whenever they mentioned their wartime experiences, a string of expletives—in heavily accented European voices—ensued. This was in contrast to Alice, a pianist whose endless optimism came to symbolize the triumph of good over evil. She was a survivor of both Nazism and Communism, and her life exemplified Mark Twain's quotation,

"Anger is an acid that can do more harm to the vessel in which it is stored than to anything on which it is poured." Despite the murder of her mother and husband, and her imprisonment along with her young son in Terezin, she refused to hate: "Hatred brings hatred. I never hated, never, never." Perhaps her refusal to give in to rancor, and her passion for music, were the secret to her longevity; she passed away at age 110. Her resistance to enmity was echoed by a woman from another place, Fannie Lou Hammer, whose life was lived under the shadow of Jim Crow. She similarly stated, "Ain't no such thing as hate. I can't hate anybody and hope to see God's face." In a similar vein, Lizzie Velazquez turned the other cheek to her tormentors, and in the process helped change the attitudes of her bullies. Their magnanimity leaves me humbled.

The entries many can relate to are on dys*func*tional families. Leo Tolstoy stated in the preface to *Anna Karenina*, "All happy families are all alike; each unhappy family is unhappy in its own way." Some of the ladies' families were the stuff from the pen of Dickens but it is, after all, sorrow that makes for the best ink. One would be hard-pressed to find upbringings as bizarre as those experiences by Amy Tan, Carrie Fisher, Jeanette Walls, Jeanette Winterson, and Leah Vincent, who came from families unhappy in their own ways. Their relatives could be described by the old nursery rhyme, "One flew east and one flew west and one flew over the cuckoo's nest." Their greatness is that rather than crumbling, they not only survived, but prevailed—a testament to their indomitable spirits.

A parable that ties in with the fleeting nature of both sorrow and pain comes from King Solomon. He tasked Benaiah, the captain of his guards, with an impossible task: "Bring me a ring that can make a happy person sad and a sad person happy." The Captain searched all the market stalls of Jerusalem and those in foreign lands before he despaired of success. At this juncture, he encountered an old man who took a simple gold band and carved on it the words, "Gam Zeh Ya'avor"—"This too shall pass."

A common thread that bids the disparate individuals profiled can be summed up in Fannie's words, "I was sick and tired of feeling sick and tired." *Still I Rise* is more than biographies of intrepid women who have enabled their daughters to stand with straighter spines. It also doubles as an instruction for lives well-lived.

ACKNOWLEDGEMENTS

The most difficult part of writing *Still I Rise* is the Acknowledgements page; the chapters focus on others; on this page, myself. That being said, first and foremost, I want to thank my literary agent, Roger Williams, for birthing our second book together. I love words but cannot find adequate ones to express my appreciation for his unwavering belief and enthusiasm. It was my most fortunate day when our paths crossed. To borrow Roger's signature sign-off, "Namaste."

I also want to express my appreciation to my editor Brenda Knight for championing my book, for always being encouraging and positive. *Still I Rise*, from start to finish, has been a labor of love. It also gave me something to believe in at a difficult juncture, and by learning about these indefatigable ladies, it helped me combat my own demons. As I read in a Facebook post from "Curly Bee," "Something will grow from all you are going through. And it will be you."

A nod must also go to my husband, Joel Geller, for understanding that for the past several years, my significant other has been my laptop. I must also mention my daughter, Jordanna. Throughout the roller coaster ride of my writing career—for each of my five books—she was my sounding board and one-woman cheerleader. She exemplifies the saying that a good friend doubles one's joy and halves one's sorrow. Lastly is a tribute to my mother, Gilda Wagman. Although she may not have read my books, she was always my steadfast advocate. It is her gift of love that helped me, to varying degrees, to survive my own cuckoo's nest.

A last shout out to my coterie of friends who, understanding writing is whatever wind I have beneath my wings, have been supportive. A quotation by Madeleine Albright exemplifies female solidarity—and its mirror opposite: "There's a special place in Hell for women who do not support other women." This concept was recently brought to the forefront through the Women's March and the omniscient sea of pussy hats.

Amy Tan said her addiction to eBay was an impediment to writing; mine is Facebook. However, as writing is a solitary pursuit, it helped connect me during the long hours of solitary confinement.

Sending a book out is akin to a child leaving the nest; a mixture of the bitter and the sweet. It is my hope that my book will help readers *to still rise*. I would love to hear from you, and, if the spirit moves you, to post a review on Amazon.

Facebook: https://www.facebook.com/marlene.wagman.5
Email: onceagaintozelda@hotmail.com
Webpage: http://www.marlenewagmangeller.com/

Marlene Wagman-Geller
San Diego, California, 2017

Mother to Son

Well, son, I'll tell you:

Life for me ain't been no crystal stair.

It's had tacks in it,

And splinters,

And boards torn up,

And places with no carpet on the floor—

Bare.

But all the time

I'se been a-climbin' on,

And reachin' landin's,

And turnin' corners,

And sometimes goin' in the dark

Where there ain't been no light.

So, boy, don't you turn back.

Don't you set down on the steps.

'Cause you finds it's kinder hard.

Don't you fall now—

For I'se still goin', honey,

I'se still climbin',

And life for me ain't been no crystal stair.

—Langston Hughes

BIBLIOGRAPHY

Chapter 1

Brace, Marianne. "Waxing Mythical: The life and legend of Madame Tussaud by Kate Berridge." *Independent*, August 26, 2006. http://www. independent.co.uk/arts-entertainment/books/reviews/waxing-mythical-the-life-and-legend-of-madame-tussaud-by-kate-berridge-413583.html

Gross, John. "Waxworks that Never Wane." *The Telegraph*, Jan. 12, 2003. http://www.telegraph.co.uk/culture/4729626/Waxworks-that-never-wane.html

Leafloor, Liz. "The Bloody History of a Waxworks Museum: Madame Tussaud and Her Eerie Creations." *Epoch Times,* Feb. 19, 2015. http:// www.theepochTimes.com/n3/1256069-the-bloody-history-of-a-waxworks-museum-madame-tussaud-and-her-eerie-creations/

Sonin, Adam. "Madame Tussaud: A career in wax carved out during the French Revolution." *Ham & High,* Jan. 21, 2014. http://www.hamhigh. co.uk/news/heritage/madame_tussaud_a_career_in_wax_carved_out_during_the_french_revolution_1_1800798

Chapter 2

Cohen, Sascha. "Helen Keller's Forgotten Radicalism." *Time, Inc.*, June 26, 2015. http://Time.com/3923213/helen-keller-radicalism/

Greene, Bob. "Her Life Was Not a Joke." *Chicago Tribune*, May 11, 1992. http://articles.chicagotribune.com/1992-05-11/features/9202110905_1_keller-family-helen-keller-jokes

"Helen Keller." Wikipedia. Retrieved July 10, 2016. Wikimedia Foundation, Inc. https://en.wikipedia.org/wiki/Helen_Keller

Kendrick, Walter. "Her Hands Were a Bridge to the World." *The New York*

Times, Aug. 30, 1998. http://www.nyTimes.com/1998/08/30/books/her-hands-were-a-bridge-to-the-world.html

Salter, Mary Jo. "The Achiever: Helen Keller." *The New York Times*, Nov. 24, 1996. http://www.nyTimes.com/1996/11/24/magazine/the-achiever-helen-keller.html

Slagle, Alton. "Helen Keller lived a life that triumphed over darkness." the Daily News, June 3, 1968. <http://www.nydailynews.com/news/national/helen-keller-lived-life-triumphed-darkness-article-1.2689443>

Slotnik, Daniel E. "Waltzing with Helen Keller." The *New York Times*. June 1, 2016. https://www.nyTimes.com/interactive/projects/cp/obituaries/archives/helen-keller

Shattuck, Roger. "A World of Words." *The New York Review of Books*, Feb. 26, 2004. http://www.nybooks.com/articles/2004/02/26/a-world-of-words/

Waxman, Olivia B. and Liz Ronk. "See Helen Keller and the Leaders She Inspired." *Time, Inc.*, Jun 27, 2016. http://Time.com/4360595/helen-keller-birthday-the-unconquered-documentary-life-magazine/

Whitman, Alden. "Helen Keller, 87, Dies." *The New York Times*, June 2, 1968. http://www.nyTimes.com/learning/general/onthisday/bday/0627.html

Chapter 3

Foderaro, Lisa W. "Alcoholics Anonymous Founder's House Is a Self-Help Landmark." *The New York Times*, July 6, 2007. http://www.nytimes.com/2007/07/06/nyregion/06aa.html

Gilbert, Matthew. "A Hallmark story of alcoholism." *The Boston Globe*, April 24, 2010. http://archive.boston.com/ae/tv/articles/2010/04/24/a_hallmark_story_of_alcoholism_in_when_love_is_not_enough/

"Lois Burnham Wilson Dies; Founded Al-Anon for Alcoholics' Families." *Los Angeles Times*, Oct. 8, 1988. http://articles.laTimes.com/1988-10-09/news/mn-5528_1_alcoholics-anonymous

"Lois M." Wikipedia, Inc. Retrieved August 17, 2016. https://en.wikipedia. org/wiki/Lois_W.

"Lois' Story." Stepping Stones Foundation. Retrieved August 15, 2016. http://www.steppingstones.org/loisstory.html

McNamara, Mary. "Television review: 'When Love Is Not Enough' on CBS." *Los Angeles Times*, April 24, 2010. http://articles.latimes.com/2010/ apr/24/entertainment/la-et-lois-wilson-20100424

Mulderig, John. "When Love Is Not Enough: The Lois Wilson Story, April 25, CBS." *Catholic News Service,* April 13, 2010. http://www.catholicnews. com/services/englishnews/2010/-when-love-is-not-enough-the-lois-wilson-story-april-25-cbs.cfm

Stasi, Linda. "'Love' Drunk." *New York Post*, April 23, 2010. http://nypost. com/2010/04/23/love-drunk/

Pace, Eric. "Lois Burnham Wilson, Founder of Al-Anon Groups, Is Dead at 97." *The New York Times*, Oct. 6, 1988. http://www.nyTimes. com/1988/10/06/obituaries/lois-burnham-wilson-a-founder-of-al-anon-groups-is-dead-at-97.html

Prager, Richard. "A Rich History of AA's Cofounder." *MichaelPrager.com.* Retrieved August 15, 2016. http://michaelprager.com/My-Name-Is-Bill-Bill-Wilson-His-Life-and-the-Creation-of-Alcoholics-Anonymous-Susan-Cheever-book%20review

Chapter 4

Agard, Chancellor. "The Mystery of Hattie McDaniel's Missing Oscar – and the Incredible Life of the First African-American Oscar Winner." *People,* Sept. 23, 2016. http://people.com/awards/oscars-2016-6-things-to-know-about-hattie-mcdaniel/

Als, Hilton. "Mammy for the Masses." *New Yorker*, Sept. 26, 2005. http:// www.newyorker.com/magazine/2005/09/26/mammmy-for-the-masses

Curtis, Mary C. "SAG Awards: From Hattie McDaniel to Viola Davis, still winning for playing 'The Help'." *Washington Post*, Jan. 30, 2012. https://www.washingtonpost.com/blogs/she-the-people/post/from-hattie-mcdaniel-to-viola-davis-still-winning-for-playing-the-help/2012/01/30/gIQAT3WTcQ_blog.html?utm_term=.ac4b92feef79

"Hattie McDaniel becomes the first black actor to win an Oscar." *Chicago Tribune*. Retrieved June 15, 2016. http://www.chicagotribune.com/sns-black-history-moments-pg-003-photo.html

"Hattie McDaniel loved her role as 'Mammy' in 'Gone With the Wind'." WN.com. Retrieved June 15, 2016. https://article.wn.com/view/2014/03/23/Hattie_McDaniel_loved_her_role_as_Mammy_in_Gone_With_the_Win/

Witheridge, Annette. "'I'd rather make $700 a week playing a maid than working as one': How the FIRST black Oscar winner dealt with being segregated from white Gone with the Wind co-stars at Academy Awards." *The Daily Mail,* Feb. 25, 2016. http://www.dailymail.co.uk/news/article-3462821/I-d-make-700-week-playing-maid-working-one-Hattie-McDaniel-black-Oscar-winner-Mammy-Gone-Wind-segregated-Clark-Gable-white-actors-Acade

Chapter 5

"Alice Herz-Sommer – obituary." *The Telegraph*, Feb. 24, 2014. http://www.telegraph.co.uk/news/obituaries/10657632/Alice-Herz-Sommer-obituary.html

Andersono, Martin. "Alice Herz-Sommer: Pianist and oldest Holocaust survivor who became a symbol round the world of optimism and tolerance." *Independent*, Feb. 24, 2014. http://www.independent.co.uk/news/obituaries/alice-herz-sommer-pianist-and-oldest-holocaust-survivor-who-became-a-symbol-round-the-world-of-9150253.html

Gardner Jr., Ralph. "Urban Gardner: Examining a Life Well Lived." *The Wall street journal.* Feb. 26, 2014. <https://www.wsj.com/articles/SB10001424052702304255604579407313580583416>

Fox, Margalit. "Alice Herz-Sommer, Who Found Peace in Chopin Amid Holocaust, Dies at 110." *New York Times*, Feb. 27, 2014. https://www.nyTimes.com/2014/02/28/world/europe/alice-herz-sommer-pianist-who-survived-holocaust-dies-at-110.html>?_r=0

Heathcote, Charlotte. "Life is good says Holocaust survivor Alice, 106." *Express*, Nov. 14, 2010. http://www.express.co.uk/expressyourself/211886/Life-is-good-says-Holocaust-survivor-Alice-106

Hennessy, Val. "Heavenly music that saved Alice from Hell." *Mail Online*, July 31, 2007. http://www.dailymail.co.uk/home/books/article-472091/Heavenly-music-saved-Alice-Hell.html

JTA, jpost.com staff. "Documentary On Oldest Holocaust Survivor Wins Oscar A Week After Her Death." *The Jerusalem Post*, March 3, 2014. http://www.jpost.com/Arts-and-Culture/Entertainment/Documentary-on-oldest-Holocaust-survivor-wins-Oscar-a-week-after-her-death-344091

Kennedy, Maev. "Alice Herz-Sommer: 'Everything we experience is a gift we should pass on.'" *The Guardian*, Feb. 24, 2014. https://www.theguardian.com/world/2014/feb/24/oldest-holocaust-survivor-dies-aged-110

Langer, Emily. "Alice Herz-Sommer, concert pianist and Holocaust survivor, dies at 110." *The Washington Post*, Feb. 26, 2014. https://www.washingtonpost.com/world/europe/alice-herz-sommer-concert-pianist-and-holocaust-survivor-dies-at-110/2014/02/26/f3f38f40-9e6a-11e3-a050-dc3322a94fa7_story.html>?utm_term=.dedea59a7762

Nupen, Christopher. "Alice Herz-Sommer obituary." *The Guardian*. Feb. 24, 2014. <https://www.theguardian.com/world/2014/feb/24/alice-herz-sommer>

"Oldest Holocaust survivor, Alice Herz-Sommer, dies at 110." *BBC*, Feb. 23, 2014. http://www.bbc.com/news/world-europe-26318383

Pempel, Kacper. "World's Oldest Holocaust Survivor, Alice Herz-Sommer, Dies In UK." *Newsweek*. Feb. 24, 2014. http://www.newsweek.com/worlds-oldest-holocaust-survivor-alice-herz-sommer-dies-uk-230019

Quinn, Ben. "Alice Herz-Sommer: pianist and oldest known Holocaust survivor dies aged 110." *The Guardian*, Feb. 23, 2014. https://www. theguardian.com/world/2014/feb/23/alice-herz-sommer-holocaust-survivor-dies

Ross, Alex. "The Woman Who Remembers Mahler." *New Yorker*, Nov. 26, 2013. http://www.newYorker.com/culture/culture-desk/the-woman-who-remembers-mahler

Stoessinger, Caroline. "A Pianist Who Survived Hitler Plays Today at 110." *Wall Street Journal*, Nov. 25, 2013. <https://www.wsj.com/articles/SB1000 1424052702303289904579196034133385774>

Chapter 6

Bernstein, Adam. "Irena Sendler, 98; Saved Children in WWII." *Washington Post*, May 13, 2008. http://www.washingtonpost.com/wp-dyn/content/article/2008/05/12/AR2008051202751.html

"Dead at 98: Heroic Irena Sendler, who helped save 2,500 Jewish children from the Nazis." *The Daily Mail,* May 12, 2008. http://www.dailymail. co.uk/news/article-565969/Dead-98-Heroic-Irena-Sendler-helped-save-2-500-Jewish-children-Nazis.html

Dear, Suzanne Gelleri. "Irena Sendler." *The Telegraph*, May 12, 2008. http://www.telegraph.co.uk/news/obituaries/1950450/Irena-Sendler.html

Easton, Adam. "Holocaust heroine's survival tale." *BBC News*, March 3, 2005. http://news.bbc.co.uk/2/hi/europe/4314145.stm

Fox, Michael. "Modesty is the M.O. for Polish heroine Irena Sendler." *San Francisco Jewish Community Publications Inc.*, April 21, 2011. http:// www.jweekly.com/article/full/61518/modesty-is-the-m.o.-for-polish-heroine-irena-sendler

Harding, Louette. "Irena Sendler: A Holocaust heroine." *Mail Online*, Aug. 1, 2008. http://www.dailymail.co.uk/home/you/article-1037057/Irena-Sendler-Holocaust-heroine.html

"Irena Sendler." *The Economist,* May 22, 2008. http://www.economist. com/node/11402658

"Irena Sendler of Poland, Nobel Peace Prize, a real winner." *Citizen Wells*, Feb. 20, 2008. https://citizenwells.com/tag/irena-sendler-of-poland/

Jones, Maggie. "The Smuggler." *The New York Times Magazine,* Dec. 24, 2008. http://www.nytimes.com/2008/12/28/magazine/28sendler-t.html

Miller, Stephen. "Irena Sendler, 98, Saved 2,500 Children From Nazis." *New York Sun.* May 13, 2008. http://www.nysun.com/obituaries/irena-sendler-98-saved-2500-children-from-nazis/76346/

Quetteville, Harry de. "Poland honours heroine who saved children." *The Telegraph,* March 15, 2007. http://www.telegraph.co.uk/news/ uknews/1545602/Poland-honours-heroine-who-saved-children.html

Rabinowitz, Dorothy. "Against the Darkness." *The Wall Street Journal*, April 17, 2009. https://www.wsj.com/articles/SB123991537451426695

Stromme, Lizzie. "Irena Sendler: The Holocaust heroine who saved 2500 Jewish children from Nazi evil." *Express*, Sep. 13, 2016. http://www. express.co.uk/news/history/710220/Irena-Sendler-Holocaust-heroine-saved-2500-Jewish-children-Nazi

Vinciguerra, Thomas. "The Lives of Others." *New York Times*, Oct. 30, 2016. https://www.nytimes.com/2016/10/30/books/review/red-bandanna-tom-rinaldi-and-more.html

Weinblatt, Charles S. "Irena's Children: The Extraordinary Story of the Woman Who Saved 2,500 Children from the Warsaw Ghetto." *New York Journal of Books*. Retrieved Aug. 10, 2016. http://www.nyjournalofbooks. com/book-review/irenas-children-woman-warsaw-ghetto

Woo, Elaine. "WWII savior of young Jews." *Los Angeles Times*, May 13, 2008. http://articles.la*Times*.com/2008/may/13/local/me-sendler13

Chapter 7

Casey, Constance. "BOOK REVIEW: A Woman Who Got Tired of Being Pushed: THIS LITTLE LIGHT OF MINE: The Life of Fannie Lou Hamer by Kay Mills." *Los Angeles Times*, Jan. 01, 1993. http://articles.la*Times*.com/1993-01-01/news/vw-2930_1_fannie-lou-hamer

DeMuth, Jerry. "Fannie Lou Hamer: Tired of Being Sick and Tired." *The Nation*, April 2, 2009. https://www.thenation.com/article/fannie-lou-hamer-tired-being-sick-and-tired/

Joiner, Lottie L. "Remembering Civil Rights Heroine Fannie Lou Hamer: 'I'm Sick and Tired of Being Sick and Tired.'" *The Daily Beast*, Sept. 2, 2014. http://www.thedailybeast.com/articles/2014/09/02/remembering-civil-rights-heroine-fannie-lou-hamer-i-m-sick-and-tired-of-being-sick-and-tired.html

Johnson, Thomas A. "Fannie Lou Hamer Dies; Left Farm To Lead Struggle for Civil Rights." *New York Times*, March 15, 1977. http://www.ny*Times*.com/1977/03/15/archives/fannie-lou-hamer-dies-left-farm-to-lead-struggle-for-civil-rights.html>?_r=0

Marsh, Charles. "God's Long Summer: Stories of Faith and Civil Rights." *The Washington Post*, 1997. http://www.washingtonpost.com/wp-srv/style/longterm/books/chap1/godslongsummer.htm

Yaeger, Lynn. "Celebrating Fannie Lou Hamer, Heroine of the 1964 Democratic National Convention." *Vogue*, July 25, 2016. http://www.*Vogue*.com/article/celebrating-fannie-lou-hamer-1964-dnc

Chapter 8

Alter, Alexandra. "Author, Poet Maya Angelou Dies." *The Wall Street Journal*, May 28, 2014. https://www.wsj.com/articles/author-poet-maya-angelou-dies-1401285606

Associated Press. "Maya Angelou dead at 86." *New York Post*. http://nypost.com/2014/05/28/maya-angelou-dead-at-86/

Brown, Emma. "Maya Angelou, writer and poet, dies at age 86."
The Washington Post, May 28, 2014. https://www.washingtonpost.
com/entertainment/maya-angelou-writer-and-poet-dies-at-age-
86/2014/05/28/2948ef5e-c5da-11df-94e1-c5afa35a9e59_story.
html>?utm_term=.adeoa8c29b4b

Fox, Margalit. "Maya Angelou, Lyrical Witness of the Jim Crow South,
Dies at 86." *New York Times*, May 28, 2014. https://www.nytimes.
com/2014/05/29/arts/maya-angelou-lyrical-witness-of-the-jim-crow-
south-dies-at-86.html

Gross, Robert A. "Newsweek's Original Review Of Maya Angelou's 'I
Know Why The Caged Bird Sings.'" *Newsweek*, May 28, 2014. http://
www.newsweek.com/newsweeks-original-review-i-know-why-caged-bird-
sings-252587

Julianelli, Jane. "Remembering Maya Angelou." *Harper's Bazaar*, May 28,
2014. http://www.harpersbazaar.com/culture/art-books-music/a2442/
maya-angelou-bazaar-november-1972/

Little, Anita. "Still We Rise: Remembering Maya Angelou." *Ms. Magazine*,
May 28, 2014. http://msmagazine.com/blog/2014/05/28/still-we-rise-
remembering-maya-angelou/

Schultz, Laura. "May Angelou: A biography of an Award-winning Poet and
Civil Rights Activist." *New York Journal of Books*. Retrieved Aug. 12, 2016.
http://www.nyjournalofbooks.com/book-review/maya-angelou-biography-
award-winning-poet-and-civil-rights-activist

Vilkomerson, Sara. "Maya Angelou: An obituary for a literary giant."
Entertainment Weekly, May 28, 2014. http://ew.com/article/2014/05/28/
maya-angelou-obituary/

Woo, Elaine. "Maya Angelou, who vividly detailed the black experience,
dies at 86." *Los Angeles Times*, May 28, 2014. http://www.la*Times*.com/
local/obituaries/la-me-maya-angelou-20140529-story.html

Chapter 9

"Dr. Ruth Westheimer Biography." *Biography.com*. Retrieved Oct. 10, 2016. http://www.biography.com/people/dr-ruth-westheimer-9542073#synopsis

Geller, Laura. "The Long Life of a Short Woman: All In A Lifetime by Dr. Ruth Westheimer." *Los Angeles Times*, Jan. 10, 1988. http://articles.latimes.com/1988-01-10/books/bk-34531_1_ruth-westheimer

Kamin, Debra. "Let's talk about sex, bubbe." *The Times of Israel*, June 27, 2013. http://www.timesofisrael.com/lets-talk-about-sex-bubbe/

Krug, Nora. "Dr. Ruth, 87, still shocking us with her sex talk." *The Washington Post*, June 3, 2015. https://www.washingtonpost.com/news/arts-and-entertainment/wp/2015/06/03/dr-ruth-87-still-shocking-us-with-her-sex-talk/?utm_term=.3bf58f9b00dc

Mano, Keith. "Good Sex!" *People*, April 15, 1985. http://people.com/archive/cover-story-good-sex-vol-23-no-15/

McGrath, Nick. "Dr Ruth Westheimer: My family values." *The Guardian*, Nov. 9, 2012. https://www.theguardian.com/lifeandstyle/2012/nov/10/dr-ruth-westheimer-my-family-values

Morris, Bob. "AT HOME WITH: Dr. Ruth Westheimer; The Bible as Sex Manual?" *New York Times*, Dec. 21, 1995. http://www.nyTimes.com/1995/12/21/garden/at-home-with-dr-ruth-westheimer-the-bible-as-sex-manual.html>?pagewanted=all

Musleah, Rahel. "Ruth Westheimer." *Hadassah Magazine*. Retrieved Oct. 10, 2016. http://www.hadassahmagazine.org/2015/01/05/ruth-westheimer/

Chapter 10

Bennetts, Leslie. "Joan Rivers's Remarkable Rise to (and Devastating Fall from) Comedy's Highest Ranks." *Vanity Fair*, Nov. 3, 2016. http://www.vanityfair.com/hollywood/2016/11/joan-rivers-last-girl-before-freeway-excerpt

Bennetts, Leslie. "The Triumph of Joan Rivers." *Dailyworth*, Nov. 15, 2016. https://www.dailyworth.com/posts/4395-how-joan-rivers-reinvented-her-career-in-middle-age

Carlson, Michael. "Joan Rivers Obituary." *The Guardian*, Sept. 4, 2014. https://www.theguardian.com/stage/2014/sep/04/joan-rivers-obituary-limelight

Cavendish, Dominic. "Joan Rivers: the world will be a duller place without her." *The Telegraph*, Sept. 4, 2014. http://www.telegraph.co.uk/culture/comedy/comedy-news/11076323/Joan-Rivers-the-world-will-be-a-duller-place-without-her.html

Claire, Marie. "Inside the fascinating life of the unforgettable Joan Rivers." *Marie Claire*, June 9, 2016. http://www.marieclaire.co.uk/entertainment/people/inside-the-turbulent-life-of-the-brilliant-joan-rivers-6525

Cole, Stephen. "Can Joan Rivers still talk?" *The Globe and Mail*, Jan. 17, 2011. http://www.theglobeandmail.com/arts/film/can-joan-rivers-still-talk/article562221/

Collins, Scott, David Colker and Amy Kaufman. "Joan Rivers dies at 81; driven diva of stand-up comedy, TV talk." *Los Angeles Times*, Sept. 4, 2014. http://www.laTimes.com/local/obituaries/la-me-joan-rivers-20140904-story.html

Connelly, Sherryl. "Joan Rivers' extreme highs and lows detailed in 'Last Girl Before Freeway,' Leslie Bennetts' biography on comedy legend." *New York Daily News*, Oct. 29, 2016. http://www.nydailynews.com/entertainment/joan-rivers-highs-lows-detailed-girl-freeway-article-1.2850177

Dargis, Manohla. "A New Biography of Joan Rivers." *New York Times*, Nov. 28, 2016. https://www.nyTimes.com/2016/11/28/books/review/joan-rivers-biography-last-girl-before-freeway-leslie-bennetts.html>?_r=0

Eckel, Sara. "Joan Rivers: Feminist icon?" *The Washington Post*, Dec. 2, 2016. https://www.washingtonpost.com/opinions/joan-rivers-feminist-icon/2016/12/02/870f6648-9556-11e6-bc79-af1cd3d2984b_story.html>?utm_term=.7422a855e2db

Felsenthal, Julia. "A New Biography Reveals the Agony and the Ecstasy of Joan Rivers." *Vogue*, Nov. 12, 2016. http://www.Vogue.com/article/joan-rivers-last-girl-before-freeway-leslie-bennetts-interview

Hesketh-Harvey, Kit. "Joan Rivers: My loyal, mad, generous, galactic friend." *The Telegraph*, Sept. 5, 2014. http://www.telegraph.co.uk/culture/comedy/comedy-news/11077240/Joan-Rivers-My-loyal-mad-generous-galactic-friend.html

"Joan Rivers." *The Economist*, Sept. 13, 2014. http://www.economist.com/news/obituary/21616858-joan-rivers-americas-most-abrasive-comedienne-died-september-4th-aged-81-joan-rivers

"Joan Rivers was the queen of American comediennes, noted for her acerbic, backbiting humour." *Dbsjeyaraj.com*, Sep. 24, 2014. http://dbsjeyaraj.com/dbsj/archives/32937

Krug, Nora. "What Joan Rivers didn't take to the grave, according to her daughter's new book." *The Washington Post*, April 22, 2015. https://www.washingtonpost.com/news/arts-and-entertainment/wp/2015/04/22/what-joan-rivers-didnt-take-to-the-grave-according-to-her-daughters-new-book/?utm_term=.5112f6eb6a21

McFadden, Robert D. "Joan Rivers, a Comic Stiletto Quick to Skewer, Is Dead at 81." *New York Times*, Sept. 4, 2014. https://www.nyTimes.com/2014/09/05/arts/television/joan-rivers-dies.html

Meryman, Richard. "Joan Mourns Edgar." *People*, Aug. 31, 1987. http://people.com/archive/cover-story-joan-mourns-edgar-vol-28-no-9/

Miller, Julie. "Joan Rivers, Pioneering Comedian, Dies at 81." *Vanity Fair*, Sept. 1, 2014. http://www.vanityfair.com/hollywood/2014/09/joan-rivers-died-age-81

Murphy, Tim. "Joan Rivers on the Eve of Her Roast: 'God Has Given Us This Gift of Humor. Animals Don't Laugh.'" *New York Magazine*, Aug. 7, 2009. http://nymag.com/daily/intelligencer/2009/08/joan_rivers_on_the_eve_of_her.html

Noonan, Peggy. "Joan Rivers: The Entertainer." *The Wall Street Journal*, Sept. 5, 2014. http://blogs.wsj.com/peggynoonan/2014/09/05/joan-rivers-the-entertainer/

Parry, Ryan. "Joan Rivers had to woo daughter back after Melissa blamed her for her father's suicide." *Daily Mail*, Nov. 11, 2016. http://www.dailymail.co.uk/news/article-3899152/Elite-private-schools-3-million-wedding-Fashion-Police-guilt-ridden-Joan-Rivers-woo-daughter-Melissa-blamed-comic-father-s-suicide-cut-mom-life.html

People Staff. "Joan Rivers." *People*, Dec. 26, 1983. http://people.com/archive/joan-rivers-vol-20-no-26/

Riedel, Joan. "Joan Rivers' biggest regret revealed" *New York post*. Oct. 25, 2016. <http://nypost.com/2016/10/25/joan-rivers-biggest-regret-revealed/>

Rosin, Hanna. "Mean Girl." *Slate.com*. Retrieved Oct 20, 2016. http://www.slate.com/articles/double_x/doublex/2014/09/joan_rivers_relentless_filthy_and_honest_about_being_a_woman_video.html

Rothman, Lily. "Joan Rivers Joked About Death — Along With Everything Else." *Time*, May 16, 1994. http://time.com/3259746/joan-rivers-jokes/

Schulman, Michael. "Postscript: Joan Rivers (1933-2014)" *The New Yorker*. Sept. 4, 2014. <http://www.newYorker.com/culture/culture-desk/postscript-joan-rivers>

Silverman, Stephen M. "Joan Rivers Dies at 81." *People Celebrity*. Sept. 23, 2016. <http://*people*.com/celebrity/joan-rivers-dead/>

Silverman, Stephen. "Melissa Rivers Bids Farewell to Her Mother's Casket." *People*, Sept. 23, 2016. http://people.com/celebrity/melissa-rivers-bids-farewell-to-her-mothers-casket/

Van Meter, Jonathan. "Joan Rivers Always Knew She Was Funny." *New York Magaine*, May 23, 2010. http://nymag.com/movies/features/66181/

Van Meter, Jonathan. "Joan Rivers Always Knew She Was Funny." *Vulture. com*, Sept. 4, 2014. http://www.vulture.com/2014/09/joan-rivers-always-knew-she-was-funny.html

Whitworth, Melissa. "Joan Rivers: the queen of comedy reflects on her past." *The Telegraph*, Sept. 4, 2014. http://www.*telegraph*.co.uk/culture/film/starsandstories/8096974/Joan-Rivers-the-queen-of-comedy-reflects-on-her-past.html

Wolcott, James. "The Joan Rivers Biography That Captures Her Many, Many Ups and Downs." *Vanity Fair*, Nov. 3, 2016. http://www.vanityfair.com/hollywood/2016/11/joan-rivers-biography-last-girl-before-freeway

Chapter 11

Barnes, Brooks. "From Footnote to Fame in Civil Rights History." *New York Times*, Nov. 25, 2009. http://www.nyTimes.com/2009/11/26/books/26colvin.html

Conniff, Ruth. "Mothers of Intervention." *New York Times*, May 8, 2009. http://www.nyTimes.com/2009/05/10/books/review/Conniff-t.html>?_r=0

Gray, Eliza. "Before Rosa Parks, There Was Claudette Colvin." *Newsweek*, March 1, 2009. http://www.newsweek.com/rosa-parks-there-was-claudette-colvin-76163

MacPherson, Karen. "Children's Corner: Award-winning book a riveting account of teen's fight against segregation." *Pittsburgh Post-Gazette*, Dec. 1, 2009. http://www.post-gazette.com/life/my-generation/2009/12/01/Children-s-Corner-Award-winning-book-a-riveting-account-of-teen-s-fight-against-segregation/stories/200912010211

MacPherson, Karen. "Kids books: A riveting account of teenage girl's fight against segregation." *The Seattle Times*, Dec. 5, 2009. http://www.seattletimes.com/entertainment/books/kids-books-a-riveting-account-of-teenage-girls-fight-against-segregation/

O'shaughnessy, Patrice. "Claudette Colvin: A civil rights pioneer gets due recognition." *New York Daily News*, June 7, 2009. http://www. nydailynews.com/news/world/claudette-colvin-civil-rights-pioneer-due-recognition-article-1.377988

Ross, Janell. "Rosa Parks is the name you know. Claudette Colvin is a name you probably should." *The Washington Post*, Dec. 1, 2015. https:// www.washingtonpost.com/news/the-fix/wp/2015/12/01/rosa-parks-the-name-you-know-claudette-colvin-the-one-too-many-dont/?utm_ term=.1984a9fb9e78

Sawyer, Jenny. "Claudette Colvin: twice Toward Justice." *Christian Science Monitor*, March 18, 2009. http://ezorigin.csmonitor.com/Books/Book-Reviews/2009/0318/claudette-colvin-twice-toward-justice

"She would not be moved." *The Guardian*, Dec. 15, 2000. https://www. theguardian.com/theguardian/2000/dec/16/weekend7.weekend12

Chapter 12

Bradshaw, Peter. "Loving review: civil rights tale marries heartfelt drama with too much restraint." *The Guardian*, May 16, 2016. https://www. theguardian.com/film/2016/may/16/loving-review-civil-rights-tale-marries-heartfelt-drama-with-too-much-restraint

Coleman, Arika L. "What You Didn't Know About Loving v. Virginia." *Time*, June 10, 2016. http://time.com/4362508/loving-v-virginia-personas/

Curtis, Mary C. "Is 'The Loving Story' over, even now?" *The Washington Post*, Feb 13, 2012. https://www.washingtonpost.com/blogs/she-the-people/post/is-the-loving-story-over-even-now/2012/02/13/ gIQAkrqECR_blog.html>?utm_term=.27e050908604

Dominus, Susan. "The Color of Love." *New York Times Magazine*, Dec. 23, 2008. http://www.nyTimes.com/2008/12/28/magazine/28loving-t.html

Dowd, Kathy Erich. "The Real Story Behind Loving: How an Interracial Couple's Landmark Fight for Their Right to Wed Made History — and Inspired the Film Earning Oscar Buzz." *People*, Oct. 26, 2016. http:// people.com/movies/richard-mildred-loving-real-story/

Ebert, Roger. "Loving." *RogerEbert.com*, Dec. 4, 2016. http://www.rogerebert.com/reviews/loving-2016

Fish Ph.D, Jefferson M. "The Loving Story—a valentine from HBO." *Psychology Today*, Feb. 17, 2012. https://www.psychologytoday.com/blog/looking-in-the-cultural-mirror/201202/the-loving-story-valentine-hbo

Margolick, David. "A Mixed Marriage's 25th Anniversary of Legality." *New York Times*, June 12, 1992. http://www.nyTimes.com/1992/06/12/news/a-mixed-marriage-s-25th-anniversary-of-legality.html>?pagewanted=all

Martin, Douglas. "Mildred Loving, Who Battled Ban on Mixed-Race Marriage, Dies at 68." *New York Times,* May 6, 2008. http://www.nyTimes.com/2008/05/06/us/06loving.html

"Mildred Loving." *The Economist*, May 15, 2008. http://www.economist.com/node/11367685

Newbeck, Phyl. "Mildred Loving." *The Guardian*, May 6, 2008. https://www.theguardian.com/world/2008/may/07/usa.humanrights

Newbeck, Phyl. "Mr. and Mrs. Loving." *Style Weekly*, Aug. 18, 2004. http://www.styleweekly.com/richmond/mr-and-mrs-loving/Content?oid=1360711

Scheffler, Ian. "Lovings At Home." *New Yorker*, Feb. 13, 2012. http://www.newYorker.com/culture/photo-booth/lovings-at-home

Senna, Danzy. "Behind the Scenes of Loving, the Most Beautiful Love Story Ever Told." *Vogue*, Oct. 17, 2016. http://www.Vogue.com/article/loving-movie-joel-edgerton-ruth-negga-director-jeff-nichols

Stanley, Alessandra. "Scenes From a Marriage That Segregationists Tried to Break Up." *New York Times*, Feb. 13, 2012. http://www.nyTimes.com/2012/02/14/arts/television/the-loving-story-an-hbo-documentary.html

Stewart, Jocelyn Y. "She won battle to legalize interracial marriage." *Los Angeles Times*, May 07, 2008. http://articles.laTimes.com/2008/may/07/local/me-loving7

Stuever, Hank. "HBO's 'The Loving Story': A resilient romance that changed history." The Washington Post. Feb. 13, 2012. <https://www.washingtonpost.com/entertainment/tv/hbos-the-loving-story-a-resilient-romance-that-changed-history/2012/02/09/gIQAPYT8BR_story.html>?utm_term=.426c65be5d52>

Viner, Brian. "A poignant tale with heartrendingly fine performances worthy of an Oscar win - and the Cannes Film Festival's coveted Palme D'Or: BRIAN VINER reviews Loving." *Daily Mail*, May 16, 2016. http://www.dailymail.co.uk/tvshowbiz/article-3593593/A-poignant-tale-heartrendingly-fine-performances-worthy-Oscar-win-Cannes-Film-Festival-s-coveted-Palme-D-BRIAN-VINER-reviews-Loving.html

Wiegand, David. "'The Loving Couple' review: interracial pioneers." *SFGate*. Feb. 14, 2012. http://www.sfgate.com/news/article/The-Loving-Couple-review-interracial-pioneers-3313006.php

Wilkinson, James. "The incredible true story of the interracial couple whose powerful love destroyed America's segregation laws - and inspired the most talked-about film at Cannes." *Daily Mail*, May 17, 2016. http://www.dailymail.co.uk/news/article-3596079/The-incredible-true-story-interracial-couple-powerful-love-destroyed-America-s-segregation-laws-inspired-talked-film-Cannes.html

Zorthian, Julia. "The History Behind Loving Day." *Time*, June 10, 2016. http://*Time*.com/4364686/loving-day-loving-v-virginia/?iframe=true&preview=true

Chapter 13

Beech, Hannah. "Aung San Suu Kyi: Burma's First Lady of Freedom." *Time*, Dec. 29, 2010. http://content.Time.com/Time/magazine/article/0,9171,2040197,00.html

Clapp, Priscila. "Aung San Suu Kyi's Workaround Revolution." *The Daily Beast*, April 19, 2016. http://www.thedailybeast.com/articles/2016/04/20/aung-san-suu-kyi-s-workaround-revolution.html

Connelly, Karen. "The Lady and The Peacock, by Peter Popham." *The Globe and the Mail*, Sept. 6, 2012. http://www.theglobeandmail.com/arts/books-and-media/the-lady-and-the-peacock-by-peter-popham/article548907/

Daily Mail Reporter. "Aung San Suu Kyi's tears as she meets British son she hasn't seen for ten years." *Daily Mail*, Nov. 23, 2010. http://www.dailymail.co.uk/news/article-1332241/Aung-San-Suu-Kyis-tears-meets-son-Time-years.html

Foster, Stephanie. "The Lady and the Peacock : Aung San Suu Kyi and the Politics of Burma." *The Huffington Post*, June 17, 2012. http://www.huffingtonpost.com/stephenie-foster/aung-san-suu-kyi-biography_b_1425811.html

Frayn, Rebecca. "The untold love story of Burma's Aung San Suu Kyi." *The Telegraph*, Dec. 11, 2011. http://www.telegraph.co.uk/news/worldnews/asia/burmamyanmar/8948018/The-untold-love-story-of-Burmas-Aung-San-Suu-Kyi.html

Freeman, Joe. "Aung San Suu Kyi's visit with her son and grandchildren is a poignant reminder of what she has sacrificed." *The Washington Post*, Sept. 14, 2016. https://www.washingtonpost.com/news/worldviews/wp/2016/09/14/aung-san-suu-kyis-visit-with-her-son-and-grandchildren-is-a-poignant-reminder-of-what-she-has-sacrificed/?utm_term=.c502bbb5bf1f

Hammer, Joshua. "A Free Woman." *New Yorker*, Jan. 24, 2011. http://www.newYorker.com/magazine/2011/01/24/a-free-woman

James, Randy. "Aung San Suu Kyi." *Time*, May 15, 2009. http://content.Time.com/Time/world/article/0,8599,1898692,00.html

Mydans, Seth. "Aung San Suu Kyi, Long a Symbol of Dignified Defiance, Sounds a Provocative Note." *New York Times*, Nov. 17, 2015. https://www.nyTimes.com/2015/11/18/world/asia/myanmar-aung-san-suu-kyi.html>?_r=0

Petrou, Michael. "REVIEW: The Lady and the Peacock: The Life of Aung San Suu Kyi." *MacLean's*, Feb. 16, 2012. http://www.macleans.ca/culture/books/review-the-lady-and-the-peacock-the-life-of-aung-san-suu-kyi/

Popescu, Lucy. "The Lady and the Peacock: The Life of Aung San Suu Kyi, By Peter Popham." *Independent*, Nov. 17, 2011. http://www.independent.co.uk/arts-entertainment/books/reviews/the-lady-and-the-peacock-the-life-of-aung-san-suu-kyi-by-peter-popham-6263578.html

Popham, Peter. "Burma: How Aung San Suu Kyi will help govern country despite being barred from presidency." *Independent*, March 6, 2016. http://www.independent.co.uk/news/world/asia/burma-how-aung-san-suu-kyi-will-help-govern-country-despite-being-barred-from-presidency-a6915561.html

Popham, Peter. "'The Lady and the Peacock': Peter Popham's Biography Reveals the Real Aung San Suu Kyi." *The Daily Beast*, March 29, 2012. http://www.thedailybeast.com/articles/2012/03/29/the-lady-and-the-peacock-peter-popham-s-biography-reveals-the-real-aung-san-suu-kyi.html

"The Lady and The Peacock: The Life of Aung San Suu Kyi – review." *Evening Standard*, Oct. 13, 2011. http://www.standard.co.uk/lifestyle/books/the-lady-and-the-peacock-the-life-of-aung-san-suu-kyi-review-6453103.html

Chapter 14

Fox, Margalit. "Patty Duke, Child Star and Oscar Winner, Dies at 69." *New York Times*, March 29, 2016. https://www.nyTimes.com/2016/03/30/arts/television/patty-duke-dies.html

"From the *PEOPLE* Archive: Inside Patty Duke's Life and 'Heartbreaking' Youth as a Child Star." *People*, March 29, 2016. http://*people*.com/movies/inside-patty-dukes-life-and-heartbreaking-youth-as-a-child-star/

"Patty Duke 1946 - 2016: Child star battled her demons." *Sunday Express*, April 1, 2016. http://www.express.co.uk/news/obituaries/657324/Patty-Duke-1946-2016-death-Patty-Show-Oscar-Helen-Keller

"Patty Duke, actress – obituary." *The Telegraph*, March 30, 2016. http://www.telegraph.co.uk/obituaries/2016/03/30/patty-duke-actress---obituary/

Smith, Nigel. "Patty Duke, Oscar-winning actress and former child star of TV show, dies at 69." *The Guardian*, March 29, 2016. https://www.theguardian.com/film/2016/mar/29/patty-duke-the-miracle-worker-dies-at-69

Tribune News Service. "Oscar-winning actress Patty Duke is dead at 69." *The Chicago Tribune*, March 29, 2016. http://www.chicagotribune.com/entertainment/tv/ct-patty-duke-dead-20160329-story.html

Wloszczyna, Susan. "Patty Duke: 1946-2016."*RogerEbert.com*, March 29, 2016. http://www.rogerebert.com/balder-and-dash/patty-duke-1946-2016

Yahr, Emily. "Patty Duke: The original survivor of dysfunctional child stardom." *The Washington Post*, March 29, 2016. https://www.washingtonpost.com/news/arts-and-entertainment/wp/2016/03/29/patty-duke-the-original-survivor-of-dysfunctional-child-stardom/?utm_term=.0fb28055d336

Chapter 15

Bertodano, Helena de. "Amy Tan: a life that's stranger than fiction." *The Telegraph*, Nov. 11, 2003. http://www.telegraph.co.uk/culture/books/10417111/Amy-Tan-a-life-thats-stranger-than-fiction.html

Gray, Paul. "Books: The Joys And Sorrows Of Amy Tan." *Time*, Feb. 19, 2001. http://content.Time.com/Time/magazine/article/0,9171,999251,00.html

Hoggard, Liz. "The Opposite of Fate." *The Guardian*, Nov. 22, 2003. https://www.theguardian.com/books/2003/nov/23/fiction.features1

Jaggi, Maya. "Ghosts at my Shoulder." *The Guardian*, March 2, 2001. https://www.theguardian.com/books/2001/mar/03/fiction.features

Jones, Vanessa E. "Her Mother Was Her Muse." *The Chicago Tribune*, March 7, 2001. http://articles.chicagotribune.com/2001-03-07/features/0103070014_1_amy-tan-daisy-tan-joy-luck-club

Kelly, Drew. "Amy Tan on Joy and Luck at Home." *The Wall Street Journal*, July 30, 2014. https://www.wsj.com/articles/amy-tans-joy-and-luck-1406742990

w, Julie. "How Stories Written for Mother Became Amy Tan's Best Seller." *New York Times*, July 4, 1989. http://www.nytimes.com/1989/07/04/books/how-stories-written-for-mother-became-amy-tan-s-best-seller.html

Mason, Deborah. "A Not-So-Dutiful Daughter." *New York Times*, Nov. 23, 2003. http://www.nyTimes.com/2003/11/23/books/a-not-so-dutiful-daughter.html

May, Meredith. "Amy Tan's inspiration is always close to home." *SFGate,* Nov. 23, 2013. http://www.sfgate.com/books/article/Amy-Tan-s-inspiration-is-always-close-to-home-5006764.php

Mulkerrins, Jane. "Amy Tan: a life that's stranger than fiction." *The Telegraph*, Nov. 2, 2013. http://www.telegraph.co.uk/culture/books/10417111/Amy-Tan-a-life-thats-stranger-than-fiction.html

Chapter 16

Bazelon, Emily. "The Making of a Justice." *New York Times*, Jan. 18, 2013. http://www.nyTimes.com/2013/01/20/books/review/my-beloved-world-by-sonia-sotomayor.html

"Before judgment days." *The Economist*, Feb. 2, 2013. http://www.economist.com/news/books-and-arts/21571112-americas-first-hispanic-supreme-court-justice-recounts-her-youthful-struggles

Bello, Grace. "My Beloved World." *The Christian Science Monitor*, Jan. 15, 2013. http://www.csmonitor.com/Books/Book-Reviews/2013/0115/My-Beloved-World

Connelly, Sherryl. "Book review: 'My Beloved World,' by Sonia Sotomayor." *New York Daily News*, Jan. 6, 2013. http://www.nydailynews.com/entertainment/music-arts/book-review-beloved-world-article-1.1230649

Cunningham, Laura Shaine. "'My Beloved World,' by Sonia Sotomayor." *SFGate*, Feb 22, 2013. http://www.sfgate.com/books/article/My-Beloved-World-by-Sonia-Sotomayor-4301509.php

Iassovoli, Brenda. "A Justice Like No Other." *Time for Kids*, Sept. 18, 2009. http://www.timeforkids.com/news/justice-no-other/171201

Kakutani, Michiko. "The Bronx, the Bench and the Life in Between." *The New York Times*. Jan. 21, 2013. <http://www.nyTimes.com/2013/01/22/books/my-beloved-world-a-memoir-by-sonia-sotomayor.html>

Lithwick, Dahlia. "Book review: 'My Beloved World' by Sonia Sotomayor." *The Washington Post*, Jan. 11, 2013. https://www.washingtonpost.com/opinions/book-review-my-beloved-world-by-sonia-sotomayor/2013/01/11/7a93dcd6-55cd-11e2-bf3e-76c0a789346f_story.html>?utm_term=.9921482e4a70

Stolberg, Sheryl Gay. "Sotomayor, a Trailblazer and a Dreamer." *New York Times*, May 26, 2009. http://www.nyTimes.com/2009/05/27/us/politics/27websotomayor.html

Chapter 17

Barber, Lynn. "Wishful Drinking by Carrie Fisher – review." *The Telegraph*, Dec. 11, 2008. http://www.*telegraph*.co.uk/culture/books/bookreviews/3707859/Wishful-Drinking-by-Carrie-Fisher-review.html

Cavina, Michael. "As iconic Princess Leia, Carrie Fisher was a life force to be reckoned with." *The Washington Post*, Dec. 27, 2016. https://www.washingtonpost.com/news/comic-riffs/wp/2016/12/27/as-iconic-princess-leia-carrie-fisher-was-a-life-force-to-be-reckoned-with/?utm_term=.10a1fa59abe0

Conrad, Peter. "Shockaholic by Carrie Fisher - Review." *The Guardian*, Nov. 10, 2011. https://www.theguardian.com/books/2011/nov/10/shockaholic-carrie-fisher-review

David, Anna. "Carrie Fisher Forever Changed the Way People Talk About Addiction." *Time*, Dec. 27, 2016. http://Time.com/4618670/carrie-fisher-addiction-books/

Downes, Lawrence. "The Honesty of Carrie Fisher." *New York Times*, Dec. 28, 2016. https://www.nyTimes.com/2016/12/28/opinion/the-honesty-of-carrie-fisher.html

Durst, Will. "'Shockaholic,' by Carrie Fisher: review." *SFGate,* Nov. 6, 2011. http://www.sfgate.com/books/article/Shockaholic-by-Carrie-Fisher-review-2323976.php

Gilbert, Matthew. "'Wishful Drinking' a guided tour through a dysfunctional past." *The Boston Globe*, Dec. 10, 2010. http://archive.boston.com/ae/tv/articles/2010/12/10/fishers_wishful_drinking_a_guided_tour_through_a_dysfunctional_past/

Italie, Hillel. "No one could make us laugh through pain like Carrie Fisher." *Star Tribune*, Dec. 27, 2016. http://www.startribune.com/no-one-could-make-us-laugh-through-pain-like-carrie-fisher/408447105/

Itzkoff, Dave. "Carrie Fisher, Child of Hollywood and 'Star Wars' Royalty, dies at 60." *New York Times*, Dec. 27, 2016. https://www.nyTimes.com/2016/12/27/movies/carrie-fisher-dead-star-wars-princess-leia.html

Larson, Sarah. "Carrie Fisher's Powerful Force." *New Yorker*, Dec. 28, 2016. http://www.newYorker.com/culture/culture-desk/carrie-fishers-powerful-force

McGrath, Charles. "Princess Leia's Wit Tames the Dark Side." *New York Times*, Jan. 1, 2009. http://www.nyTimes.com/2009/01/02/books/02book.html

Stack Liam. "Carrie Fisher: A Look at Her Life Beyond 'Star Wars.'" *New York Times*, Dec. 27, 2016. https://www.nyTimes.com/2016/12/27/movies/carrie-fisher-a-look-at-her-life-beyond-star-wars.html

Sturges, Fiona. "The Princess Diarist by Carrie Fisher review – fame, sex and Harrison Ford." *The Guardian*, Dec. 20, 2016. https://www.theguardian.com/books/2016/dec/20/princess-diarist-carrie-fisher-review-harrison-ford

Chapter 18

Akbar, Arifa. "Why be happy when you could be normal? by Jeanette Winterson." *The Independent*, Oct. 27, 2011. http://www.independent.co.uk/arts-entertainment/books/reviews/why-be-happy-when-you-could-be-normal-by-jeanette-winterson-2377134.html

Feay, Suzi. "'Winterson-world was bonkers!'" *The Independent*, April 7, 2012. http://www.independent.co.uk/arts-entertainment/books/features/winterson-world-was-bonkers-7626801.html

"Jeanette Winterson: I've found happiness after a life of despair." *Belfast Telegraph*, June 4, 2012. http://www.belfasttelegraph.co.uk/woman/life/jeanette-winterson-ive-found-happiness-after-a-life-of-despair-28756702.html

Joughin, Sheena. "Why Be Happy When You Could Be Normal? by Jeanette Winterson, review." *The Telegraph*, Nov. 25, 2011. http://www.telegraph.co.uk/culture/books/biographyandmemoirreviews/8899342/Why-Be-Happy-When-You-Could-Be-Normal-by-Jeanette-Winterson-review.html

"Londoner's Diary: Wedding bells chime for Susie Orbach and Jeanette Winterson." *Evening Standard*, March 12, 2015. http://www.standard.co.uk/news/londoners-diary/londoners-diary-wedding-bells-chime-for-susie-orbach-and-jeanette-winterson-10307701.html

Ramaswamy, Chitra. "Interview: Jeanette Winterson, writer." *The Scotsman*, Nov. 1, 2011. http://www.scotsman.com/lifestyle/interview-jeanette-winterson-writer-1-1938801

Sayers, Valerie. "Books." *The Washington Post*, April 2, 2012. https://www.washingtonpost.com/entertainment/books/2012/04/02/gIQAYlesrS_story.html>?utm_term=.a4ca7ecbeb42

"The Long View: A Q & A with Writer Jeanette Winterson." *Vogue,* March 5, 2012. http://www.vogue.com/article/the-long-view-an-interview-with-writer-jeanette-winterson

Chapter 19

Chisholm, Anne. "The things that pass as normal." *The Telegraph*, May 7, 2005. http://www.telegraph.co.uk/culture/books/3642071/The-things-that-pass-as-normal.html

Glazebrook, Olivia. "Learning How to Swim." *The Spectator*, April 30, 2005. http://www.spectator.co.uk/2005/04/learning-how-to-swim/

Hazlick, Denise. "Life in 'Glass Castle' only made Walls stronger." *Today*, Mar. 20, 2006. http://www.today.com/popculture/life-glass-castle-only-made-walls-stronger-2D80555381

McLaren, Leah. "Why we love books about kids in peril (Jeannette Walls knows)." *The Globe and the Mail*, June 14, 2013. http://www.theglobeandmail.com/arts/books-and-media/book-reviews/why-we-love-books-about-kids-in-peril-jeannette-walls-knows/article12562668/

Migration. "Author Jeannette Walls discusses the liberating power of secrets unveiled." *The Denver Post*, May 1, 2016. http://www.denverpost.com/2012/01/05/author-jeannette-walls-discusses-the-liberating-power-of-secrets-unveiled/

Mondloch, Helen. "Transcending the Worst of Times." *Northern Virginia Magazine,* Oct. 1, 2015. http://www.northernvirginiamag.com/entertainment/entertainment-features/2015/10/16/transcending-the-worst-of-Times/

"One child's life in poverty is the reality of 'The Glass Castle'." *Daily Emerald*, April 6, 2006. http://www.dailyemerald.com/2006/04/06/one-childs-life-in-poverty-is-the-reality-of-the-glass-castle/

People Staff. "Picks and Pans Review: The Glass Castle." *People*, April 4, 2005. http://people.com/archive/picks-and-pans-review-the-glass-castle-vol-63-no-13/

Prose, Francine. "'The Glass Castle': Outrageous Misfortune." *New York Times*, March 13, 2005. http://www.nytimes.com/2005/03/13/books/review/the-glass-castle-outrageous-misfortune.html

"That's my Mom. The last time I saw her, she was rummaging through the trash for food." *The Guardian*, April 2, 2005. https://www.theguardian.com/books/2005/apr/03/biography.features

Windolf, Jim. "A Secret Of Her Own." *Vanity Fair,* April 1, 2005. http://www.vanityfair.com/hollywood/2005/04/jeannette-walls-msnbc-gossip-past

Witchel, Alex. "How Jeannette Walls Spins Good Stories Out of Bad Memories." *New York Times Magazine*, May 24, 2013. http://www.nyTimes.com/2013/05/26/magazine/how-jeannette-walls-spins-good-stories-out-of-bad-memories.html

Chapter 20

"J.K. Rowling Biography." *Biography.com*. Retrieved June 1, 2016. http://www.biography.com/people/jk-rowling-40998#fame-and-fortune

"The JK Rowling story." *The Scotsman,* June 16, 2003. http://www.scotsman.com/lifestyle/culture/books/the-jk-rowling-story-1-652114

Wagman-Geller, Marlene. *Once Again to Zelda: The Stories Behind Literature's Most Intriguing Dedications*. New York: Perigree Trade, 2008.

Chapter 21

Adato, Allison. "Against the Odds." *People*, Aug. 11, 2003. http://people.com/archive/against-the-odds-vol-60-no-6/

"Author of 'Seabiscuit' endures rough ride." *The Washington Times*, July 10, 2003. http://www.washingtonTimes.com/news/2003/jul/10/20030710-120521-6344r/

Frey, Jennifer. "Despite Illness, Author Pushed to the Finish Line." *Los Angeles Times*, Sept 16, 2007. http://articles.laTimes.com/2001/mar/27/news/cl-43092

Gell, Aaron. "Chronic Fatigue Syndrome: A Celebrated Author's Untold Tale." *Elle*, Dec. 2, 2010. http://www.elle.com/beauty/health-fitness/advice/a2458/chronic-fatigue-syndrome-a-celebrated-authors-untold-tale-517101/

Hesse, Monica. "Laura Hillenbrand releases new book while fighting chronic fatigue syndrome." *The Washington Post*, Nov. 28, 2010. http://www.washingtonpost.com/wp-dyn/content/article/2010/11/28/AR2010112803533.html

Hylton, Will S. "The Unbreakable Laura Hillenbrand." The *New York Times* Magazine. Dec. 18, 2014. <https://www.nyTimes.com/2014/12/21/ magazine/the-unbreakable-laura-hillenbrand.html>?_r=0>

Jacobs, Sally. "Illness made Laura Hillenbrand a long shot to finish the acclaimed book 'Seabiscuit.' *The Massachusetts CFIDS/ME & FM Association*, Dec. 7, 2015. https://www.masscfids.org/resource-library/7-coping/58-illness-made-laura-hillenbrand-a-long-shot-to-finish-the-acclaimed-book-qseabiscuitq

Jaffe, Jody. "Brave Hearts." *Bethesda Magazine*, March-April 2005. http://www.bethesdamagazine.com/Bethesda-Magazine/January-December-2006/Brave-Hearts/

McElwaine, Sandra. "Laura Hillenbrand's Acclaimed Bestsellers Haven't Changed Her." *The Daily Beast*, Dec. 21, 2011. http://www.thedailybeast. com/articles/2011/12/21/laura-hillenbrand-s-acclaimed-bestsellers-haven-t-changed-her.html

Sheldon, Michael. "A Dead Horse Rescued Me." *The Telegraph*, Sep. 3, 2004. http://www.*telegraph*.co.uk/women/womens-health/3309988/A-dead-horse-rescued-me.html

Chapter 22

Carpentier, Megan. "Tammy Duckworth shows her strength in Senate fight: 'These legs don't buckle." *The Guardian*, Aug. 25, 2016. https://www. theguardian.com/us-news/2016/aug/25/tammy-duckworth-senate-race-illinois-profile

Davey, Monica. "Tammy Duckworth Unseats Mark Kirk in Illinois Senate Race." *New York Times*, Nov. 8, 2016. https://www.nyTimes. com/2016/11/09/us/politics/illinois-senate-tammy-duckworth.html

McElwaine, Sandra. "Tammy Duckworth on Gun Control, Women in Combat." *The Daily Beast*, Feb. 9, 2013. http://www.thedailybeast.com/ articles/2013/02/09/tammy-duckworth-on-gun-control-women-in-combat.html

Nelson, Rebecca. "The Dark Humor of Tammy Duckworth, Iraq War Hero and Gun Control Advocate." *GQ.com*, Sept. 29, 2016. http://www.gq.com/story/tammy-duckworth-iraq-war-hero-and-gun-control-advocate-interview

Perlman, Seth. "G.O.P. Senator Under Fire After Insulting Veteran's Racial Heritage." *Vanity Fair*, Oct. 27, 2016. http://www.vanityfair.com/news/2016/10/mark-kirk-tammy-duckworth-veteran-debate

Riopell, Mike. "10 years after losing her legs, Duckworth returns to flying." *The Daily Herald*, April 29, 2015. http://www.dailyherald.com/article/20141111/news/141119848

Riopell, Mike. "How two helicopter crews got Duckworth out of Iraq." *The Daily Herald*, Nov. 12, 2014. http://www.dailyherald.com/article/20141111/news/141119763/

Riopell, Mike. "The day Capt. Tammy Duckworth was shot down." *The Daily Herald*, Nov. 14, 2014. http://www.dailyherald.com/article/20141111/news/141119904/

Weinstein, Adam. "Nobody Puts Tammy Duckworth in a Corner." *Mother Jones*, September/October 2012. http://www.motherjones.com/politics/2012/08/tammy-duckworth-versus-joe-walsh-congress

Chapter 23

Alexander, Harriet. "The Ohio kidnappings: Mother Courage." *The Telegraph*, Aug. 3, 2013. http://www.telegraph.co.uk/news/worldnews/northamerica/usa/10220400/The-Ohio-kidnappings-Mother-Courage.html

Aradillas, Elaine. "Michelle Knight: Inside My New Life." *People*, Sept. 23, 2016. http://people.com/celebrity/michelle-knight-kidnapping-victim-writes-memoir-about-survival/

Aradillas, Elaine. "Why Cleveland Kidnapping Survivors Amanda Berry and Gina DeJesus Don't Speak with Fellow Victim Michelle Knight." *People*, April 23, 2015. http://people.com/crime/cleveland-kidnapping-survivors-dont-speak-to-michelle-knight/

Associated Press in Cleveland. "Cleveland escapee Michelle Knight: 'Take the bad in life and replace it'." *The Guardian*, March 15, 2015. https://www.theguardian.com/us-news/2015/mar/15/cleveland-kidnapping-michelle-knight

Associated Press in Cleveland. "Cleveland kidnapping victim Michelle Knight 'forgives' abductor Ariel Castro." *The Guardian*, May 5, 2014. https://www.theguardian.com/world/2014/may/05/cleveland-kidnapping-michelle-knight-ariel-castro-forgives

Christie, Joel. "'I'm able to talk about it now without crying': Michelle Knight reveals she has a boyfriend and how she's healing from 'house of horrors' abuse." *The Daily Mail*, April 15, 2015. http://www.dailymail.co.uk/news/article-3041049/I-m-able-talk-without-crying-Michelle-Knight-reveals-boyfriend-s-healing-house-horrors-abuse.html

Collman, Ashley. "'He's with me all the time and supports everything that I do': Michelle Knight speaks out about new boyfriend in interview on the second anniversary of her escape from Cleveland house of horrors." *The Daily Mail*, May 7, 2015. http://www.dailymail.co.uk/news/article-3072021/He-s-Time-supports-Michelle-Knight-speaks-new-boyfriend-interview-second-anniversary-escape-Cleveland-house-horrors.html

Davidson, Amy. "Michelle Knight, Missing." *New Yorker*, May 9, 2013. http://www.newYorker.com/news/amy-davidson/michelle-knight-missing

Evans, Sophie Jane. "'Every rose is for every abortion I had there': Michelle Knight tells the harrowing stories behind each of her tattoos - which she got after being rescued from 'house of horrors.'" *The Daily Mail*, Sept 6, 2015. http://www.dailymail.co.uk/news/article-3223921/Every-rose-abortion-house-Michelle-Knight-tells-harrowing-stories-tattoos-got-house-horrors-rescue.html

Hampson, Sarah. "Survivor of unspeakable horror, Michelle Knight refuses to be defined by captivity." *The Globe and Mail*, May 18, 2014. http://www.theglobeandmail.com/arts/books-and-media/survivor-of-unspeakable-horror-michelle-knight-refuses-to-be-defined-by-captivity/article18726841/?page=all

Hattenstone, Simon. "Kidnapped a block from home. Eleven years Ariel Castro's captive. How Michelle Knight survived." *The Guardian*, May 10, 2014. https://www.theguardian.com/world/2014/may/10/michelle-knight-ariel-castro-how-i-survived

Hattenstone, Simon. "Michelle Knight survived 11 horrific years as a prisoner at the hands of monster Ariel Castro in a terrifying house of horrors." *The Daily Telegraph*, May 14, 2014. http://www.dailytelegraph.com.au/news/michelle-knight-survived-11-horrific-years-as-a-prisoner-at-the-hands-of-monster-ariel-castro-in-a-terrifying-house-of-horrors/news-story/72dc4b62215628041b8f7475e13d427a

Jalabi, Raya. "Michelle Knight on Ariel Castro: my abduction didn't define who I am." *The Guardian*, May 7, 2014. https://www.theguardian.com/world/2014/may/06/michelle-knight-remember-me-as-a-victor-not-a-victim

Jones, Abigail. "Life After 11 Years Of Captivity, Rape And Torture: Michelle Knight's Story." *Newsweek*, Sept. 3, 2015. http://www.newsweek.com/2015/09/11/michelle-knight-survival-ariel-castro-captivity-368058.html

Li, David K. "Michelle Knight: I hid from rescuers." *The New York Post*, May 7, 2014. http://nypost.com/2014/05/07/michelle-knight-part-of-me-died-to-survive-kidnap-hell/

Pelisek, Christine. "The Forgotten Victim: Cleveland's Michelle Knight." *The Daily Beast*, May 9, 2013. http://www.thedailybeast.com/articles/2013/05/09/the-forgotten-victim-cleveland-s-michelle-knight.html

Stephenson, Hannah. "Knight is 'letting go of the hate' and putting nightmare abduction behind her." *Irish Examiner*, June 18, 2014. http://www.irishexaminer.com/lifestyle/features/knight-is-letting-go-of-the-hate-and-putting-nightmare-abduction-behind-her-272393.html

Chapter 24

Bronner, Sasha. "Leaving Her Ultra-Orthodox Past Meant More Than Losing Her Family. It Meant Redefining Her Womanhood." *The Huffington*

Post, July 23, 2015. http://www.huffingtonpost.com/entry/escaping-her-ultra-orthodox-past-meant-redefining-what-it-means-to-be-a-woman_us_55b01a38e4b08f57d5d3a26b

Cahalan, Susannah. "NYC woman finds redemption after shunned by family." *New York Post*, Jan. 25, 2014. http://nypost.com/2014/01/25/nyc-woman-finds-redemption-after-shunned-by-family/

Daily Mail Reporter. "The remarkable journey of Orthodox Jewish woman cast out into a life of poverty by her family after buying a tight sweater at 17... who then went on to graduate Harvard." *Daily Mail*, Jan. 26, 2014. http://www.dailymail.co.uk/news/article-2546290/Orthodox-Jewish-woman-shunned-family-age-17-graduates-Harvard.html

Deneson, Amy. "My goddamn Flesh." *Brooklyn Rail,* Sept. 5, 2014. http://brooklynrail.org/2014/11/books/my-goddamn-flesh

Feith, Gena. "Book Review: 'Cut Me Loose' by Leah Vincent." *The Wall Street Journal*, Jan. 17, 2014. https://www.wsj.com/articles/SB10001424052702304549504579320683901880384

McDonough, Megan. "Book review: 'CUT ME LOOSE Sin and Salvation After My Ultra-Orthodox Girlhood,' by Leah Vincent." *The Washington Post*, May 9, 2014. https://www.washingtonpost.com/opinions/review-cut-me-loose-sin-and-salvation-after-my-ultra-orthodox-girlhood-by-leah-vincent/2014/05/09/a09be8b2-af7f-11e3-95e8-39bef8e9a48b_story.html>?utm_term=.c0d6261b3144

Meyers, Dvora. "Why I Chose My Own Name: Leah Vincent's Journey Out of Ultra-Orthodoxy." *Elle,* Jan. 16, 2014. http://www.elle.com/culture/books/reviews/a12649/leah-vincent-profile/

Pitz, Marylynne. "How Leah Vincent, a Squirrel Hill rabbi's daughter, built a new life after leaving her family." *Pittsburgh Post-Gazette*, May 14, 2014. http://www.post-gazette.com/ae/books/2014/05/14/How-a-rabbi-s-daughter-built-a-new-life-after-leaving-her-ultra-orthodox-family-in-Squirrel-Hill/stories/201405140008

Shuman, Sam. "Interview: Leah Vincent." *Jewish Book Council*, Feb. 25, 2014. http://www.jewishbookcouncil.org/_blog/The_ProsenPeople/post/interview-leah-vincent/

Vincent, Leah. "Adrift Too Long, Searching for a Navigator." *New York Times*, Jan. 16, 2014. https://www.nyTimes.com/2014/01/19/fashion/adrift-too-long-searching-for-a-navigator.html>?_r=0

Vincent. Leah. "From good girl to prostitute: My path from ultra-Orthodox Judaism to Craigslist sex ad." *Salon*, Feb. 2, 2014. http://www.salon.com/2014/02/03/from_good_girl_to_prostitute_my_path_from_ultra_orthodox_judaism_to_craigslist_sex_ad/

Vincent, Leah. "My Post-Ultra-Orthodox Wedding." *The Daily Beast*, March 21, 2014. http://www.thedailybeast.com/articles/2014/03/21/the-right-wedding-for-two-rebels.html

Chapter 25

Bronner, Sasha. "How Being Called The 'World's Ugliest Woman' Transformed Her Life." *The Huffington Post,* Oct. 20, 2015. http://www.huffingtonpost.com/entry/how-being-called-the-worlds-ugliest-woman-transformed-her-life_us_56213be0e4b02f6a9

Associated Press. "'I know what it is to be bullied': How 'world's ugliest woman' Lizzie Velasquez is turning her story into a documentary to help others overcome their tormentors." *Daily Mail*, May 23, 2014. http://www.dailymail.co.uk/femail/article-2637461/Worlds-ugliest-woman-pursues-anti-bullying-film.html

Associated Press. "'World's ugliest woman raises money for anti-bullying film." *New York Daily News*, May 23, 2014. http://www.nydailynews.com/life-style/world-ugliest-woman-raises-money-anti-bullying-film-article-1.1803788

Hawkins, Kathleen. "Lizzie Velasquez: 'Online bullies called me the world's ugliest woman.'" *BBC News,* March 14, 2015. <http://www.bbc.com/news/blogs-ouch-30948179>

Jaworowski, Ken. "Review: 'A Brave Heart: The Lizzie Velasquez Story,'
One Woman's Push for Acceptance." *New York Times*, Sept. 24, 2015.
https://www.nyTimes.com/2015/09/25/movies/review-a-brave-heart-the-
lizzie-velasquez-story-one-womans-push-for-acceptance.html

Katz, Brigit. "They called her the 'Ugliest Woman in the World.' Now, Lizzie
Velásquez is fighting back." *Women in the World*, March, 2015. http://
nytlive.nyTimes.com/womenintheworld/2015/03/20/they-called-her-the-
ugliest-woman-in-the-world-now-lizzie-velasquez-is-fighting-back/

Layton, Lyndsey. "Once bullied, now empowered, Lizzie Velasquez
lobbies Capitol Hill." *Washington Post*, Oct. 27, 2015. https://www.
washingtonpost.com/local/education/once-bullied-now-empowered-
lizzie-velasquez-lobbies-capitol-hill/2015/10/27/8f6c8ece-7ce3-11e5-afce-
2afd1d3eb896_story.html>?utm_term=.28a4b6771005

Lemire, Christy. "A Brave Heart: The Lizzie Velasquez Story." *RogerEbert.
com*, Sept. 25, 2015. http://www.rogerebert.com/reviews/a-brave-heart-
the-lizzie-velasquez-story-2015

Neumaier, Joe. "Web sensation ready for her closeup in 'A Brave Heart:
The Lizzie Velasquez Story': movie review." *New York Daily News,* Sept.
24, 2015. http://www.nydailynews.com/entertainment/movies/web-
sensation-ready-closeup-brave-heart-review-article-1.2373026

Noble, Freya. "'I didn't know how I was going to pick myself up': Woman
ridiculed online as 'the world's ugliest woman' tells how she fought back
against the bullies." *Daily Mail*, Sept. 9, 2016. http://www.dailymail.co.uk/
news/article-3780933/How-world-s-ugliest-woman-Lizzie-Velasquez-
fought-against-bullies.html

Price, Lydia. "How Lizzie Velasquez, Once Called 'World's Ugliest Woman,'
Is Fighting Bullies with Her New Film." *People*, Sept. 24, 2015. http://
people.com/celebrity/lizzie-velasquez-releases-a-brave-heart/

Strauss, Bob. "Dealing with disorder, Lizzie Velasquez displays 'A Brave
Heart.'" *Los Angeles Daily News,* Sept. 22, 2015. <http://www.dailynews.
com/arts-and-entertainment/20150922/dealing-with-disorder-lizzie-

velasquez-displays-a-brave-heart>

Taylor, Ella. "Film Review: 'A Brave Heart: The Lizzie Velasquez Story.'" *Variety*, Sept. 18, 2015. http://variety.com/2015/film/reviews/film-review-a-brave-heart-the-lizzie-velasquez-story-1201597202/

Velasquez, Lizzie. "Lizzie Velasquez: My Anti-Bullying Story." *The Daily Beast*, Sept. 25, 2015. http://www.thedailybeast.com/articles/2015/09/25/lizzie-velasquez-my-anti-bullying-story.html

ABOUT THE AUTHOR

Marlene Wagman-Geller received her BA from York University and her teaching degree from the University of Toronto and San Diego State University. She made the great sacrifice of leaving her Winter Wonderland for Southern California and currently teaches high school English in National City, California. The author of five books, her work has been reviewed in the *New York Times, Chicago Tribune,* and *Washington Post.*